THE SEDUCTION OF SPACE

THE SEDUCTION OF SPACE

Cruising French Cinema

JULES O'DWYER

University of Minnesota Press | Minneapolis | London

A section of chapter 2 was published in a different form as "Coming and Going: Nolot, Barthes, and the *Porn Theater*," *Discourse* 42, no. 3 (2021): 259–80; published with permission of Wayne State University Press. Portions of chapter 4 were published in a different form as "*Histoire(s) de l'art*: The Queer Curation of Vincent Dieutre," *Alphaville* 16 (2018): 53–66; and "Cruising, Cinema, and Colonial Vestiges, or *Les lieux de drague comme lieu de mémoire*," in *Queer Realms of Memory: Archiving LGBTQ Identities in the French National Narrative*, ed. Siham Bouamer, Denis M. Provencher, and Ryan Schroth (Liverpool: Liverpool University Press, forthcoming).

Published by the University of Minnesota Press
111 Third Avenue South, Suite 290
Minneapolis, MN 55401-2520
http://www.upress.umn.edu

ISBN 978-1-5179-1683-1 (hc)
ISBN 978-1-5179-1684-8 (pb)

A Cataloging-in-Publication record for this book is available from the Library of Congress.

Printed on acid-free paper

CONTENTS

Introduction. Paris's Cinematic Exploits: From *Flânerie* to Cruising 1

1. The Seduction of Space in French Queer Film and Theory 21

2. Coming and Going in Jacques Nolot's Cinema 47

3. *Quartiers chauds:* Loitering, Queer Zones, and Banlieue Aesthetics 85

4. A Queer Window onto the World? Vincent Dieutre's Documentary Frames 113

5. Sex beyond the City: Alain Guiraudie's Rural Erotics 151

ACKNOWLEDGMENTS 187

NOTES 191

INDEX 217

Introduction

PARIS'S CINEMATIC EXPLOITS
FROM *FLÂNERIE* TO CRUISING

> Like those wandering souls who go in search of a body,
> he enters—as he pleases—into each man's personality.
>
> —Charles Baudelaire

Scene One (Central Paris)

In the opening scene of Olivier Ducastel and Jacques Martineau's 2016 film *Paris 05:59: Théo & Hugo* (in French, *Théo et Hugo dans le même bateau*), a camera lingers in the spaces of a dimly lit sex club—L'Impact—in central Paris. We pan from the right, by the bar area, to a group of men on the left. The camera glides between bodies bathed in electric blue light, capturing the shimmering contours of male forms in neon chiaroscuro. The dexterous camera work in this scene seems, in fact, to recall the sociosexual practice for which this particular bar is best known: cruising. In its suggestive congruence of form and content, *Paris 05:59* exemplifies a contention that was first articulated in the gay film criticism of Bruce Brasell and will be subsequently revised and expanded on in the pages that follow: namely, that cinematic cruising not only refers to a sexual practice that is depicted narratively, but also designates, more fundamentally, a queer optic or "way of seeing."[1] Gary Needham and Cüneyt Çakırlar suggest in a close formal analysis of the film that we cannot fully appreciate the affective and erotic bonds that Ducastel and Martineau lay bare here without paying attention to techniques of editing. The refusal of point-of-view shots contributes to the film's "indistinct and anonymous register," one that resists the reification of individual identities and relinquishes "subject/object and self/other distinctions."[2] As they note, the film's formal syntax—its capacity to assemble bodies in various spatial and temporal configurations—is pressed into service to articulate what Leo Bersani, himself drawing on the late writing of Michel Foucault, termed "new relational modes." This line of thinking opens up fertile avenues of investigation into queer sex, cinematic spatiality, and—perhaps most crucially—their intersections.

Returning to the opening scene of *Paris 05:59,* we follow one man's movement downstairs—marked by a suggestive chromatic shift from blue to red—as he ventures into the club's dark room. Every corner and crevice is populated by bodies that coalesce in different forms of erotic communion. Concatenated limbs writhe to the pulse of electro. The striking use of chiaroscuro demands of the film's spectator an attentive gaze—one capable of disaggregating bodies in the dark recesses of the club, isolating them from the amorphous abstractions of the mise-en-scène. The mobile camera continues to explore the traffic of gazes, mediating the dense force field of attractions before eventually homing in on the eponymous characters, Théo and Hugo (played by Geoffrey Couët and François Nambot). Although both are initially engaged in sex acts with different partners, their gazes meet from across the room and quickly interlock in rapt attention, anticipating their own position at the fulcrum

Figure 1. *Paris 05:59: Théo and Hugo* (Olivier Ducastel and Jacques Martineau, 2016). Protagonists Théo (Geoffrey Couët) and Hugo (François Nambot) encounter each other in the midst of a neon-drenched dark room.

of the scene. The ensuing sex scene moves us from the midst of the darkroom to a more ambiguous space whose spatiotemporal coordinates are harder to parse. Detached from the previous backdrop, Théo and Hugo's bodies are bathed in white light. The diegetic music becomes muffled; the soundscape is shorn of high frequencies, leaving us with a stirring, growling bassline. The men gravitate toward each other and engage in a sex scene (oral sex, followed by anal penetration) that unfolds over eight minutes, before then returning upstairs and leaving the club together.

Caught in a state of mutual captivation, they cycle around northeastern Paris in the dead of night, weaving in and out of the empty streets. But it later transpires, midconversation, that Théo did not use a condom, which leads Hugo to disclose his seropositive status. They rush to the neighboring Hôpital Saint-Louis, where Théo is administered antiretroviral drugs (postexposure prophylaxis), before returning to the streets to wander, eat, and chat until sunrise. Although their final conversation gestures proleptically to the idea of some future together (whether as friends, sex partners, a couple, or even—Hugo jokes wryly—future ex-partners), their fate is left open. Ducastel and Martineau are mindful of the normative trappings of narrative resolution, which risks eclipsing the ethics of promiscuity so deftly articulated earlier in the film.

While this necessarily telescoped summary perhaps fails to convey the film's unfolding in real time, it underscores the important shifts in affective tone and relational register. Over the course of *Paris 05:59,* we move from the anonymous intimacies of public sex to a fragile sense of solidarity in the face of adversity, toward a projected future that may or may not assume the couple form. These shifts correspond, moreover, to key changes in location: from the neon charge of the underground sex club to the stark sterility of the clinical encounter, from the break of dawn on Parisian streets to Hugo's sheets. By entwining processes of social, sexual, and spatial exploration as the narrative unfolds, Ducastel and Martineau invite spectators to consider questions that anticipate the central preoccupation in this book. Namely, how might a focus on sexual practices allow us to understand how cinematic spaces and queer geographies take shape? Is the moving image particularly well suited to capturing the furtive, fleeting, and evanescent moments of the cruising encounter—which Mark W. Turner reminds us are "not intended to be captured"[3]—or might cinema's predication on indexical capture constitute an unethical intrusion into what queer art historian John Paul Ricco terms the "commerce of anonymity"?[4]

The Spaces of French Queer Cinema

This book considers scenes of cruising in contemporary French cinema as privileged examples of both social and spatial exploration. And in so doing, it gently contests a tendency that has grown pronounced over recent years to turn the notion of "queer space" into a buzzword that, once divested of a substantive engagement with the problematics of sexuality, might be ushered into the altogether politer realm of geometric abstraction (or as I formulate it, "queer space" as resistance to the "straight line"). This metaphorical tendency, particularly marked in recent film scholarship, has an unfortunately ironic consonance with the all-too-material processes of sanitization and gentrification that have afflicted many physical queer spaces over recent decades. This book's call to renew queer cinema scholarship's attention to the messy politics of sex—an impetus that underwrites many of its claims in more or less subtle ways—is not intended to act as a reductive gesture. Rather, my aim is to expand the reader's field of vision and provide them with more tools for conceptual analysis as they explore the rich nexus of sexuality, spatiality, and the moving image.

While film and media studies has recently witnessed a renewed interest in questions of space, place, and embodiment on the one hand, and a keen interest in queer sexualities, counterpublics, and relational practices on the other, the conceptual convergences of these two areas require further theorization. By way of a response to this gap, *The Seduction of Space* brings to the fore the work of French gay filmmakers including Jacques Nolot, Sébastien Lifshitz, Christophe Honoré, Vincent Dieutre, and Alain Guiraudie, who, similarly to Ducastel and Martineau, turn to the spatial practice of cruising to explore the formal, textual, and geographic construction of cinematic space as well as France's social landscapes. This book explores a varied cinematic corpus, drawing on examples spanning from the *court métrage* to the feature film, from fiction to creative documentary. The filmmakers whom I engage experiment conspicuously with ideas of space and place to frame and explore queer ways of being in the world. Certain recurring invocations of specific sites and settings—the film auditorium in the cinema of Nolot, the streetscape in Dieutre, the rural lakeside settings in the oeuvre of Guiraudie—invite a reappraisal of associated film-theoretical discourses in ways that puts the politics of sexuality center stage. The aim of this book, therefore, is twofold. First, it seeks to stimulate a series of encounters among film theory, queer studies, and spatial thought to generate more rigorous and expansive understandings of queer cinematic space. Second, it aims to bring to the fore the work of several filmmakers who have yet to receive adequate scholarly attention outside the rarefied circles of French queer film culture.

My appeal to "space" as a guiding analytic is motivated by several overlapping concerns. The first of these relates directly to the contexts of modern and contemporary France in which my intervention is grounded. In the recent volume *France in Flux,* Edward Welch notes that "space and territory have had an overdetermined role in the French social and political imaginary" since the founding of the Republic.[5] Spatiality, that is, provides an important analytic prism through which to understand social, political, and cultural life in France. James F. Austin makes the related point that "given its prestige, financial importance, and enormous cultural resonance in France, the cinema is well poised to engage in a spatial politics, to be an art of space producing its own space of spaces, and thus potentially redefining the space of France and the francophone world."[6] In addition to the context-specific argument that Austin wants to make, and which I go on to discuss below, his broader contention that cinema not only *registers* spaces but *produces* new spaces of experience anticipates the second reason for my conceptual emphasis.

Cinema enjoys a privileged relation to realism and the perceptual; it documents the material contours of the geophysical world on the one hand and elucidates the subjective lives of its characters or creators on the other. Film's unparalleled capacity to mediate (in the sense of both negotiating and making visible) these two registers is of particular importance to a discussion of queer spatiality. On one level, cinema fulfills the vital purpose of committing to memory those physical settings and social scenes that are either transient or temporary (and as the HIV/AIDS crisis taught us so brutally, those incipient spaces of sociality irretrievably lost to the ravages of time, illness, and gentrification.) On another level, queer filmmakers have increasingly harnessed the multisensory potentiality of the medium to think about the perceptual coordinates of queer life, to articulate a subjective sense of being (and being *differently*) in the world. Understanding cinematic space in expansive terms—as comprising "the field of the screen, the psychological space of the actor, the area of experience and geography that the film covers"[7]—I move across various registers to address not only how the erotic body articulates itself in and through space, but also the multiple ways filmmakers play with cinematic form to reorient spectatorial perception.

The prism of space also acts as a discursive fulcrum for the two other fields that I engage in this study: modern French thought and queer theory. To trace the nexus of spatiality and sexuality on film is both to encounter the notion of experiential space (or what Henri Lefebvre calls *lived* space) and to "engage in a spatial politics"—an activity that has been central to French social and political thought, as Welch and Austin both suggest. The relationship between sexuality and space has also preoccupied queer theorists and social geographers, who have turned their attention to such varied topics as gay cruising and cultures of public sex; the historical formation of gay districts and concomitant politics of erotic "dezoning"; the diverging experience of queers in urban and rural contexts; the intersecting roles that gender, sexuality, and race play in the constitution of queer zones; economies of sex tourism, both past and present; and the geopolitics of same-sex expression within an uneven globalized frame. Moreover, recent years have seen growing appeals to "space" as a heuristic that serves articulate ideas and ideals about representational equity and spatial justice in academic and activist circles alike; just consider the discursive currency of terms such as "(de)centering," or phrases such as "taking up space" within the cultural idioms of the day. It is my contention that this alignment of what Lefebvre terms "experiential space" and "representational space," or this wedding of the phenomenological to the political, simultaneously recalls, reframes, and lends urgency to earlier traditions of spatial theorizing, which I engage afresh in the chapters that follow. This book's title is intended both to recall Lefebvre's magnus opus and to twist it to perverse effect; *The Seduction of Space* figures an invitation to take seriously the role of queer sexual desire in the production of spatial relations.

To offer a brief illustration of how spatiality and sexuality impinge on the more immediate contexts of French cinema and culture, it might be useful to revisit the example with which I opened. In *Paris 05:59,* questions of queer sex and cinematic space interact and overlap in multiple, and mutually illuminating, ways. In formal terms, we have already considered how choices of editing, lighting, and mise-en-scène in the film's underground club scene help to both emphasize the porous relations between bodies and redistribute patterns of intimacy. This resists the proprietary claims that some bodies make on other bodies and eschews a monogamous optic. Indeed, Ducastel and Martineau's decision to set their opening scene in a sex club gestures even more explicitly to the ways erotic practices shape social and institutional spaces. In *The Production of Space,* Lefebvre writes that "the spatial practice of a society *secretes* that society's space."[8] Far from some neutral, apolitical, and unremarkable backdrop against which transpires the experience of everyday life (Lefebvre's own choice metaphor here is the "blank page"), space is fundamentally dynamic; it is shaped by the practices of the public that gather in a given location. *Paris 05:59* also shows us how preventative measures against the risks of a more literal secretion also spurs a shift in the film's spatial and emotional registers. By foregrounding the use of antiretroviral technologies in the hospital scene, the filmmakers make viewers cognizant of the history and practice of HIV/AIDS prevention that, even in an age of pre- and postexposure prophylaxis, continues to complicate the sense of frictionless promised in, and by, the previous site of sexual encounter.

By choosing to set their film within (and below) the streets of Paris, Ducastel and Martineau invite us to consider how ideas of sociosexual itinerancy map onto broader genealogies of spatial exploration in French culture. Consider the film's tagline, which suggestively ties the erotic acts of *Paris 05:59* to the spatial and temporal coordinates of Paris: "Théo et Hugo s'embrassent à Château d'Eau. Ils baisent au premier Métro" (The couple kiss at Chateau d'Eau station, and they fuck in the early hours of the morning at a time that coincides with the opening of the subway). As the ad copy suggests, the circulation of bodies in the film and the circadian rhythms of the city are synergistically entwined. Ducastel underscores the central role the French capital plays by saying in an interview that the film is "a love letter to the eastern Paris that we inhabit."[9]

Moreover, the film's foregrounding of Parisian space speaks to questions of not only topophilia but also cinephilia. Situating the film within the broader constellations of French art cinema, Ducastel has remarked on its formative influences and citational strategies. The temporality of the film (an hour and a half in length, unfolding in real time) and its Parisian location recall two earlier works that explore gender, sexuality, and spatial movement through the French capital: Agnès Varda's New Wave classic *Cléo from 5 to 7* (*Cléo de 5 à 7,* 1962) and Jacques Rivette's meta-modernist *Céline and Julie Go Boating* (*Céline et Julie vont en bateau,* 1974).[10] Clear parallels can be drawn between *Paris 05:59* and *Cléo* in particular. In fact, an early screenplay for Ducastel and Martineau's project was given the provisional title *Théo de 4 à 6,* but the intertextual allusion was deemed "slightly too overdetermined." Just as Théo and Hugo are thrown together to navigate the delicate situation of possible exposure to HIV, so Varda's protagonist Cléo finds a partner in Antoine, an off-duty soldier who accompanies her in the second half of the film as she agonizingly waits for the result of her cancer screening. These films remind us that when faced with the specter of finitude, the contractions or distensions of subjective temporality, or *durée,* become ever more conspicuous. And in both examples, time-stamped intertitles are used to formally register the passing of hours and minutes. But I want to impress most on readers here that both films are interested not only in the *measuring of time* but also the *mapping of space.*

To follow characters wandering through the streets of Paris—even when empty or at the break of dawn—is, in some sense, always already to partake in the promiscuous traffic of cinematic intertextuality.[11] Keith Reader reminds us that "any consideration of how Paris is depicted in the cinema will necessarily be an intertextual one," while Mike Crang and Nigel Thrift concur that the "autopoietic cycling of Parisian mythology . . . makes the city itself a permanent intertextual field."[12] How, then, might a focus on gay cruising open new ways of thinking about spatiality in French cinema and thought? Or to frame this in more explicitly comparative terms: if *Cléo* is widely understood to emblematize modernist discourses of *flânerie* from a feminist point of view, then how might Ducastel and Martineau engage similar concerns from a gay male perspective? This book argues that the import of such a line of questioning remains inaccessible to us without some grounding in the cultural and intellectual contexts of France, so to grapple with these concerns in greater detail it is important to situate these examples within the broader parameters of French spatial thought.

The affective and sensuous contours of geography have constituted an abiding concern in French thought and culture since at least the seventeenth century, when Madeleine de Scudéry developed the allegorical landscapes of her Map of Tendre (Carte de Tendre). Elaborating what Giuliana Bruno terms a "spatial mapping of emotions," Scudéry's project laid the blueprint for a conceptual terrain that would later gain greater currency under the banner of "psychogeography."[13] To trace an intellectual history of spatial exploration in modern Paris is, perforce, to follow a well-trodden path of cultural references. This genealogy stems from the nineteenth-century poet Charles Baudelaire's *flâneur* (a figure that would later be revised and popularized by Walter Benjamin) and the surrealist excursions of André Breton's *Nadja* (1928), through to the principle of *dérive*—or drift—promoted by Guy Debord and the Situationist International. Across this constellation of cultural references, urban perambulation has been framed variously as a mode of attaining a deeper understanding of the rhythms and textures of a fractured and precipitous modernity, a conduit to artistic production, a leisurely form of pleasure-seeking, and a mode of political critique. These critical investments in wandering are also keenly felt in Michel de Certeau's "Walking in the City," wherein the author explores the critical possibilities of walking as a fugitive form of rhetoric, one that articulates the city's possibilities while evading the disciplinary effects of the urban planners up above.[14] While the homology between walking and writing that de Certeau explores is largely metaphorical, this relationship has more recently been concretized by Thierry Davila, whose work points to the entangled, coconstitutive processes of walking and artistic creation in late twentieth-century French art and culture.[15] It is therefore within this more expansive framework that we need to situate Ducastel and Martineau's attempt to cut against the bias of existing representations of spatial wandering.

Yet while it may be tempting to claim that *Paris 05:59* initiates a move away from those historically sedimented discourses of *flânerie* that we find emblematized in Varda's film, and toward a reappraisal of the subcultural and socially maligned practice of cruising, this line of argument requires careful qualification. First, to overstate this case is to risk both downplaying the importance gender plays in Varda's exploration of the city in *Cléo from 5 to 7*—and by extension the wide-ranging import of feminist engagements with this film—and treating these two modes of spatial navigation as fundamentally antagonistic. Indeed, if we take this example of how, to cite Mark W. Turner, "the cruiser frequently rubs up against the *flâneur*" as a metonymic expression of the wider stakes of this book, it is important to recognize that while queer sexual practices, of the kind screened in *Paris 05:59,* have yet to be acknowledged in French discourses on spatiality, such a focus ought not to come at the expense of eclipsing other vital avenues of inquiry. This includes explorations of space from feminist and trans perspectives, on which a growing body of scholarship continues apace.[16]

Relatedly, a closer look at *Paris 05:59* also underscores the shortcomings of predetermining the political valence of "marginal" spaces. Casting our minds back to the setting of the film's opening scene of the sex club, we would do well to heed Leo Bersani's judicious warning against overstating the liberatory potential of queer places and practices. Dispelling Dennis Altman's myth that gay bathhouses constitute spaces of "Whitmanesque democracy," Bersani counts such sites "among the most ruthlessly ranked, hierarchized, and competitive environments imaginable,"[17] while a related sentiment is expressed by Damon R. Young, who also evinces a healthy skepticism toward the "inherently radical–political valence" commonly imputed to "anonymous or depersonalized queer sexual practice."[18] The exploration of space and sexuality I advance in this book therefore resists the idealizing impulse that inflects so much writing on the burgeoning topic of "queer space." From the ersatz film theatres of Jacques Nolot to the troubled waters of Guiraudie's lake, the sites, spaces, and milieus in which queers dwell are just as likely to be spaces of antagonism as sites of comfort or refuge.

Scene Two (Bois de Boulogne, Outer Paris)

To provide a spatial and sociological counterpoint to Ducastel and Martineau's film that extends a very different vision of queer sexual subcultures, I briefly turn to another contemporary film that shares this investment in the erotic spaces of the French capital, but that does so within a very different formal, aesthetic, and social register. Claus Drexel's

Ladies of the Woods (*Au coeur du bois,* 2021) takes as its subject and setting the Bois de Boulogne—a vast parkland on the western edge of the French capital. In the daytime, the park is a site of leisure and sporting pursuits, from jogging to boating to horse racing. At night the expansive woodland plays host to a vast open air red-light district, and it is to this largely nocturnal activity that Drexel's documentary gravitates. Here, too, the history of French cinema has been central to the elaboration and circulation of the mythos of this Parisian space. The Bois de Boulogne has been a well-known site of sex work for over a century. However, the first cinematic insinuation of its thorny reputation is found in Robert Bresson's early film *The Ladies of the Bois de Boulogne* (*Les dames du bois de Boulogne,* 1945), in which the bourgeoise housewife Hélène tricks her estranged husband into marrying one of the eponymous ladies of ill repute, Agnès.[19] Almost sixty years later, the establishing scenes of Sébastien Lifshitz's social realist film *Wild Side* (2004) included shots of sex workers soliciting clients by a roadside in the Bois as a biographical shorthand for the backstory of Stéphanie, its transgender protagonist. For, as many televisual exposés since the 1990s have labored to show, the Bois de Boulogne now largely serves sex workers, many of whom are transgender women or *travestis* who hail from Latin America and former French colonies. While much popular televisual coverage of these cruising zones and places of sex work often crudely reproduces the exhibitionism it moralistically seeks to denounce, Drexel's creative documentary—which interleaves talking head interviews with vignettes of the natural environment—grants the necessary space, both physical and discursive, for the subjects to recount their experiences of the woods on their own terms.

The opening sequence is shot from the woodland looking out onto the Parisian skyline. The yellowing maple trees tell us that autumn is approaching. The park is bathed in an amber light. The roaming spotlight of the Eiffel Tower up above signals that we are on the edges of Paris—a city where the relation between center and periphery is rigidly formalized and rigorously maintained. A somber song, or Portuguese *fado,* is sung by one of the documentary's subjects:

> Things well considered, we all have our fate [*fado*]
> And one born ill fated, a better fate will not have

If this song hinges on the double meaning of the word *fado* (naming both the genre of this song and the notion of fate—*fatum* in Latin—from which its name is derived), then in the context of Drexel's film these words accrue a further subtextual valence: the ineluctable "fate" of which the woman sings attains a surplus meaning. By gesturing allegorically to ideas of gendered embodiment (the "unluckiness" of those for whom their gender does not match their assigned sex at birth), the song signals proleptically the film's thematic focus on what Emmett Harsin Drager and Lucas Platero have termed "liminal travesti geographies": the gendered, social, and spatial coordinates of bodies relegated to "the margins of time and place."[20]

We later learn that the trajectory from Latin America to Europe—one common to many of the sex workers in the film—is catalyzed by questions of gendered expression. A Peruvian woman explains in an interview that when she was young, she felt a better life in Europe was beckoning her: "I would see transsexual people who would arrive in Peru on holiday; beautiful women with feminine bodies, beautiful cars, a big house, and all of that. I thought that I might be able to do the same as them." Yet, while for many the French capital represented the hope for a livable life (metonymized visually by the roaming spotlight of the Eiffel Tower above), this liberal promise would later ring hollow. The coconstitutive effects of queerphobia, racism, linguistic barriers, and hostile immigration policing mean that the film's subjects are only able to earn a living outside the formal economy, on the fringes of the socially and legally permissible. The documentary alternates between explorations of the spatial politics of the parkland terrain (we come to learn that the discrete plots or places are organized along lines of nationality, seniority, and gender) and autobiographical accounts of the women who work there, pointing to the interplay of two spatial registers—the local and the global—which, as Karl Schoonover and Rosalind Galt powerfully argue, have grown increasingly crucial to the thinking of gender and sexuality within an expanded frame.[21]

In their groundbreaking volume *Queer Ecologies,* Catriona Mortimer-Sandilands and Bruce Erikson single out the urban park as exemplary space from which to consider historically how "landscapes have been organized to produce and promote (and prohibit) particular kinds of sexual identity and practice."[22] They write that "the naturalization (of apparently fragile) heterosexuality in the midst of a perceived proliferation of deviant sexual types and expressions began, in the mid- to late-nineteenth century, to create social anxiety about the state of white European masculinity, and the parks movement was heavily influenced by a desire to shore it up."[23] Although they are addressing an American context, these words resonate strikingly in our present discussion of the Bois de Boulogne. The park's landscaping was undertaken during Baron Haussmann's renovation of Paris in the mid-nineteenth century. Made to the measure of a bourgeois male subject, the plan's conservative ideals of spatial reordering, sanitizing, and biopolitical management were all too apparent. Yet, it is ironically the very grandeur and expansiveness of this park (roughly a tenth of the size of the capital and comparable in size to one of Paris's twenty arrondissements) and its varied landscapes (from lakes and lawns to dense woodlands far from prying eyes) that, far from shoring up normative roles, unwittingly make room for sex workers to conduct their business in relative discretion. The women of the woods partake in the spatial practice that Michel de Certeau describes in *The Practice of Everyday Life* as the "tactic" of poaching—a counterpurposing of spaces and resources to new ends.[24]

Through a combination of interviews and static shots lingering on the temporary architectures erected in the woodland, the film shows how tents and screens are used to elicit the gaze of the potential client while also allowing the women to evade the unwelcomed attention of law enforcement. We are told that these interactions are always calculated

Figure 2. *The Ladies of the Wood* (Claus Drexel, 2021). Sex workers in mobile brothels park up on the curb of the Bois de Boulogne.

according to a dialectical logic of solicitation and discretion. Often in very concrete ways, the women's space-making practices serve to delimit public, private, and erotic spheres. But just as the film is irreducible to its sociological import or prurient logics of confession, the use of space is not just purpose-driven and instrumentalized. We come to learn that the spaces of the wood contain ever-shifting architectures and that the dynamic light levels contain a strikingly expressive potential.

In a discussion of how the woodland's wild architectures form a proscenium for the film's trans aesthetic, Lena Haque notes that through cinematographic techniques of lighting and framing, "the woodland is transformed: it is no longer simply the frontier between the city and the space of relaxation for wealthy Parisians, but the wild territory of fantastic creatures who seem to have grown between the roots like flowers that roam freely around their territory."[25] The aesthetics of fantasy and fabulation that radiate across the mise-en-scène (e.g., the shrubbery bathed in the glow of amber light, the saturated neon colors that light up campervans) also acts as a form of generic resistance to the conventional trappings of cinema verité or sociological "realness" that, as Jules Gill-Peterson has powerfully argued, reveal to us more about the "desires and projective expectations" of cinema's audiences than trans or *travesti* sex workers themselves.[26] The forest space—its theatricality, mutability, and capacity for aesthetic reshaping or landscaping—plays a key role in the film's ambition to reimagine documentary aesthetics in ways that feel neither dispassionately sterile nor gawkishly prurient.[27] Moreover, the film's poetic depiction of its material surroundings allows Drexel to sidestep the essentialist trappings of discourses on nature that continue to act as a bone of contention in queer and trans ecological critique. *Ladies of the Wood* provides an object lesson in queer cinema's capacity to imbue the geophysical world with new significations.

Speaking strictly in terms of time and space, not a lot separates Ducastel and Martineau's *Paris 05:59* from Drexel's *Ladies of the Wood*. There exists five years between the films' theatrical releases and five and a half miles between the films' locations, to be precise. Yet the sexual geographies these two Parisian films present, and the questions they invite, diverge considerably. While this book is not comparative in its method, I nonetheless want to consider how French film's dense network of intertexts and common geographic reference points encourage us to bring cinematic objects into conversation. This allows us to reflect on the unevenness of France's sexual geographies and the frictionless access to space that is granted to some bodies and denied to others. On the one hand, this book is interested in treating cinema as a powerful representational index that can tell us much about questions of spatial justice (or the question of who enjoys "the right to the city," to invoke Lefebvre). But this book also explores the queer affordances and potentialities of cinematic form—its ability to "take place," reconfigure its spatiotemporal coordinates, invest places with new meanings, and shine new light on familiar locations—quite literally in the case of both examples above. Cinematography, I argue, is a crucial tool in the counternormative repurposing of space and place.

The Map and the Territory

To establish the parameters of the sexual geographies I explore in this book, it is useful to revisit a key insight from Michel de Certeau. In "Walking in the City" he advances the idea that the spatial practices of the mobile urban subject have an *enunciative* function. The walker's movements produce "a rhetoric of walking" that can be deciphered by semiologists of space and theorists of the everyday; these movements "encode" information about them and their desires (whether conscious or unconscious); and the "text" they produce as they weave throughout the city's streets comes to be informed by social and embodied particulars. Although there are clear shortcomings to this homology between walking and writing (not least its predication on able-bodiedness), I invoke this idea to clarify and qualify my book's own orientation toward certain social geographies, cinematic spaces, and cultural objects—one that is no doubt informed by my own subject position as a white gay man. By taking the spatial practice of *cruising* as its guiding motif and conceptual point of departure, this book often leads us toward scenes of public sex and, by extension, a largely (though not exclusively) gay male lifeworld. To avoid any ambiguity, this book represents *a* journey through, rather than *the* account of, French queer cinema—and I want to insist here on the attenuating force of the indefinite article.

Given that a conceptual focus on space runs the risk of precluding historical considerations, a brief note on the periodization of my corpus is necessary.[28] This book focuses primarily on work produced in the last thirty years. Many of the filmmakers I discuss in the following chapters came of age in the 1970s and 1980s but started making films from the late 1990s and early 2000s onward—a period that exists at one remove from the most acute phase of the HIV/AIDS crisis in France but continues to exist under its penumbral shadow. So, while the formal experimentation of earlier figures such as Jean Genet, Chantal Akerman, and Cyril Collard are undoubtable touchstones for many of the filmmakers discussed here, they do not constitute this book's primary objects. This book combines its discussions of the minor works of filmmakers who are internationally renowned (e.g., Christophe Honoré) with work by filmmakers, such as Jacques Nolot and Vincent Dieutre, who have yet to receive their rightful place in queer and French film history. To make space for this lesser-known work, I foreground the autobiographical particulars of some of these queer auteurs and largely sidestep the work of more well-known directors such as François Ozon, Céline Sciamma, and Robin Campillo, who have all benefited from more extensive scholarly engagement. It will not have escaped some readers' attention, however, that the spatial idiom that I invoke above ("making space") conceals an important irony: namely, that the cinematic corpus I assemble often *reflects,* rather than *disrupts,* a white gay male hegemony. My intention is to read cinematic texts against the grain to critically reflect on the fault lines that emerge in French gay culture, particularly the question of race. As such, I hope readers find in this book an important critique of the racial blind spots that continue to make the terrain of French queer cinema an uneven space, and one that *reflects on* those structural iniquities that mean queer filmmakers of color continue not to have much space.

This book's account of how sexuality informs and inflects our understanding of cinematic space rests at the intersection of multiple disciplines. Chapter 1 therefore provides an overview to the theoretical frame that underpins the rest of the study. While the three fields I engage with in this book—film studies, queer theory, and spatial thought—are initially presented discretely, the chapter goes on to bring them into dialogue to reveal their respective blind spots and mutual resonances. I argue that while a "French" influence might be detected at the substrate of both queer theory and contemporary sociopolitical thinking on space, the surprising paucity of French-authored scholarship operating at the nexus of sexuality and space is itself symptomatic of the uneasy place that questions of sex and gender occupy within the nation's illustrious spatial tradition. Drawing attention to the gaps and omissions in spatial thought, this book suggests that France's cultural production—and more specifically, its cinema—both provides an opportunity to move beyond these shortcomings and sheds light on contemporary political and aesthetic concerns. The subsequent chapters address work by queer filmmakers, paying particular focus to locations in which scenes of cruising take place: from the movie theater to the museum, from Paris's central streetscapes to its banlieues, from abandoned factories to lush lakefronts.

Across four core chapters, I consider how specific invocations of place in cinema present opportunities to revisit key discussions in film and queer theory. This is notably the case in chapter 2, which looks at the work of Jacques Nolot. I begin by reading Nolot's *Porn Theatre* (*La chatte à deux têtes,* 2002), a film that explores cruising and sex work in a movie theater in Paris's Pigalle red-light district alongside the film theory of his onetime lover, Roland Barthes. Such a reading seeks to queerly revivify the ossified terrain of 1970s apparatus theory by drawing attention to the historical continuum between homosocial practices of cinemagoing and cultures of public sex. The second part of the chapter moves away from spaces of film exhibition(ism) and public sex and toward the private sphere to consider the roles material objects and domestic spaces play in Nolot's *Before I Forget* (*Avant que j'oublie,* 2007). Just as the turn-of-the-century porn theater presents us with a dialectical image, an archive of queer sociality underwritten by historical loss, his apartment similarly acts as a repository of a life in decline.

Racial exclusion surfaces conspicuously in Nolot's final film. In one scene, the filmmaker presents a sexual transaction with a young North African hustler in Paris. In another, we listen to wealthy white Parisian men project their sexual fantasies onto the space of the banlieue, the primary site of social and geographical exclusion in contemporary France. Chapter 3 explores these dynamics in greater depth. First, I turn to Sébastien Lifshitz's *Open Bodies* (*Les corps ouverts,* 1998) to explore how cruising, and the cognate term "loitering," attain a different valence when used to describe the movements of racialized bodies. I then travel across the boulevard Périphérique—the ring road that separates Paris from its much-maligned suburbs—to explore Christophe Honoré's *Man at Bath* (*Homme au bain,* 2010). This short film, in which the generic codes of postcolonial pornography and art cinema promiscuously intermingle, allows us to think about the aesthetic and social codes that underwrite both the French tradition of the *cinéma de banlieue* and ethical concerns about the eroticization of France's social and urban margins.

Chapter 4 turns to experimental documentary filmmaking. It centers on the work of Vincent Dieutre, a filmmaker whose penchant for travel is felt across the entirety of his filmography. Space is a notable feature in Dieutre's work: some of his films are tightly focused on specific urban locations (notably Paris and Rome), while some of his travelogues trace queer geographies across Europe. The chapter begins by discussing his own neighborhood, the eponymous Parisian district of *Bonne nouvelle* (2001), to explore the fraught relationship between queerness and multiculturalism presented in this short film. Second, I offer a detailed account of *Tenebrae Lessons* (*Leçons de ténèbres,* 1999), a film that takes us across various cities in Europe to offer a wide-ranging meditation on gay aesthetics, curatorial practice, and sexual and archival cruising. The final part of this chapter, on the 2013 first-person documentary *Jaurès,* returns us to the urban fabric of Paris. The film is framed almost entirely from the aperture of an apartment window. Dieutre's architectural focus on an urban intersection invites us to consider processes of, and discourses on, queer cinematic worldmaking alongside the notion of intersectionality. This remains a sticking point within French political discourse due to its perceived incompatibility with Republican ideals. A reading of the film against the grain of its filmmaker's intention allows us to think more expansively about sexuality's relation to other matrices of power and its role in accounts of spatial injustice. Through the bias of Dieutre's films, I continue to rethink the representational politics of urban marginality, focusing particularly on the entanglement of geopolitical and racial alterity.

Chapter 5 considers representations of queer sex beyond the city by way of Alain Guiraudie's cinema. Here I explore how the southwestern director's work throws into acute relief the urban bias that has overwhelmingly characterized representations of French queer life. First, I look at his early short films to suggest that while they lack any concrete engagement with same-sexual desire we can nonetheless sense Guiraudie working through, in an embryonic form, his later interests in cruising and homosocial bonding. Such themes are at play in *That Old Dream*

That Moves (*Ce vieux rêve qui bouge,* 2001), set in a steel factory shortly destined for decommission. This critically neglected example of "slow cinema" explores the erotic and economic forces that intertwine to produce normative masculinities in a postindustrial setting. Finally, I turn to the lakeside setting of his 2013 breakthrough thriller *Stranger by the Lake* (*L'inconnu du lac*) to analyze the surprising ecological dimensions of sociosexual practices. Drawing on recent ecological discourses that contest the "antisocial" turn in queer theory, this chapter considers how an optics of cruising might reattune spectators to the richness of the material world. Cruising need not be conceived of as the unique preserve of the urban subject; the slower temporalities and sense of spatial expansiveness associated with Guiraudie's film invite different, though equally suggestive, forms of deliberative spectatorship.

The arc of this book follows a roughly centrifugal movement. It moves from Paris—which has long been considered the epicenter of French queer cinema—through to semirural sites of postindustrial entropy, before terminating its southward trajectory in a rural lakeside setting in Provence. To set in motion this book's multileveled exploration of *spatiality* and *sexuality,* and to clear the ground for the cinematic exploration to follow, I now turn to explore both of these terms (and their fertile intersections) as "traveling concepts" that circulate across a number of cultural contexts and disciplinary fields—from French cultural studies and queer theory and geography, onward into the realm of film and media.[29]

1

THE SEDUCTION OF SPACE IN FRENCH QUEER FILM AND THEORY

> A whole history remains to be written about spaces—which would at the same time be the history of powers (both of these terms in the plural)—from the great strategies of geopolitics to the little tactics of habit.
>
> —Michel Foucault

French

From the spiral escargot that curls from Paris's epicenter and unfurls toward its outer limits, and the hard-edged *hexagone* that delimits the "metropolitan" territory, through to the idea of the Francosphère, France's geographies, histories, and mythologies are often articulated with recourse to spatial figures. Yet while shapes are often used to describe the territory in ways that feel innocuous or merely descriptive, this belies the fact that these tropes perform the political work of shaping France's social and cultural landscapes. Consider, for example, how the notion of the "hexagon," whose origins stem back to the late eighteenth century, now provides a common byword for France's mainland territory, having migrated from the realm of "geographic observation" to the annals of "cultural history."[1] The sharp-angled hexagon exists in tension, both geometrically and geographically, with the more soft-edged, nebulous, and diffuse concept of the Francosphère. A contemporary revision of the idea of "la Francophonie" (a previously favored concept whose territorial claim was expressed in linguistic terms that had grown increasingly untenable), the Francosphère names a broader sphere of cultural and geopolitical influence. And despite the concerted efforts to redefine it, its contours still bear residual traces of France's colonial past. Such examples highlight the subtle but wide-ranging influence of spatial tropes in the nation's imaginary; both are inextricably entwined with the exercise of power in France, its distribution of political capital, and attendant logics of inclusion and exclusion.

Shaped by the legacies of Jacobinism, France's administrative organization is characterized by a strong and robust statist tradition that asserts Paris as its cultural and political core. Even within the greater Parisian region, the boulevard Périphérique—the capital's outer ring road, erected in 1958 at the start of the Fifth Republic—creates a further distinction between central Paris (known anachronistically as "Paris *intra-muros*" or an "intramural" Paris) and the suburbs or banlieue that entrenches both racial tensions and socioeconomic fault lines. In his work on spatiality and justice, Mustafa Dikeç notes that the banlieue "no longer serves merely as a geographical reference or an administrative concept, but stands for alterity, insecurity and deprivation."[2] This view that tallies with author François Maspéro's description of the boulevard Périphérique in Dantean terms, as "a circular purgatory, with the paradise of Paris at its center."[3]

France's fondness for spatial metaphor is perhaps matched by its proclivity for abstract thought. But lest we assume that these tropes exist in a discursive realm at one remove from concrete realities, we need look no further than the architectural fabric of modern Paris—both the Haussmannian facades of the city and the concrete *cordon sanitaire* that delimits it—to find a materialization of the state's ambition for political regulation. Given that the ideals of the modern French nation are wrought by steel and chiseled in stone, an interrogation of its built environments must, perforce, offer us an insight into its ideological makeup.

In *Thinking Space* Michael Crang and Nigel Thrift place special emphasis on France as a producer and exporter of spatial theory by foregrounding the intellectual legacy of both its spatial theorists (e.g., Henri Lefebvre and Michel de Certeau) and its more poetic thinkers (from Gaston Bachelard to Georges Perec) on the broader "spatial turn" in the humanities. Drawing particular attention to the French capital, they suggest that Paris acted as a discursive fulcrum point for, and physical home to, spatial thinkers and practitioners whose intellectual contributions and enduring legacies would radiate far beyond the hexagon. If social theory has long been "haunted" by the "spectre [of] nineteenth-century Paris" as they contend, then the question of social space continues "to revolve around, return to, and [be] orchestrated by arguments grounded in the history of the Parisian metropolis."[4]

Offering further weight and texture to these contentions, Kristin Ross elaborates a theory of the "spatial event" to offer an account of how symbolic and material forces shape France's culture and its political imaginary. She situates the unfolding events of the Paris Commune against a wider geopolitical backdrop, describing the 1870s as comprising "two very significant *spatial* movements or events. It was the decade that saw the formation of a consciousness conducive to producing a colonialist, expeditionary class. The speed and mathematical directness with which the railroad proceeds through space, joining together previously inaccessible places as coordinate in a systematized grid, had already begun, within Europe, to make space *geographic*. Throughout the 1870s France prepared to accelerate that movement in to a geopolitical one, to expand and project onto a global scale Haussmann's inter-urban 'fantasy of the straight line.'"[5] Ross's influential study, *The Emergence of Social Space,* from which the above passage is drawn, intercalates a number of spatial registers: a bottom–up politics of contestation emerging from Paris's streets, political "fantasies" of urban planning and infrastructure, and the geopolitics of empire. Together they helped to forge the distinctive political imaginary of modern France while also speaking to broader structural forces that are far from exclusive to the country. (Indeed, when shorn of its final sentence, this passage might well be taken as a description of unfolding of urban modernity writ large.) "The post-Haussmann social division of the city" raises for her the question of "who, among its citizens, has a 'right to the city'"—a phrase that registers her intellectual debt to Lefebvre. Ross's description of the antagonism between new radical political formations (those emblematized by the Paris Commune) and disciplinarian modes of urban reorganization (the social blueprint that was concretized in Haussmann's Paris), enjoins us to consider questions of spatiality in political terms and, by extension, to reframe the political in distinctly spatial terms. For if late nineteenth-century Paris offered a historical instantiation of what Ross terms the "emergence of social space," then it is only in the France of the mid-twentieth century that we would see the emergence of a sustained theoretical idiom through which such a phenomenon might be analyzed.

In their volume, Crang and Thrift ask us to consider a question that will inform the methodological backbone of this book: what happens when we "think through the places, and the imaginations of places, that produce spatial theory?"[6] Put another way, while the work of theory often aspires toward abstraction—ridding itself of concrete particulars and contingent details in a bid to proffer a universalizing claim—there is much to be gleaned by resituating these discourses in the national contexts from which they emerge. Theoretical concerns with space have been at the forefront of the French national imaginary since the 1950s, when the subject started to receive sustained treatment from several diverse conceptual vantage points: from Situationists to phenomenologists, from state architects to anthropologists of the everyday.

Henri Lefebvre's magnum opus, *The Production of Space,* serves as an important touchstone in critical theories of space. The study offers novel understandings of how space is both conceptualized and actualized that leaves a lasting contribution to intellectual thought in a way that resonates far beyond the immediate remit of Marxist geography. Here Lefebvre exceeded the bounds of discrete disciplines as he sought to elaborate a "pluridisciplinary" method appropriate to his multifaceted object of study. Drawing particular attention to what he called *l'espace vécu,* or lived space, he sought to analyze spatial relations at the level of the perceiving subject, thereby marking a decisive rupture with the apolitical abstractions of Euclidean geometric space. Far from constituting a neutral backdrop to our engagement with the world, space, as per Lefebvre's understanding, is the "product" of complex social, political, and cultural forces. More specifically, its ontology comprises a complex admixture of three key elements: the aforementioned *espace vécu* as it is revealed to a sensing subject through spatial practices, embodied experience, and sensory phenomena; *l'espace perçu*—"representations of space" as they are formally abstracted, codified, and rendered legible through processes of mapping; and *l'espace conçu*—the mental spaces of representation, connotation, and ideology that become superimposed onto the geophysical world. Though Lefebvre notes the attendant risks of "introducing divisions and so defeating the object of the exercise, which is to rediscover the unity of the productive process," the three constitutive aspects of space need to be understood relationally, advancing the pursuit of what James Williams calls "a unitary theory of space, or 'spatiology,' involving a rapprochement between physical space . . . , mental space . . . , and social space."[7] Rather than laying claim to a field, Lefebvre opened up a rich site of inquiry that I'll describe for the purposes of my argument as French spatial theory—a term I use to name a loose body of thought whose adherents had shared interests in the theorization of the everyday, whose shared lineages of political contestation stemmed from 1871 to 1968, and who were in part products, and critics, of the symbolic overdeterminism of France, whether understood as a geographic territory or a geopolitical abstraction.[8]

Another indispensable figure here is Michel de Certeau, whom Verena Andermatt Conley describes as both a "foil and complement to Lefebvre."[9] While de Certeau's own theory of space can't be absorbed seamlessly into the triadic schema set out above, we can broadly deduce that his definition of space as a dynamic site of lived experience and political potentiality hews closely to the notion of Lefebvre's *espace vécu,* whereas his description of place implies an "indicator of stability" and fixity that aligns with the register of *espace perçu.* A distillation of de Certeau's interest in space can be found in "Walking in the City," an essay written under the sign of semiotic theory. While I recognize that by alighting on this text I am guiding readers toward a work whose status as well-trodden terrain is perhaps rivaled only by the urban metropolis of Manhattan that de Certeau describes, I momentarily dwell on a passage to bring into view another important element of spatial theorizing germane to the present discussion: the notion of spatial practices. Taking the dense fabric of Lower Manhattan as his object, de Certeau considers urban space from two diverging perspectives. The first, glimpsed from the vantage point of the World Trade Center, lends the city a monolithic, static character. The second, street-level perspective aligns with the "ordinary practitioners" of the city, who "write" the city's text through the practice of walking, thus enunciating the possibilities of spatial governance.[10] De Certeau explains, "If it is true that a spatial order organizes an ensemble of possibilities (e.g., by a place in which one can move) and interdictions (e.g., by a wall that prevents one from going farther), then the walker actualizes some of these possibilities. In that way, he makes them exist as well as emerge. But he also moves them about and invents others, since the crossing, drifting away, or improvisation of walking privilege, transform or abandon spatial elements."[11] In this description of the stark socioeconomic stratification of Manhattan, which he evocatively describes as "a texturology in which extremes coincide," de Certeau harnesses the political connotations of verticality before describing the emergent conditions of possibility for a ground-level politics that reshapes and reformulates the spatial order from the bottom up.[12] In contradistinction to the coolly detached "strategies" of urban planners as they are elaborated from on high, he emphasizes the tactics of the street dwellers who, in Crang's words, "take the predisposition of the world and make it over."[13] Born out of necessity, tactics emerge at the grassroots level to negotiate alternative uses of urban space. De Certeau's emphasis on the tactics and praxis of everyday life offers an important rejoinder to the abstractions of spatial strategies. In essence, not only is space not given to us as a Kantian *a priori,* but the spatial practices of mobile subjects entail world-making capacities; built into his political ontology of space, like that of Lefebvre, is a capacity for reshaping, carving out, contesting a dominant spatiotemporal order. (This tendency to conceive politics *spatially* anticipated what Dikeç would go on to term the "ruptural politics" of more recent philosophers like Jacques Rancière.)

The French spatial theory that emerged from the post-1968 period sought to recast the sites of everyday life—spaces that, by virtue of their ordinariness, are susceptible to the ideological creep of depoliticization—as a field of ideological coordinates constantly engaged in a dialectical tug of war between the spatial practices of populations and the representations of space proffered by "planners, urbanists, technocratic subdividers," and between mobile bodies and a static built environment.[14] There was, however, a limitation to this body of thought: while class served as the primary lens through which spatial experience became differentiated, concerns with other social particulars and forms of difference largely fell by the wayside. What, if anything, does French spatial theory have to tell us about questions of sexuality, among other vectors of lived experience that organize, differentiate, and orient bodies in space?

Crang writes of de Certeau that his "peripatetic intellectual wanderings need to be read as a refusal of disciplinary authority, continually destabilizing boundaries."[15] Given that I am interested in moving away from general accounts of lived space and toward those informed by sexuality, I note how the suggestive spatial language deployed to describe the theorist's epistemological errancy here might be read as an invitation to stray, waywardly, into other conceptual fields that are similarly marked by a foundational "refusal of disciplinary authority" and invested in "destabilizing boundaries." This is to say, we might recognize here certain pronounced affinities with the lineaments of queer theory.

The myriad questions that come into view when we refract French spatial theory through the prism of sexuality appear to be far reaching: Do these thinkers offer any answers to Phil Hubbard's question of why the "actions of urban designers, planners and governors produce particular types of city in which some sexual predilections and tastes are catered for, but others excluded"?[16] Do questions of marginality—understood along the axes of gender, race, or sexuality—substantively inform responses to Lefebvre's question of "who has the right to the city"? At first glance, however, sexuality does not appear to be addressed substantively in this body of thought. While Lefebvre and de Certeau both focus on the body's role in spatial perception and production, the question of how sexual nonnormativity and embodied differences inform and inflect understandings of spatiality remain a critical blind spot.[17]

Michael Brown characterizes passing references to sexuality in Lefebvre's *The Production of Space* as "random," "desultory," and "complicit in heteronormativity," while Claire Colebrook's reading of de Certeau similarly notes a lack of engagement with sex.[18] Similar criticisms extend to the work of a second generation of spatial theorists emerging in the wake of French spatial theorists. In a discussion of the field of postmodern geography (a loose group of prominent theorists including Edward Soja and David Harvey, who were active in the 1990s and often considered the intellectual progeny of Lefebvre), Victor Burgin notes how questions of fantasy and desire—both of which are central to the Lefebvrian category of *l'espace perçu*—remain occluded.[19] In a similar vein, J. Jack Halberstam highlights the "active exclusion of sexuality as a category of analysis [for these theorists] precisely because desire has been cast by neo-Marxists as part of a ludic body politics that obstructs the 'real' work of activism."[20] Halberstam's argument, which points to a broader tension in cultural geography, lays bare an implicit politics of epistemological value whereby "hard" categories of sociological difference such as class supersede "softer" considerations, such as sexuality, which are considered secondary. By diagnosing these tendencies, we indeed find echoes of a common refrain in queer theory, from Gayle Rubin's landmark pronouncement that "the time has come to think about sex" despite the topic's routine characterization as "a frivolous diversion from the more critical problems of poverty," through to Judith Butler's equally forceful imperative to analyze sexuality outside the sphere of the "merely cultural" to which it is routinely relegated.[21]

Before we consider these lines of argument in more detail, I return briefly to address the intellectual contexts of France, given that questions of national specificity are often lost in more general discussions of the "spatial turn." I argue that the primacy of class as an analytic lens in postmodern geography that Halberstam highlights also bears the residual trace of a distinctly French conception of spatial politics. The very arrangement of Paris—that privileged site for the "production" of spatial theory, as per Crang and Thrift—is itself a negative index of a long tradition of class-based contestation. The wide boulevards of Haussmann's modern renovation of Paris, for example, are a material manifestation of the need to control and quell protests, or *manifestations,* arising in the city. Given that street-based protests, and the "ruptural" politics to which they give rise, are deeply etched into the national psyche, it thereby makes sense that the dominant way of imagining spatial politics that we find in work by Lefebvre and de Certeau, among others, are shaped by, and figure a response to, this class-based tradition. To take Halberstam's critique in yet another dimension: the occlusion of sexuality from the remit of spatial inquiry tallies, moreover, with a characteristically French hostility to the politics of difference, insofar as the very notion of identity-based rights chafes against the abstract ideals of the French Republic. In effect, the reappraisal of France's illustrious tradition of spatial thought through the lens of such "epiphenomenal" categories as sexuality not only brings into view the normative investments of its key theorists, such as Lefebvre, de Certeau, and their intellectual heirs; but also exposes the identitarian fault line in France's political discourse tout court.

While the abovementioned appraisals of the occlusion of sexuality within the oeuvre of Lefebvre and de Certeau are largely accurate and evenhanded, they do not yield a complete picture. For while their work is riddled with blind spots, it nonetheless offers us the conceptual tools to enact a mode of autocritique. Interestingly, the scant references to desire that Lefebvre *does* make in *The Production of Space* preempts the later concerns of queer theorists in surprising ways. Writing against the creeping hegemony of "abstract space," which Lefebvre laments as one of the more deleterious effects of capitalist modernity, he writes of how the "sensory," "sensual," and "sexual" are allowed to exist only within the "narrowest leeway [of] representational spaces"—that is to say, within the marginal spheres of artistic or (merely) cultural production.[22] He goes on to note, in a striking passage, that "a characteristic contradiction of abstract space consists in the fact that, although it denies the sensual and the sexual, its only immediate point of reference is genitality: the family unit, the type of dwelling . . . fatherhood and motherhood, and the assumption that fertility and fulfilment are identical."[23] While there is a risk in overstating the queer implications of his statement, Lefebvre's acknowledgment of a sphere of pleasures outside the social scripts of what would later come to be known as "reproductive futurity" leaves open the possibility of a more thoroughgoing, and less debilitatingly normative, application of his thought.[24] Similarly, while Colebrook argues that "sex" is "a case not tackled by Certeau," this is not to say that scholars working in queer studies have not sought inspiration from his thought. In fact, the act of weaving the fraught question of sexuality into the very fabric of de Certeau's work might be seen, wittingly or unwittingly, to replicate the very notion of the "tactics" the theorist so deftly outlines elsewhere. In the first volume of *The Invention of Everyday Life,* de Certeau advocates the practice of "poaching" (*la perruque*), a tactic of resistance whereby the minoritarian subject pilfers preexisting materials and resources with a view to repurposing them to new ends. In a metareflexive gesture, then, the conceptual tools gleaned from French spatial thought might themselves be creatively repurposed to attend to its own sexual blind spots. We need look no further than George Chauncey's historical reappraisal of New York—the very textual ground of de Certeau's most famous analysis—from the perspective of its vibrant queer scenes. Implicitly invoking the idea of poaching as a clandestine and inconspicuous mode of spatial appropriation, Chauncey here shows how queers "reterritorialized the city in order to construct a gay city in the midst of (and often invisible to) the normative city."[25]

In the postwar intellectual milieu I'm interested in sketching here, the figure who comes the closest to offering a thoroughgoing meditation on spatiality and sexuality is Foucault, whose notion of the heterotopia, developed in his seminal essay "Of Other Places," entails significant possibilities for thinking space queerly. This purposefully capacious term names an ensemble of sites and spaces that, according to Foucault, are both anchored in the real work but rework and contest its dominant spatial, temporal, and sociocultural norms in various ways. In the essay, Foucault considers spatiotemporal relations within the *longue durée* of Western thought, arguing that while temporal concerns weighed heavy on the episteme of the nineteenth century, "the present epoch will perhaps be above all the epoch of space."[26] The perspicacity of this statement is not only borne out in the work of Foucault's contemporaries but is further amplified in light of the "spatial turn" that touched on many disciplines in the humanities and social sciences following (and no doubt partially as a result of) the essay's publication. While we can identify certain similarities between the essay and Lefebvre's conception of spatiality, such as his critique of commonsense understandings of space as "homogenous and empty," and resonances between his meditations on "countersites" and de Certeau's reflections on tactics, spatial contestation, and minoritarian dwelling, Foucault's originality lies in his understanding of space's fundamentally *relational* nature, and his interest in how disciplinary architectures shape the human subject. In an apt summary of this essay's enduring legacy (and one that looks beyond its hallowed status as the urtext of postmodern geography) James S. Williams writes that he "leaves open the possibility of a new kind of 'spaceplay' capable of generating new practices, identities and subjectivities."[27]

Though sex surfaces only fleetingly in the essay (the brothel is mentioned as an archetypical heterotopia), such "new practices" would later surface in an addendum to his thinking on space and relationality. In a string of posthumously published interviews conducted in the late 1970s and early 1980s, Foucault spoke with atypical candor about the politics of queer subcultural practices. In "The Gay Science," he discussed the need for relational experimentation and "unexpected combinations and fabrications of pleasure" as an ethical imperative to figure alternative modes of relational possibility. Meanwhile, in the later "Friendship as a Way of Life," he noted that homosexuality constituted a "historic occasion to reopen affective and relational virtualities, not so much through the intrinsic qualities of the homosexual but because the 'slantwise' position of the latter, as it were, the diagonal lines he can lay out in the social fabric allow these virtualities to come to light."[28] The implications of this enigmatic statement—in particular its invocation of the formal correspondences between homosexual practices and spatial orientations—has spurred much thinking at the nexus of space and sexuality. The motif of obliqueness has figured as a touchstone for queer theorists from Sara Ahmed and Leo Bersani to John Paul Ricco, each of whom note the fortuitous connection between Foucault's invocation of "slantwise" positionalities and the spatial valence of the term "queer."[29] Further impressing on us the need to reread Foucault as a thinker of both sexuality and spatiality, Philip Howell makes a compelling case for geographers to take literally Foucault's invocation of "sites of sexuality," or spaces in which sexual and gendered norms attain an "affective intensification"; while Paul B. Preciado draws on Foucault to understand the built environment as a social *dispositif* for sexual and gendered regulation.[30] Phil Hubbard, who has traced these two privileged objects of Foucauldian inquiry, space and sexuality, in tandem across the philosopher's oeuvre, argues that they are not only complementary, but also consubstantial: "To paraphrase Michel Foucault," he notes, "a history of sexualities is therefore a history of spaces."[31]

Before I consider the more recent queer theories of space that have emerged out of these discourses—which will entail a transatlantic move from the intellectual milieu of post-1968 Paris to the American academy (a move that is interestingly prefigured by the geographic trajectory of Foucault's own life)—I return briefly to the national context of France to consider how questions of sexuality and queerness might cast new light on this chapter's opening lines. If Lefebvre taught us to remain alert to the mobilization of spatial rhetoric, especially as it is pressed in the service of political power, then how might these critical insights be brought to bear on an understanding of present-day France?

Where better to start than with the first spatial figure we encountered in this chapter: the hexagon. A preeminent symbol within the "mental space" of the French nation, the hexagon is by its nature an exclusionary trope insofar as it refers solely to the country's metropolitan territory (i.e., France's outer territories, many of which were gained through colonial expansion, do not figure on this mental map). Yet the notion of the hexagon in France's geopolitical imaginary also informs the country's sexual geographies, as Mehammed Amadeus Mack has recently shown. In *Sexagon: Muslims, France, and the Sexualization of National Culture,* he returns to the hexagon to mount a critique of how France's logics of inclusion and exclusion—the shape of its territory—are also informed by questions of sexuality: "[France's] borders increasingly have come to be defined through values such as gay-friendliness, secular feminism, and metrosexuality, on the one hand, and the condemnation of immigrant and working-class machismo on the other."[32] Using one of the privileged symbols of the Republic against itself, Mack's idea of the "sexagon" describes how modern France's increasing appeal to the language of sexual liberalism to delineate ideas of nationhood and belonging can serve as an alibi for strategies of exclusion. Transposing a line of argument that first crystallized in Jasbir Puar's influential critique of homonationalism onto an understanding of contemporary French society and culture, he draws attention to how the turn to champion sexual diversity ought not to be understood as a discourse of inclusion, but rather is symptomatic of the suppression or displacement of other forms of difference, notably race and religion. As Mack explains, "Sexual vocabularies became the best platform in postmulticulturalist Europe to symbolically strip those who had always become French of their 'Frenchness.'"[33] These structural tensions are played out at a number of sites and scales, from the banlieue to the real and imagined spaces of the French postcolony.

Queer

Just as spatial metaphors are often mobilized to lend symbolic weight to France's political structures, so the language of spatiality suffuses discourses of sexuality. To take an obvious example, we might consider the connotations of social propriety and moral rectitude attached to the term "straight" as opposed to its more oblique counterpart "queer," or indeed the semantically freighted concept of the closet (in French, *le placard*) that frames understandings of sexual self-nomination according to a binary opposition between "in" or "out," disclosure or concealment. While some spatial metaphors are relatively persistent, such as the closet—which, according to Eve Kosofsky Sedgwick's field-defining analysis, operates synecdochally to highlight the discursive production of sexual subjecthood—others are more malleable and readily redeployed to address new contexts and social formations. For example, while the spatial practice of cruising has long referred to the physical movement of bodies partaking in a choreography of sexual conquest, the term has acquired a new valence in light of shifting patterns of sexual consumption. Cruising's definitional expansion reflects a broader shift in focus away from physical spaces and their attendant sociospatial apparatuses to newly emerging virtual spheres. In French, *la drague numérique* (cybercruising) refers to a panoply of ways of seeking out and engaging with queer bodies, providing modes of erotic communion that need not even be predicated on physical touch. Though we ought, rightly, to be wary of leveling the specificities of spatial motifs as we move between language areas (there exist important nuances between the English *cruising* and the French *drague,* as urban anthropologist Emmanuel Redoutey has shown), many spatial tropes operate across linguistic registers given that they pertain to the category of "orientational metaphors" which, as George Lakoff and Mark Johnson argue, are not wholly arbitrary by virtue of their grounding "in both physical and cultural experience."[34] How, then, has a concern with nonnormative sexualities come to impinge on the field of human geography? And, in a reverse gesture, how the language of spatiality has come to inform queer theory?

Above I suggested that while an underlying motivation of French spatial theory was to complicate dominant understandings of space by affording greater attention to lived experience and minority practices, certain biases and blind spots have left this ambition unfulfilled. Yet the task of "putting sexualities on the map," to borrow the phrase of David Bell and Gill Valentine, requires careful consideration, not least because there exists a clear tension between the definitional fixity of "homosexual" and the fluidity of "queer," and because the ambition to "map" sexualities raises fundamental ethical and methodological questions about how or why nonnormative sexualities should be mapped.[35] For, as Mack demonstrated above, the corrective action of "tacking" queer sexualities onto geography in an effort to more accurately reflect the variegation of social space runs the risk of elucidating only a single dimension of nonnormative experience, all the while eclipsing others. (And on this point, Puar goes further, arguing that "claiming of space—any space, even the claiming of queer space—is a process informed by histories of colonization.")[36]

The growing interest in the nexus of sexuality and space over recent decades has spurred diverse research agendas across a number of fields: from anthropology to human geography, from queer theory to ecocriticism. Entire subdisciplines have been formed to gain critical purchase on this nexus, from empirical work on the "geographies of sexuality" through to more speculative work in queer theory. The mid to late 1990s saw a steady stream of research into sexuality from within the field of human geography. Bell and Valentine's *Mapping Desire,* which represents one of the first encounters between geography and the then-emerging field of queer theory, was indeed born out of a critical frustration with earlier work from the 1970s and 1980s in the field of "gay and lesbian geographies."[37] Multidisciplinary in its ambition, it sought to "think about the ways in which the spatial and the sexual constitute one another."[38] Engaging a broadly Lefebvrian understanding of spatial production, Bell and Valentine argued that the presence "of queer bodies in particular locations forces people to realize . . . that the space around them [has] been produced as (ambiently) heterosexual, heterosexist and heteronormative."[39] Within this spatial schema the queer body came to serve a largely heuristic function, signaling a dehiscence in an otherwise normative social fabric. Though a valuable initial reflection on the intersections of sexuality and human geography, *Mapping Desire* would likely strike the present-day reader as an index of its time, both in terms of its impassioned appeal for a queer "politics of transgression," and also insofar as its conception of queer spaces, places, and environment as de facto resistant exhibits an idealism that clearly predates Lisa Duggan's coinage of the term "homonormativity."[40] What emerges in this text, and the critical moment it came to capture, is an incommensurability between geography's epistemological investments, which we might characterize as a positivistic propensity toward mapping, and queer theory's deconstructive drive, which can be understood as broadly anti-empiricist. Over time, the subfield of "geographies of sexuality" would increasingly draw insight from queer theory, leading to the refinement of its conceptual apparatus. For example, the field saw a gradual shift of emphasis away from the site-specific "mapping" to work on sexuality and the spatial distribution of power in a Foucauldian vein, and a concomitant move away from an interest in the ipseity of "place" toward more speculative questions of space. As Larry Knopp explains, invoking de Certeau's place/space distinction, "The fixity and certainty inhering in most dominant ontologies of 'place' is rejected by many queers who instead favour a mobility and placelessness due to the possible violence and exclusion that could surface as a result of being visibly marked out."[41]

From Geographies of Sexuality to "Queer Space"

The "spatial turn" in queer theory, which emerged in tandem with advances in geographic inquiry, might be understood less as a corrective to the omissions of prior scholarship, as we saw in the field of human geography, and more as a response to a burgeoning interest in how sociosexual practices unfold in space and time. An important text in setting this agenda was Leo Bersani's 2002 essay "Sociability and Cruising," which took up the late Foucault's interest in how "relational system[s] can be reached through sexual practices" and explored this through an appeal to the practice of cruising, whose ethical lure (and conceptual traction) lay in its capacity to engender forms of sexual sociability and impersonal intimacy far beyond the normative purview of heterosexual culture.[42] As Heather Love writes of Bersani, he was "concerned with social relations, and particularly with how structured, hierarchical relations unfold in social space," a concern similarly at stake in Lauren Berlant and Michael Warner's "Sex in Public," which similarly positioned queer sexualities and their subcultural expressions in contradistinction to the heteronormative backdrop of the social sphere.[43] What these thinkers sought to diagram in these early interventions into queer space was, to invoke Foucault, "a view of cultural life underneath the ground of our sexual choices."[44]

The topic of sex—whether in its capacity to assemble counterpublics or to shatter subject positions—was central to early explorations of spatial perception and relational practices in queer theory. Exemplary in this regard is the work of John Paul Ricco, whose *The Logic of the Lure* (2003) offered one of the first sustained explorations of the entwinement of queer sexuality, spatiality, and the social in general, and the ethics of cruising in particular. In an implicit rejection of previous (misguided) attempts by geographers to statistically "map" queer demographies or fashion unstable and provisional forms of sociality into legible configurations of "community," Ricco elaborated a "promiscuous methodology" that he saw befitting of his fleeting, contingent, and ephemeral subject.[45]

He proposed an analytical mode that was itinerant, transitive, and (in a nod toward Judith Butler) "without proper object[s]." Rather than excavating homosexual "content," Ricco sought to diagram the structuring logic of queer eroticism. *The Logic of the Lure* moves peripatetically between art installations and moving image media that stage ethical and aesthetic questions about how to give form to experiences of anonymous sex, especially works responding visually to the disappearance of people, places, and social milieus as a direct result of the AIDS epidemic. Through a relational approach to theorizing what Leo Bersani and Ulysse Dutoit elsewhere termed "a community grounded in anonymity," he sought to navigate the tricky path between the expansiveness of theoretical speculation and the imperative to respond justly to the historically specific.[46]

Yet while *The Logic of the Lure* can be read as an early contribution to the theorization of queer space, it is important to note that its author is not uncritical of this designation. Sensitive to the semantic and syntactical permutations of the term "queer," whose etymological relation to spatiality I consider below, Ricco notes in a retrospective reappraisal of the field of inquiry he helped to forge that "'Queer Space,' in seeking an alignment of subject and predicate—'space' and 'queer'—was *definitional* in its intention and effects, whereas the kind of 'Queer Sex Space Theory' that I was writing was *conceptual:* i.e. irreducible to any definition of queer/sex/space, and conditioned by its relation to other concepts bound to historical, economic, social and political contexts."[47] By pointing to the ways "queer space" can be either hollowed out or overcathected, Ricco here flags two important methodological points I take as instructive. First, there is the question of queer's proximity to questions of nonnormative sexuality. By untethering "queer" from historical contexts and sexual practices, the term might be understood positively, insofar as it exceeds particularity, or negatively, in as much as the term risks becoming evacuated of meaning (a charge I will address shortly). Second, through the conflation of subject and predicate, the abbreviation of "queer space" tends to dissimulate the term's own discursivity, subsequently gaining "epistemological authority through its designation of an object of enquiry."[48]

The text that arguably cemented "space" and "time" as crucial analytics in queer theory was J. Jack Halberstam's *In a Queer Time and Place*

(2005). "Queer space" refers here to "the place-making practices within postmodernism in which queer people engage and it also describes the new understandings of space enabled by the production of queer counterpublics."[49] While Halberstam's understanding of counterpublicity is indebted to Samuel Delany's accounts of urban queer subcultures, it also diverges from prior work by harnessing the decentering energies of "queerness" to shift its purview beyond the urban metropolis, notably by focusing on nonurban and rural spaces. Explicitly invoking the legacies of the French spatial thinkers I considered in some detail above, the book mounts an incisive challenge to post-Lefebvrian strains of "postmodern geography." While Halberstam welcomes the generative effects of postmodernity's splintering of spatiotemporal integrity, especially insofar as it raises the possibility of carving out alternative spatiotemporal frames, he also highlights the inadequate attention to gender and sexuality in this field.

Perhaps the most prominent example of contemporary scholarship on the relationships among gender, sexuality, space, and embodiment is Sara Ahmed's *Queer Phenomenology* (2006). In the field of film and media studies, Ahmed's text is cited widely, and with approbation. *Queer Phenomenology* offers a bold critique of the normative blind spots of the phenomenological tradition, notably its presumptive grounding in the experience of a body that goes unmarked by embodied differences and social particulars. She enjoins us to "rethink the phenomenality of space—that is how space is dependent on bodily inhabitance"—by granting increased attention to the role of sexuality, race, and gender in an understanding of spatial perception.[50] Particularly germane to the present discussion is her argument that "bodies are sexualized through how they inhabit space," and her subsequent exploration of how such "orientations 'exceed' the objects they are directed towards, becoming ways of inhabiting and coexisting in the world."[51] The notion of "orientation," which she draws from Michael Moon, provides the conceptual linchpin of Ahmed's argument.[52] The term's polyvalence is rhetorically indispensable because it allows the author to link the three elements of her argument: *spatial orientation,* which prompts engagement with ideas of embodiment, proprioception, and phenomenology; *sexual orientation,* which refers to erotic object choices that a deviant body may be drawn to; and the geopolitically loaded figure of "the Orient," which Ahmed uses to point toward a broad constellation of sites of cultural, racial, and geographic alterity. *Queer Phenomenology* invites its readers to think of sexuality and race as entwined and coconstitutive elements that shape both the production and apprehension of social space. As Ahmed writes, "Orientations shape not only how we inhabit space, but how we apprehend this world of shared inhabitancy, as well as 'who' or 'what' we direct our energy and attention toward."[53] On the one hand, her understanding of social space ought to be welcomed for its robustly intersectional rebuttal to the spatial theorists I addressed above. Yet the rhetorical means by which she draws queerness and spatiality together—primarily her reliance on spatial tropes—deserves closer scrutiny.

Above I note that the way that we talk about sexuality is often articulated through spatial idioms. Yet, while many spatiosexual terms fit into George Lakoff and Mark Johnson's category of "orientational metaphors," Ahmed makes a critical turn to the metaphoricity of orientation *itself*. *Queer Phenomenology* is a text that summons the rhetorical suggestiveness of spatial tropes and privileges the notion of the "slantwise" relation to which Foucault alluded above. Consider, for instance, the central motif of the "straight line" within the book's schema. Straight lines geometrically encode heterosexuality both metaphorically and metonymically; Ahmed writes, "In being straight, for example, one's desire follows a straight line."[54] Straight lines not only attain an explicitly spatiotemporal dimension but go on to accrue an implicitly normative valence too. Ahmed discusses the various ways social subjects are expected to "fall into line" with the "straight" path of a predetermined life trajectory—namely, heteronormatively sanctioned teleologies of sexual and social reproduction. Notwithstanding any specific objections we might have to the applicability of Ahmed's description to diverse queer contexts—such as the teleological imperatives of gay hookup culture that, far from resonating with Sedgwick's famous characterization of queer movement as "recurrent, eddying, *troublant*," seem to exert a decidedly straightforward thrust through reticulated networks of digital others—I am most interested here in the argumentative strategies Ahmed deploys, and their purchase on (or resistance to) questions of sexuality.[55] Spatial tropes, particularly linear ones, serve a heuristic function in *Queer Phenomenology*, allowing readers to visualize relational dynamics that might otherwise appear willfully abstract. However, their application, particularly in the realm of the visual arts, encourages a metaleptic sleight of hand whereby queerness is imputed not to the social/sexual difference that serves as the ground of nonnormative experience, but rather to the spatial token used to articulate this difference figuratively.[56] Such a mode of abstract argumentation arrogates to itself the transgressive charge of queer nonnormativity, all the while residing politely in the comfort of linear abstraction. Or to put this another way, nonnormative eroticism is evoked while coyly eschewing sex altogether.

What, then, does queer (spatial) theory teach us about (se)x? While a concern with queer sexual practices is arguably what ignited queer theory's spatial imaginary, Halberstam notes that "much of the contemporary theory seeking to disconnect queerness from an essential definition of homosexual embodiment has focused on queer space and queer practices."[57] There is a sense that this decoupling is, clearly, to be welcomed; Halberstam's own text is a timely reminder that the theorization of queer spatiality ought to extend its purview beyond cis bodies, desires, and practices. Yet *Queer Phenomenology* alerts us to the fact that there exists within discourses of queer space a propensity toward abstraction that runs the risk of becoming disconnected not only from homosexuality, but from sexual practices tout court.[58] Or as James Penney writes, subjecting the text to its own internal logic of rhetorical recursiveness, "Ahmed's own orientation toward the term 'orientation' effectively desexualizes it."[59]

The call to move *beyond* any given topic has long constituted a common refrain in queer theory. Michael Warner argues that developments in the field frequently unfold dialectically; they "often begin by distancing themselves from what they take to be a narrower version of queer theory."[60] This move can be seen, for example, in a polemical position piece written by Natalie Oswin arguing that queer geography ought to effect a "deconstructive move" to "re-orientate queer studies within geography by highlighting the ways in which a queer approach can be deployed to understand *much more than the lives of 'queers.'*"[61] While it is undoubtedly true that theorizations of social space ought to consider sexuality alongside other forms of difference, I suggest here that such putatively progressive appeals for a capacious movement *beyond* sexuality entails a risk of effecting a more conservative move *away* from it too.

In this respect, the discourse on queer spatiality that emerged in the early to mid 2000s played out locally several tensions that queer theory has sought to grapple with more generally. The embattled history of queer theory, and the charge of its propensity toward abstraction, is perhaps too well-known to fully rehearse here. Having coined the term "queer theory" in a 1991 issue of *differences,* Teresa de Lauretis would largely disavow it in the pages of the same journal some three years later.[62] In 1996 Leo Bersani's *Homos* would voice reservations about the field's gravitation away from questions of nonnormative eroticism. Taking aim at Michael Warner's definition of queer as a "resistance to regimes of the normal," Bersani wondered whether an understanding of "queer" that "delineat[ed] political rather than erotic tendencies" might bypass sexuality altogether.[63] Similar arguments would surface throughout the years, from David Halperin's warning against a creeping normativity in queer studies that seeks to "despecify the lesbian, gay, bisexual, transgender, or transgressive content of queerness, thereby abstracting 'queer' and turning it into a 'generic badge of subversiveness,'" to the searing critique of queer studies' own aversion to sex proposed by Oliver Davis and Tim Dean more recently.[64]

There is undoubtedly much to say about these arguments, not least that they orbit around the foundational aporias of queer theory (the unsettled question of the field's search for an "object," the viability of a coalitional politics predicated on antinormativity, and the tension between the ineluctable historic residue of a narrow "gay and lesbian studies" and the progressive ambition for a queer "beyond"). But I flag them up here to encourage a critical reading of queer spatial theory, and its own propensity toward abstraction (i.e., the slantwise versus the straight line) or the occlusion of sex (a "re-orientation" of queer studies to address "much more than the lives of 'queers'"), within broader intellectual parameters. Through this book's focus on scenes of cruising, my own contribution might thus be read as an explicit parti pris. *The Seduction of Space* does not shy away from the messy question of eroticism, not least because—as Lefebvre is apt to remind us—any account of social space that traffics in tropological abstractions and grows untethered from lived experience is necessarily impoverished.

In the intellectual genealogy I sketched out above, I made the case that while French thinkers inaugurated and popularized modes of inquiry into space, their own respective blind spots received greater attention in the English-speaking world. A similar tendency might also be seen in queer theory, whose theoretical language derived in part from French post-structuralist thought before attaining a more ostensibly political valence in its Anglo-American incarnation. While the overstating of similarities between these two dovetailing trajectories is to court charges of oversimplification and anachronism—not least because, as François Cusset has demonstrated, the sobriquet "French theory" is only retrospectively conferred onto a body of work whose influence took root in the U.S. academy in the 1980s—such parallels remain instructive for at least two reasons. First, they highlight the significant and constitutive role of Foucault's thought in setting the agendas of both fields. And second, they bring into view the spatial trajectory of queer studies itself.

Much ink has been spilled in recent years about queer theory's fate in France. Despite the significant role that French thinkers played in laying the epistemic groundwork for queer theory, as well as the more general contribution of twentieth-century artists to the exploration of sexuality's vicissitudes, France has until recently remained a "barren ground for the flourishing of queer theory."[65] Accordingly, accounts of queer theory's "difficult" reception in France are often figured in the optative mood. Oliver Davis and Hector Kollias, for instance, tell a story of missed encounters, "belated" returns, and breakdowns in linguistic and intergenerational transmission, while Tim Dean notes that the very question of queer theory's "return" to France "evokes a complex problematic of translation, including yet-to-be mourned losses that have been sustained through the wear-and-tear of multiple journeys, over the years, from French to English and now back again."[66] Attempts to move beyond this inauspicious state of affairs often take one of three forms. Some French queer scholars have seized the topic as an opportunity to address the fault lines in Republican discourse, particularly its imperviousness toward the politics of identity, and how this has created the intellectual conditions for inhospitality toward a thinking of difference. Others maintain an affective orientation toward recuperation by reappraising the work of protoqueer theorists from Monique Wittig to Guy Hocquenghem. And finally, some have stressed the specificities of a queer theory "made in France" by amplifying the voices of contemporary thinkers, such as Sam Boucier, whose work has not traveled far beyond the hexagon.

While *The Seduction of Space* is in dialogue with, and critically nourished by, such scholarship, it treads a slightly different path. Though I contribute toward the transatlantic traffic in ideas on questions of space and sexuality, it is time to explore how French cinema (rather than or in addition to French thought) might enliven these discussions in compelling ways. The chapters that follow thus find in the moving image more vernacular forms of queer theorizing, reading the spatial practices of filmmakers, actors, and spectators for the subtle modes of spatial politics they bring to light. Given that the symbolism of space so saturates French politics, culture, and society, and moreover that cinema is itself a product of these processes, what follows figures an attempt to explore how queer filmmakers contribute to the production or contestation of this spatial imaginary. Before we move squarely into the realm of film analysis, we are left with two lingering questions. First, what exactly is cinematic space? And second, how do we go about exploring the entanglement of space and sexuality by way of the moving image?

Cinema

Cinematic space is a contested category. Just as the theorization of the politics of space became a discursive battleground for French theorists, with impassioned debates erupting intermittently from numerous camps (Marxists, Foucauldians, postmodernists, etc.), so, too, the question of cinematic space has served as a proxy for debates about a range of formal, textual, or ideological commitments. To offer a flavor of these discussions (and their intractability), it might prove instructive to draw an example from the history of French film criticism. In 1969 Jacques Rivette convened a roundtable with other members of the *Cahiers du cinéma* masthead that was dedicated to the thorny issue of defining cinematic space.[67] Let us turn to the scene of the roundtable: the *Cahiers* contributors begin by conceiving of cinematic space in the aggregate, as the sum of places seen in, and engendered by, a given film. However, Sylvie Pierre swiftly cast doubts on this narrow understanding by noting that the space they are trying to apprehend depends on the primacy of vision. Jacques Aumont's subsequent focus on montage is one that starts with promise because it allows the discussion to unfold in a different direction by thinking about space as a synthetic or composite product, a "stitching together" of diverse elements. However, Pascal Kané is quick to voices his misgivings: what if an overemphasis on montage and form obscures more capacious interest in the workings of ideology? As the roundtable participants work toward a working definition of cinematic space the parameters of the term are stretched in many, sometimes contradictory, dimensions—cinematic space as screen space, narrative space, geophysical place, the sum total of objects available to (visual) perception, the relation between discrete frames, the space of ideology, et cetera—these critical efforts often stall. While the ensuing debate is interesting insofar as it produces an index of the critical and political energies of the time, and because we are given a glimpse of influential concepts in film theory (the *hors-champ,* apparatus theory) in their embryonic forms, we do not leave the roundtable with much clarity about the nature or construction of cinematic space. As Rivette notes, in summary, "Not only did we fail to answer the question of [cinematic space], but we failed to ask the question. And not only did we fail to ask the question, but we only just managed to ask ourselves how we might ask the question."[68] While it is tempting to disregard this thwarted exercise in thinking-in-common for its occasional rhetorical indulgences, the roundtable's "failure" is instructive in a negative way. What emerges from the discussion is an object lesson in how preexisting theoretical commitments orient theorists toward different (and sometimes incommensurable) conclusions, and this need not be dispiriting. Rather, this episode reminds us that in the sphere of film theory, as in practice, space is not given to us *a priori.* Rather, it comes into view according to a theorist's positionality and into being through both spatial and descriptive practices.

We might suppose that a good place to start our analysis of cinematic space is with the pedagogical tool of the frame analysis. This involves taking as our focus a still image and commenting on its mise-en-scène, perhaps taking note of the "content" of the frame or, in a reverse gesture, reducing physical things to shapes, lines, or abstractions. Yet this task will be quickly disturbed, and infinitely complicated, by even the smallest of actions: a camera's movement along the *x* or *y* axis or a change in focal point, which will make our sense of spatial volume swell or contract. Cinematic space might further be thickened by considering a range of factors, from the movement of objects or bodies which that demands on our attention, activating hitherto unnoticed realms of the cinematic image (as per André Bazin's analysis of depth of field), to the machinations of narrative that produce a spatial coherence (as per Stephen Heath). As Rivette and the other *Cahiers* discussants remind us, cinema not only passively documents images of specific places but also *constructs* spaces through the articulations of editing. While the advantage of the frame analysis, which freezes and isolates a particular image, is that this approach forms lines of continuity with other forms of pictorial analysis—such methods may be familiar to students of art history—we ought to remain cognizant of the questions of temporal flow and historicity that are also at stake in that same discipline. As Sedgwick reminds us in *Touching Feeling,* "Temporal and spatial thinking are never really alternatives to each other."[69] Williams concurs that "cinematic space is always operating within different configurations of the time–space continuum, and framing space is always making meaning at a specific moment in time."[70]

Elsewhere in his book, Williams invites us to think about spatiality as an expansive analytic category that touches on various aspects of the film experience. The film analyst's task is to "develop a multi-levelled approach [to space,] sufficiently supple and capacious to register in close-up the shifting plays of cinematic form and consciousness . . . while at the same time taking into full account the film's wider, cultural frame, i.e. its more socially, historically, and politically defined landscapes."[71] An expansive understanding of cinematic space is one that resists reducing cinema to its visual component and avoids narrowing its object of inquiry to the framed parameter of the profilmic image. Given that "cinema, in its physical latitude and plastic extension, offers a unique sensation of spatial freedom on a level at once perceptual, intellectual and affective," our thinking of cinematic space must accordingly do justice to the many facets of the film experience that Williams underscores.[72]

By way of a proleptic gesture to the next chapter, it is worth noting that "cinema" refers not only to an art form or a technical apparatus; *a* cinema is also a place, a site in which affect circulates through spectating bodies that sit side by side or occasionally brush up against one another. As Elena Gorfinkel and John David Rhodes write in *Taking Place: Location and the Moving Image,* "Cinema must, by its very nature, exhibit places to its spectators and lure its spectators to places of exhibition."[73] Their choice verb *to lure*—replete with signification—holds in tension both a positive valence (an enthrallment to the medium's monstrative capacities) and a more suspicious one (informed by ideological critiques of the spectacle). As Gorfinkel notes in her contribution to that volume and Ricco also suggests in *The Logic of the Lure,* the space of the film theater has always been a rich site of encounter for queer spectators.[74]

In order to draw together the many conceptual threads that have emerged as we follow the key terms of spatiality and sexuality across multiple disciplinary fields, histories, and geographies, I register, in closing, the ways space continues to have an alluring quality for theorists of French and queer cinemas. It is telling to note that while Nick Rees-Roberts's *French Queer Cinema* (2008) attended primarily to questions of queer cinematic representation against the unfolding sociocultural backdrop of the late 1990s and early 2000s, the 2014 addendum to this project made an explicit appeal to the language of space.[75] Exploring "new theoretical modes of enquiry, particularly the queer relational focus on spatiality and orientation," his critical eye here exceeds the scope of the previous study, paving the way for a more substantive dialogue between queer film studies and theories of embodiment.[76] This critical move is one I read as symptomatic of queer film criticism's recent shift away from a narrow representational paradigm focused on the on-screen politics of sexual identity to address broader questions of embodiment, space, and materiality. Over recent years, we have also seen spatiality emerge as an important term for thinking about the politics of sexuality in both a variegated cinematic landscape and an uneven global frame, most notably in Karl Schoonover and Rosalind Galt's *Queer Cinema in the World* (2016).[77] Put schematically, the question of *what* queer cinema is seems to have been supplanted by the question of *where* it is. And this subtle shift in perspective brings into view a wide range of questions, ranging from the spaces of queer cinema's reception and circulation to geopolitical tensions between legible (read: white, liberal) forms of queerness, and modes of nonnormative sexual or gendered expression that fail to be captured in existing vocabularies. While the remit of the present book is decidedly narrower by comparison, these questions are crucially at stake in the national context of France—a country in which the articulation of space is always already a political concern.

2

COMING AND GOING IN JACQUES NOLOT'S CINEMA

> Cinema with neither beginning nor end; where linear narrative progression is put through the stroboscopic mincing machine of people's comings and goings, their fits of pleasure.
>
> —Guy Hocquenghem

Where do we find queer sex in the cinema? When film scholars offer answers to this question they turn, more often than not, to the space of the film text, orienting themselves toward their objects of study via their elected method of close reading. But in so doing they risk overlooking another crucial dimension of the film experience: the space of film's exhibition. In the framing of this question there exists a productive ambiguity that has previously been teased out in the film-theoretical writing of Roland Barthes. "Whenever I hear the word *cinema,*" Barthes writes, "I can't help thinking *hall* rather than *film.*"[1] His deceptively simple statement enacts a parallax shift—a subtle change of point of view that brings into focus a different object. Such a statement enjoins us not only to consider queer cinema's abiding interest in sex on screen, but also the open secret that the hall has long constituted a space of erotic encounter. This shift in attention, away from the screen and toward the space of the theater and the bodies that occupy it represents just one of the ways queer spatiality figures in the work of Jacques Nolot, whom I take as my focus of this chapter.

Gay cruising operates as a crucial trope in Nolot's cinema. His investment in cruising is glimpsed in his earliest work, an eleven-minute film from 1986 titled *Manège* ("Merry-go-round" in French), in which he cruises the toilets of Paris's Gare d'Austerlitz train station before picking up a young soldier from the south of France and showing him the queer spaces of the French capital, which includes a compulsory stop at the Bois de Boulogne. As the two men follow the circuitous path of Paris's outer ring road, the boulevard Périphérique, the circular rhythms of the camera work evokes the eponymous *manège*. From this short film we adduce that Paris is Nolot's preferred playground and that his distinctive mode of filmmaking will be a cinema of sexual attractions.

Appearing in over eighty roles since his on-screen debut in 1973, Jacques Nolot occupies a long-standing but peculiarly peripheral position within France's cinematic landscape. His acting career came to prominence by way of his connection to queer director André Téchiné. Nolot acted in André Téchiné's *La matiouette ou l'arrière-pays* (1983) and *Wild Reeds* (*Les roseaux sauvages,* 1994) and was both the scriptwriter of and autofictional catalyst for Téchiné's 1991 film *I Don't Kiss* (*J'embrasse pas*). He has also worked with lesser-known filmmakers such as Paul Vecchiali (*Guys in the Cafe / Le café des Jules,* 1989), another early and significant contributor to France's cinematic exploration of the AIDS crisis. Bridging the gap between these directors and the slightly later filmmakers who would come to be associated with the millennial zeitgeist of the French *cinéma du corps,* he would go on to appear in films by Claire Denis (*I Can't Sleep / J'ai pas sommeil,* 1994; *Nénette et Boni,* 1996) and François Ozon (*Under the Sand / Sous le sable,* 2002). While there has been relatively little scholarly attention dedicated to Nolot (as either an actor or a filmmaker), the breadth and scope of his filmography is significant. Not only does his career map lines of continuity between the otherwise distinct modes of filmmaking mentioned above, but his enduring presence on film might also play a vital role in resuscitating earlier moments in French queer cinema. This is particularly true of the work of a filmmaker like Vecchiali, who continues to languish in the footnotes of cinematic history despite being the first French filmmaker to make an AIDS-related film from an explicitly gay perspective.

Speaking at the Sicilia Queer Festival in 2018 during a retrospective of his work, he stated, "I am not well known. Rather, I am often recognized."[2] The position Nolot occupies within French cinema indeed deserves further unpacking given his lesser-known status as writer and director of films in addition to his career as actor. If we first consider his presence as an actor in other directors' films we might note that while many of his roles have either been secondary characters or cameos, his presence on-screen readily exceeds the sum of its (bit) parts. James S. Williams has noted certain similarities in the characters he has embodied: charming but jaded men, often in their fifties or early sixties, who are invariably social outsiders.[3] Whether playing himself or a thinly veiled alter ego, Nolot effects an intertextual bleed from one role to another, which at times places under duress the diegetic integrity of a given film. Consider, for example, the intertextual dynamics at play in Claire Denis's *I Can't Sleep*. Midway through the film, the protagonist Daïga—a Lithuanian *émigrée* who, following the collapse of the Eastern bloc, has come to Paris to work in a hotel—is enticed by the neon hues of the beckoning street signs and explores her new neighborhood of Montmartre by night. However, it is not long before she attracts unsolicited male attention and seeks refuge in a nearby movie theater in the Pigalle red-light district. Daïga stumbles inadvertently into a porn theater, a fact that she comes to realize when confronted with the image on-screen. While we might not be able to discern these images in detail, the film can be identified as a heterosexual porn flick; the granular images, saturated palette, kitsch fur furnishings, and male hirsuteness anchor us in the visual idiom of 1970s softcore. As Daïga starts to laugh, she provokes the attention of the man in the neighboring seat—none other than Jacques Nolot—whose penetrating gaze interpellates her, suggesting that she is far from the theater's typical client. Once again, she finds herself out of place.[4]

This minor event represents just one link in a chain of alienating incidents relayed in *I Can't Sleep,* a film that deftly limns the urban contours of northern Paris with particular attention to racial, sexual, and gendered alterity. However, the deferred resonance of this scene, and the broader implication of Daïga's incursion into Nolot's homosocial milieu, can only be registered after the fact. Spectators familiar with Nolot's later work are encouraged to infer from Denis's casting of him an admittedly subterranean intertext, given that a similar porn theater in close proximity to Montmartre would later lend itself, as both subject and setting, to the second film in Nolot's own trilogy, *Porn Theatre* (*La chatte à deux têtes,* 2002). Denis's calculated enacting of Daïga's misidentification is, however, more significant than an anachronistic in-joke, a breaking of the fourth wall, or a Hitchcockian pun at one remove. For

Williams, such a scene "bespeaks [Nolot's] particular persona"—a point I am tempted to interpret in both a broad and a narrow sense.[5] First, it encapsulates the dynamics of sex and senescence that rest at the core of his later cinematic endeavors. And second, the cameo gestures proleptically to his later substantive role as a gatekeeper of the auditorium's homosocial spaces. Indeed, it is particularly telling that Williams titles his formalist account of Nolot's cinema "His Life to Film," insofar as he foregrounds the interdigitated registers of cinematic mediation and biographical reality—or the slippage from reel to real—that structure, and threaten to overdetermine, Nolot's autofictive project.[6]

Roland Barthes by Jacques Nolot

Jacques Nolot's cinema ought to be understood in dialogue with a broader constellation of queer artists and intellectuals, given that his anachronistic cinema indexes a fast-disappearing generation and Parisian milieu. His films are liberally peppered with anecdotes that serve to reinforce his position as a node in a network of prominent gay figures. Roland Barthes, whom he came to know through a mutual friend, André Téchiné, was at one time his cruising partner, and the two would encounter each other in and around the place Saint-Sulpice. In a rhetorical gesture consonant with the theme that animates my inquiry, Barthes drew on a spatial lexicon to describe Nolot, who was twenty years his junior. This designation is recounted to us by Pierre, Nolot's alter ego in *Before I Forget* (*Avant que j'oublie,* 2007), who claims that Barthes once introduced him to André Téchiné as a *roulure.* While the term commonly circulates in the French vernacular as an injurious term for a prostitute (somebody who, to adopt the similarly moralizing English idiom, "gets around"), Barthes exercised his penchant for word play by twisting, and thereby blunting, the connotative barb of his catty statement. He argued that the term was supposed to be understood with greater creative and semantic license to mean someone more generally "nomadic" or "without roots." It is through an analysis of Nolot's *Porn Theatre,* which I engage in conversation with Barthes's film theory, that I wish to pursue some of the tensions that inhere in this anecdote—one that operates in the registers of both the literal and the metaphoric, and neatly ties together both sexual and spatial practices.

Nolot's nod to Barthes's writing is prefigured in his first film, *Hinterland* (*L'arrière-pays,* 1997), which charts the filmmaker's journey to the southwestern town of his childhood following the death of his mother. While Barthes famously withheld from view the photographic referent of his mother that stands at the absent center of *Camera Lucida* (1981), his meditation on photography, Nolot's unflinching presentation of his dead mother's corpse as an explicit but nonetheless graceful reverse pietà registers itself among the film's most memorable images (due in no small part to the incomparable Agnès Godard, Nolot's cinematographer). This tension between Barthes's form of nondisclosure and the frontality of Nolot's cinema underscores a broader relation between both figures that comes to the fore with greater force in the subsequent two parts of his trilogy (*Porn Theatre* and *Before I Forget*). *Porn Theatre* presents the sociospatial obverse of Nolot's first film; it reveals a milieu more familiar to the adult Nolot, to which *Hinterland,* in its measured discretion, does not make us privy. The film is set in Le Méry, a crumbling erotic movie theater off Paris's rue de Clichy and documents the comings and goings of the theater's denizens with a combination of humor, pathos, and near-anthropological precision.

Prior even to entering the eponymous theater, there are two ways this setting connotes queer sexuality. Not only does the cinema's location in Pigalle situate the film against the backdrop of perhaps the most powerful toponymic signifier of France's sex tourism, but movie theaters have long occupied an assured place in French queer culture more generally. Consider, for instance, the not-insignificant fact that the French entry in Guy Hocquenghem's *Le gay voyage*—a 1980 atlas of gay culture, which, chapter by chapter, sets its imperious sight on a sweep of cities from Berlin to San Francisco—focuses not on the more predictable spaces of the Marais neighborhood or the insalubrious corners of the Tuileries Gardens, but the art deco movie palace Le Louxor, described as a particularly rich, vibrant, and unmistakably Orientalized sociosexual enclave.[7] As David Caron notes, "For Hocquenghem, the social function of the old theaters appears to be just as important as their sexual one. In fact, the two cannot be so easily separated, and desire without purpose allows for the perpetual reinvention of social relations as a series of seductive contacts with no future in mind."[8] One other notable example of the cinema within the French queer imaginary can be found in

Barthes's own posthumously published memoir *Incidents,* wherein he pens an essay entitled "Soirées de Paris" that offers a more introspective account of the evening he spent in Le Dragon, a gay cinema in Saint-Germain-des-Prés: "I dare not cruise my neighbour, though I probably could (idiotic fear of being rejected)."[9]

While clear parallels might be drawn between Nolot's film and Tsai Ming-liang's near-contemporaneous *Goodbye, Dragon Inn* (*Bu san,* 2003)—another example of early slow cinema that is set at the cusp of the film medium's supposed obsolescence—or Samuel Delany's anthropologically thick description of the deleterious effects of erotic rezoning in *Times Square Red, Times Square Blue,* I suggest that Barthes's short essay "Leaving the Movie Theatre" (1975) offers perhaps the most compelling urtext and theoretical reference point for Nolot's film. Although the pretext for such a reading might seem to be animated by a set of bad relations (i.e., those all-too-convenient discourses supplied to us by virtue of Barthes and Nolot's personal ties), I am primarily interested in the conceptual resonances, rather than personal relations, between them. By fleshing out (so to speak) what appears to be a missed encounter, I want to highlight with greater precision the diverging ways Barthes and Nolot configure relations between erotics and embodiment, cinematic time and space, and the sexual politics of the auditorium. By affording Nolot's little-known film the same epistemological weight as Barthes's writing I advance a contention that underpins this book as a whole: that film texts and histories of viewing practices can themselves offer substantive possibilities for queer film theory, rather than simply serving as objects to illustrate its more notorious and influential theoretical concepts.

Entering the Movie Theater

The opening shot of *Porn Theatre* presents us with a cloudy blue sky. The tranquility of the image is undercut abruptly by the subsequent shot, in which a group of pigeons flutter through the streetscape, the irruptive movement accompanied by the ambient noise of traffic. We then move indoors as the birds mill around a theater's chipped tile floor. The pigeons' movements guide the camera in an upward motion toward the box office, where we are introduced to an inattentive cashier (Vittoria

Scognamiglio) who will act as the establishment's gatekeeper. While this sequence could be understood in symbolic terms, either as postlapsarian allegory or as linguistic pun (Williams reminds us that the French *oiseau* [bird] is also a priapic signifier), this movement from outside to inside serves also to concentrate the film's spatial relations in two ways.[10] First, the shift from the boundless sky to the theater's restricted spatiality offers an unwitting index of the origins of Nolot's project. For, as James Quandt notes, Nolot's "chamber drama . . . derives quite conspicuously from a theater production," a point Nolot corroborates in a later interview as he explains that he first conceived *Porn Theatre* as a play set à huis clos, before being encouraged by producer Pauline Duhault to adapt it into a film.[11] Second, the sequence suggests an analogy between the movement of the pigeons and the exchanges we will come to witness between the theater's patrons. By abstracting these spatial practices in the opening sequence, the film encourages us to be attentive to its choreography of gestures; through the unrelenting triage of sexual types that will be at stake later in the film, Nolot goes on to offer an extended meditation on the politics of the pecking order.

A *travesti* sex worker in a yellow dress (credited simply as *l'homme à la robe jaune,* played by Olivier Torres) enters the foyer from the stairs below. His footsteps are heavy, his gait slow, and his movements exaggerated. With a wistful air of nonchalance he exchanges a few words with the cashier, checks his hair and lipstick in the glass reflection of a poster frame (a mise en abyme advertising the eponymous skin flick *La chatte à deux têtes*), and follows the next patron through the double doors and into the theater. Despite his heavy-handed solicitation, the second man does not pursue Torres, who prowls languorously down the aisle, his yellow dress matching the drab ochre of the theater's decor. The ensuing passage announces the film's preoccupation with cinematic slowness and self-reflexivity; moving with a measured pace, the camera tracks the movement of the figure in yellow through the darkness of the side aisle and toward the image on-screen. As he disappears and reappears from behind the theater's colonnades, his splintered, stroboscopic presence recalls the photogrammic structure of Muybridgean motion. He moves toward and across the pornographic image as the projector's light beam abstracts his body into a silhouette. Following a close-up of the female porn star—seemingly at the point of climax, her lips bright red and skin drained of color—the final shot pans back across the counterfield to reveal about fifteen men spread evenly across the auditorium.

I describe the opening scene in detail here in order to highlight Nolot's explicit interest in demarcating the cinema's material, architectural, and fantasmatic spaces. The scene advances from sky to ground, from outside to foyer, then from the seating of the auditorium to the screen. Despite the film's centripetal attraction toward the screen in this instance of abstraction, which threatens to collapse the distinction between diegetic pornography and the site of its reception, it nonetheless resists what Steven Marcus describes as the organizational logic of the pornotopia.[12] While the cinematic screen and the auditorium are both spaces where desire is produced and circulated, Nolot's interest lies also in thinking the limit of this coextensiveness, a task he achieves by punctuating the film's action with scenes of labor and waiting—notably that of sex work and concierge work.

Nolot's cathexis of the movie theater and his attention to the physical and phenomenological coordinates of erotic filmgoing clearly work to frame the auditorium as a space of anonymity and availability. But *Porn Theatre* further demands viewers to theorize the isomorphism

Figure 3. *Porn Theatre* (Jacques Nolot, 2002). A *travesti* in a yellow dress (Olivier Torres) approaches the movie theater screen, her face momentarily intersecting with the pornographic image.

between what José Capino has termed the "complex, mutually reinforcing internalization or externalization of both cinematic text and spectatorial presence that occurs in adult theater" beyond the "obvious and pedestrian practices of corporeal mimicry."[13] To gain a critical purchase on the asymmetrical relations between texts and spectators and come to a more nuanced understanding of the affective and relational modes the film explores, I suggest that we ought to bring in—and, by implication, bring *out*—Roland Barthes's writing on film.[14]

The Theater in Theory

Nestled among Barthes's intermittent reflections on cinema is "Leaving the Movie Theatre," in which he describes both the psychic and embodied experience of filmgoing. The essay first appeared in a 1975 special edition of the journal *Communications* dedicated to "Psychanalyse et cinéma," which also contains within its pages two examples of what can retrospectively be labeled "apparatus theory": an early version of what would become Christian Metz's *The Imaginary Signifier* and an essay by Jean-Louis Baudry on the cinematic *dispositif.* In a marked but measured opposition to these thinkers, Barthes subtly presses against the grain of much psychoanalytic film theory. Although the personal register in which he writes undercuts the false universalism often imputed to psychoanalytic film theory, the essay's confessional address—its opening line runs thus: "There is something to confess: your speaker likes to *leave* a movie theater" (345)—and its recurring motifs of mirrors, keyholes, and hypnosis suggest he is far from dispensing wholesale with a psychoanalytic image repertoire. Furthermore, the evocative account of succumbing to the charm of the image flirts with, but ultimately undercuts, earlier Situationist critiques of the spectacle. Williams notes in his sharp and impassioned exegesis of the piece that the essay slips from the third- to first-person singular to first-person plural.[15] Such a rhetorical strategy indeed typifies the deictic approach of the later Barthes and provides a stylistic analogue to the essay's subject: the "color" of the movie theater's "diffused eroticism" (346).

Although this essay has yet to find its place in scholarly accounts of the topographical in Barthes's oeuvre, spatial dynamics guide his inquiry forcefully here. He writes for instance that the word *cinema* calls to mind a place (the theater *hall*) more readily than a medium (*film*) (346). This provocatively simplistic formulation is further complicated by his coinage of the term *une situation de cinéma,* whereby the word *situation,* signifying both topos and affective disposition, points to broader ideas about how spectatorial experiences are conditioned by our specific spatiotemporal coordinates as well as the desires we entertain when we enter the theater. Such a desire, for Barthes, typically responds to a state of otium ("idleness, leisure, free time"), and the films he goes to see are rarely the "object of a veritable preliminary alert"—that is to say, precognized (345). Yet if it is a sense of openness, contingency, or even innocence that initially governs the essay's tone, this sensibility quickly attains a disarmingly erotic charge when questions of relationality are raised: "The movie house (ordinary model) is a site of availability" (even more than cruising), and the "inoccupation of bodies" he senses in the cinema best defines metropolitan "eroticism" (even more than striptease) (346).

While Nolot's film hypostasizes the connections Barthes draws between cinema's site of reception and the erotic possibilities the spaces engender, we ought not to overlook first the more coded queerness of the essay itself. Note how the cinema is framed here in contradistinction to the domestic site of televisual reception, a privatized space in which "eroticization" is necessarily foreclosed. In a queer gesture that might best be understood as articulating a proto-Edelmanian sentiment, Barthes opines that "television doomed us to the Family" (345). The dark, anonymous space of the auditorium, by contrast, opens onto a horizon of relational possibilities that stretches well beyond the bounds of the conjugal. Philip Watts has also made a strong case for the critical–theoretical prescience of the essay in more general terms. If we consider schematically the paths film theory has taken in the forty years since the piece was penned, we can surely note its brilliant flashes and moments of foresight. Watts writes that Barthes "called into question the tenets of apparatus theory quite subtly . . . not through argumentation, but through the staging of his own body."[16] As such, his writing represents "one of the very first attempts to resist what is now widely recognized as the over-reaching, universalizing gestures of Paris School apparatus theory by opening up a space to reflect on desire and on the sensuous world of the film spectator."[17] If the critical ascendance of affective and embodied film theories (as well as their privileged object in the context of French film, the *cinéma du corps*) represent some of the discourses that have since emerged in the "space" Watts describes, then Nolot's 2002 return to the apparatus and auditorium, as both physical and theoretical loci, undoubtedly complicates this periodization.

Far from disavowing its jarring historicity and succumbing to the self-effacing logic of cinematic architecture that Jocelyn Szczepaniak-Gillece terms "neutralization," the mise-en-scène of Nolot's film depicts Le Méry as a late 1970s relic in decorative terms.[18] But the anachronistic contours of the film might also be sensed in theoretical terms. Nolot's film, which appears conversant in Barthes's conceptual language, seems to resist broad teleological narratives of film theory, which tell us there is little left to learn by revisiting prior theorizations of the cinematic apparatus. A close engagement with Nolot's film therefore allows us first to expand on the sexual and spatial dynamics that informed the context in which "Leaving the Movie Theatre" was originally penned; and subsequently, by ushering these ghosts into the contemporary period, *Porn Theatre* indexes shifting approaches to public sex and tests the viability of the theater's proposed modes of relationality as a political blueprint.

Across Barthes's essay we find a suggestive triangulation of questions of desire (whether erotic, embodied, or cinematic—these are purposefully hard to disaggregate); the social, material, and relational conditions of film viewing (the nature of one's relation to the other "unoccupied" bodies that populate the room, questions of space, proxemics, and the distribution of attention); and an understanding of the apparatus as *appareil*—"the currency of a gleaming vibration whose imperious jet brushes our skull, glancing off someone's hair, someone's face" (347). Another compelling element of Barthes's account (which will assure his continued relevance as film theory grows increasingly attentive to questions of lingering, boredom, and minor affects) is that he accords similar weight to the spectator's apprehension of the screened image and the cinematic "situation" at large: the movements of bodies, ambient noises, and other contingent details of the viewing encounter. As Watts notes, this mode of fetishistic apprehension is guided by a principle of metonymy, "grounded in a hermeneutics that takes a part . . . for the whole."[19] For Barthes, cinematic pleasure is bound to a cathexis of the part object and seems to rely, somewhat counterintuitively, on two coextensive orders of sensation: a tug and pull between immersion and distraction. His theorization therefore diverges markedly from that of Baudry, who describes the spatial and perceptual fixity of the spectator as one of enchainment, capture, and captivation. Though the affective dynamics that Barthes describes have recently interested scholars such as Jean Ma and Gorfinkel, for whom this oscillating lull can be mapped onto the interstitial states of weariness and the soporific, I focus on how these forces find their more pointedly erotic expression in the cinema. For, as Barthes stresses in *The Pleasure of the Text,* "it is intermittence, as psychoanalysis has so well stated, which is erotic."[20]

Nolot's *Porn Theatre* suggestively extends Barthes's contention that the cinematic apparatus functions as a matrix of non-ocular pleasures. His film is interested, moreover, in exploring the asymmetry between viewers and film texts as well as the jarring incongruity between the diffuse homosocial eroticism of the movie theater and its putatively straight stimulus. These interrelated tensions are best emblematized in an erotic tableau presented midway through the film. Two men stare agape into the off-screen field where pornography is being screened. Their wide eyes are locked in this gaze as if to register hyperbolically the full force of spectatorial immersion. The suturing effect is called into doubt, however, as the camera pans down and we see they are flanked by a third figure (a *travesti* credited as *l'homme nu,* played by Jean-Louis Coquery) dressed in a loose robe, a red quarter-cup bra, and a suspender belt. Reclining in his seat, Coquery's body displaces the projected image as the locus of erotic entanglement. While the eyes of the male spectators are transfixed by the projected image, their hands massage the chest of the newly supine figure before edging down toward his genitals. Looking relations are clearly at stake in this scene, which figures a mise-en-abyme of pornographic spectacle. Metz's warning against the ideologically suspect fantasy of the spectator's mastery over the screened image is redoubled here, given the imbrication of both physical and projected bodies. In this scene, however, Nolot probes more concretely the limits of ocularcentrism. Framed in quasi-Bressonian close-up, the hands of these men grasp, as it were, to answer the question of how the relational aporia of the porn theater (its simultaneous invocation and disavowal of contact) might be worked out at the level of the senses.

The entanglement of bodies on display here recalls, in turn, a passage from Barthes's essay in which he writes of erotic spectatorship as the coexistence of two states of reception: the submission of the body "twice over" (349). The first state, Barthes suggests, is engrossed in—and narcissistically attached to—the profilmic image, while the second he describes as lingering, slightly disengaged, attuned to epiphenomenal detail. In "Passing Over Peripheral Detail" Roger Cardinal turns to one of Barthes's earlier essays ("The Third Meaning," 1970) to further explore the perceptual margins of the filmic experience. Here, a similarly bipartite mode of cinematic apprehension is identified and its sensory corollaries explored in further detail. The first order of viewing engages "a single-minded gaze [that] is directed toward the obvious Gestalt or figure on offer" and, upon the seizure of a focal message, "ignores its periphery."[21] The second "focusses less narrowly and instead roams over the frame, [is] sensitive to its textures and surfaces—to its ground," a mode of sensory apprehension that imbricates "habits of looking" with "habits of touching." Cardinal continues that the second "decentred sensibility is, moreover, receptive at all levels, with the result that any encouragement to attend to what lurks at the fringes of normal sight is equally an encouragement to summon up the resources of the sensory system over and beyond the visual."[22] This schema is rendered more explicit in Paul Willemen's postscript to the essay, which gestures to the productive possibilities of applying Barthes's framework to the object of pornography. Within Cardinal's schema, Willemen surmises that "the look is a signifier for the repressed desire for tactile contact and as such retains vestiges of tactility in its signifying operations."[23] This elaboration sheds light on the negotiation of these two perceptual registers—the ocular and the haptic, the distanced and the proximate—which Barthes describes tellingly as the "difficult fetishism" of spectatorship (348). Through a further fleshing out of Barthes's corporeal metaphor, Nolot brings into view the social implications of this spectatorial mode. His scene engages at least three bodies rather than one and, through its emphasis on tactility and peripheral vision, queries apparatus theory's frequent reduction of spectatorship to an asocial mastery of the visual image.

This sex scene with Coquery, however, entails a different order of interpretative "difficulty"; the scopic and sensory splintering we watch here begs the question not only of how bodies relate to one another, but of which conceptual language might best equip film theorists reading the film. If the analytic lens of haptic film theory is beset by an uncomfortable literalism here, then a recourse to object relations theory raises further questions still. The pitfalls of this interpretative quandary are indeed evident in Olivier Cheval's account of the scene, which partakes in the dubious reduction of the queer body to its constituent parts, signs in the schema of psychosexual allegory. His reading, which exhibits a clear debt to Baudry's taxonomy of the dream screen, focuses on breasts as "a partial object" involved in the "sublimation, transfer and projection" of the on-screen spectators.[24] While the prefixal weight of trans* has proven useful in recent years to forge new modes of attachment between nonnormatively gendered bodies (as Avery Tompkins notes, the asterisk habitually appended to the prefix opens the term to a broader range of identities, such as the cross-dresser), here the term is put to more dubious allegorical work.[25] For Cheval, the term is used to articulate a set of interstitial relations at once spatial (Coquery's body as existing in a space between spectator and screen), psychoanalytic (the body part as transitory object), gendered, and intersensory. While the film *does* force us to consider psychoanalytic interpretation and the tenets of apparatus theory as a convenient interpretative foil, the camera's focus on Coquery's body in the throes of sexual passion is an attempt to rescue this queer body from the lure of allegorization, rather than concede ground to the cinematic and theoretical apparatus that would be complicit in his marginalization. Put simply, the *travesti* body exists as a locus of pleasure and erotic autonomy, rather than a transitory object or supplement for the theater's more normatively gendered patrons.

If "Leaving the Movie Theatre" took aim at the limits of psychoanalytic reductionism, as Watts says, "through a staging of [Barthes's] own body," then we can in turn note how Nolot extends these questions to attend to issues of nonnormative embodiment and intercorporeal modes of spectatorship.[26] It is important to stress, though, that the vision *Porn Theatre* presents of polymorphous sexuality is neither utopian nor ethically unambiguous. The discursive address of the film might be described as "critically queer" insofar as it subjects the erotic economy of the theater to its own internal limits.[27] As the film unfolds, the politics of sexual practices is posed in an increasingly reflexive fashion: carefully choreographed scenes of group sex open to broader concerns surrounding the politics of queer counterpublics; and differences of age, gender, race, serostatus, and even gay self-nomination come to shape the implicit hierarchy of the auditorium, its force field of attractions and forms of prophylaxis. Just as the above-discussed scene pivoted between specular immersion and peripheral distraction, such a pattern operates across the film as a whole. Scenes of auditorium sex are punctuated by behind-the-scenes activities. Conversations between sex workers, interactions—ranging from the banal to the poetic—between the concierge and her clients, and the footfall of local vagrants work to undercut the cinematic spectacle, and indicate, as Williams has noted, that despite "the claustrophobia of the film's highly theatrical interior space, it does not take place in a vacuum."[28]

Through the film's relentless display of competing drives, embodied temporalities, and relational forms, the theater comes to exemplify a site of what Barthes would later call idiorrhythmia—a term he coined (from the Greek *idios,* own, and *rhuthmos,* rhythm) to explore how the individual's rhythms find a place in a wider social and spatial totality, and which Susan Harrow glosses helpfully as a "median term between aversive forms of loneliness and hyper-integrative forms of collective living."[29] Though cinema did not inform Barthes's elaboration of the term explicitly, Williams joins others in situating Barthes's "idea of an erotics of cinematic space" within his "general project in the 1970s to open up the social and collective sphere to new forms of critical enquiry."[30] Offering his own (more wry and skeptical) intervention into discourses of queer world-making, Nolot's film offers a critical—indeed crucial—reminder that these forms of imagined collectivity do not always harbor an egalitarian dimension or a utopian valence. *Porn Theatre* counters a growing tendency in recent years to frame the spaces of queer cinema's reception (its auditoria and festivals) as sites of utopian possibility, where counterpublics not only dwell but thrive. This position frequently hinges rhetorically on the strategic yoking together of utopia's two meanings—imputing to the utopia as "nonplace" (derived from the Greek *ou,* not, and *topos,* place) a positive valence (i.e., Eutopia as "ideal place"). That the social space of *Porn Theatre* oscillates ambiguously between idealism (fantasies of erotic communion, uninhibited displays of polymorphous sexualities) and realism (its cynical tenor, foregrounding of boredom, and exploration of queer inequities) gestures toward, but ultimately stops short of, this implicitly positive valorization. Nolot's skeptical stance hews closely to Kadji Amin's call for the deidealization of queer culture, theory, and practice in this regard. As Amin writes, "Deidealization deexceptionalizes queerness in order to analyze queer possibility as inextricable from relations of power, queer deviance as intertwined with normativity, and queer alternatives as not just alternatives."[31] *Porn Theatre* is similarly not blind to how Barthes's idiorrhythmic ideal must negotiate the strains, hierarchies, and inequities that come to structure the queer socius. Indeed, while it's tempting to characterize the "queerness" imputed to the theater as a general resistance to monogamy and conjugality, along with an unbridled expression of polymorphous sexuality, the auditorium also reifies a particularly masculinist and priapic economy that often markedly occludes women and *travesti* subjects.

As the film gathers pace, the spatiosexual dynamics that lay dormant in Barthes's writing are amplified, and relational possibilities are multiplied. Group sex scenes take place in the toilets and alcoves, and even the box office becomes the site of the apparatus's allegorical "queering"; the cashier eventually seduces the young projectionist (a timid but willing neophyte, played by Sébastien Viala), engineering a threesome in which, we assume, Nolot will ultimately partake as the film draws to its close. Largely consigned to the *hors-champ,* the porn that is projected seems to function merely as a pretext for cruising. Such a configuration recalls the writing of Hocquenghem, who similarly conceives of the screen as a *protection-prétexte* that "screens" the secrets of the filmgoing public and assuages their sexual anxieties.[32]

But just as spectators of Nolot's film start to question whether we in fact need moving images to sustain the theater's idiorrhythmic mode of erotic communion, he is quick to reassert the apparatus's indispensability. Increasingly caught up in the cashier's advances, the projectionist is led astray from his post in the booth. Erotic activity is held in abeyance when the film reel comes to its end and the theater's patrons are momentarily suspended in the dark. It is particularly telling that it is not the end of the screening that is experienced as an incursion, but the fact that the lights have come up. Such a reaction tallies with the emphasis Barthes himself places on lighting, rather than film screening, in addition to his invocation of the discreet yet abundant possibilities afforded to us in the dark. As his writing suggests, and Nolot's staging makes manifest, the relation between screened images and the spaces of cinema's circulation and reception is far from assured. The activities that take place in the theater's darkness exist on a spectrum, which (as Barthes's writing and the film's soporific protagonist both remind us) ranges from slumber to sex.

While Barthes's suggestive account of film spectatorship unspools a rich and tantalizing vision of erotic possibility, his writing often lingers—in a manner perhaps not dissimilar from the writer's own experiences in "Soirées de Paris"—in the optative mood, the register of subjunctive possibility. I've sought to suggest here that while *Porn Theatre* runs the real risk of flattening its urtext through this hypostatization, the film's literalism allows Nolot to expand on the questions that Barthes so creatively contoured and resituate them within broader social, spatial, and political parameters. The film ultimately effects a slippage, marking a declension from the vantage point of the first-person spectator through to intercorporeal and idiorrhythmic forms of spectatorship. Though the screened image serves as a necessary structural precondition, given that it organizes spectatorial attention, it is ultimately dethroned when Nolot turns his attention to the more peripheral sites of the toilets and the foyer. The cinema "hall" occupies a tenuous place, negotiating the hermetic enclosure of the "optical vacuum" and the expansiveness of the outside world. The film presents moments in which everyday expressions of disciplinary power (e.g., a police raid targeting clients of Arab origin) are entwined with broader problems in sociopolitical actuality (e.g., the rise of France's far-right figurehead Jean-Marie Le Pen). Such eruptions of the real put under further duress the idea that erotic movie houses are one of the last bastions of social bonding and that their spaces of interclass "contact" might act as a social balm.

While the film is implicitly underwritten by discourses on cinematic spectatorship and homosociality that came to prominence in the late 1970s, we ought not overlook how it is indelibly shaped by the ongoing effects of HIV/AIDS in contemporary France. Through a mismatch of architectural styles and narrative spaces, Nolot presents a disjunctive view of periodicity; the film's setting feels out of joint and hard to situate historically. We habitually move back and forth between two sides of a historical juncture; against a backdrop of decidedly retro décor, the film is punctuated by a string of poetic monologues of its seropositive protagonist, played by Nolot, delivered to the concierge in the theater's lobby. Multiple questions of temporality are evoked through the connotative possibilities of theatrical space. Negotiating the tensions between the auditorium's real and virtual spaces, its dynamics of labor and leisure, exposure and discretion, the theater represents a fertile site for Nolot. *Porn Theatre* explores the spaces of both literal and fantasmatic projection—registers that, while enigmatically intertwined, are frequently held in tension.

From Boredom to Bliss, Entropy to Utopia

Given that I introduced Nolot against a wider backdrop of French queer cinema, there exists an extratextual component to his film that merits reflection. Looking beyond the diegesis of the film and toward its broader relation to cinephilic discourse, how might the status of cinema itself be understood in this work? Williams figures the Parisian film theater as an emblematic site of self-reflexivity. He reads Nolot's film as an attempt to broaden the representational scope of gender and sexuality in French cinema by engaging with one of its paradigmatic spaces. Williams argues that the film theater—the "archetypal, self-reflexive site of the nouvelle

Figure 4. *Porn Theatre* (Jacques Nolot, 2002). A sweeping panning shot reveals the ochre seats of the adult movie theater following a screening. The floor is littered with tissues.

vague"—holds a privileged space in French cinematic heritage that Nolot seeks to both "excavate" and "regender."[33] I now expand the metacinematic remit of *Porn Theatre* further still by drawing out some links between Nolot's film, Barthes's thought, and a broader body of queer cinema. Due precisely to the self-reflexivity that Williams identifies, the film presents a rich chronotope that resists absorption into any one spatiotemporal, generic, or even geographic frame. Not only is it the case that Nolot "make[s] queer the very territory of French cinema" as Williams has it, but in a reverse gesture his reflexive film enjoins us to consider French cinema against a wider backdrop of queer film.

In both its superannuated decor and its use of the porn theater lobby as a rich proscenium for a dramatic exploration of gender and sexuality, Nolot's film maps lines of continuity with Marie-Claude Treilhou's *Simone Barbès or Virtue* (*Simone Barbès ou la virtue,* 1980), which was until recently consigned to film historical oblivion. Set in a porn theater south of the Seine, Les Mille Colonnes in Montparnasse, the first part of the film centers two young women, Simone and Martine, who work as ushers in a porn theater frequented largely by heterosexual men. As with *Porn Theatre, Simone Barbès* makes creative use of the lobby's vacant space and the fallow time of cinematic projection. Here, the two protagonists discuss life and love, though their conversations are routinely punctuated by the groans emanating from the porn's soundscape and disrupted by the incursion of men coming and going. While the all-male porn theater is an improbable backdrop for the film's exploration of lesbian desire, both women's shared frustration toward this environment produces something new; this generates an unlikely ground for the queer feminist politics that Treilhou explores in a nearby lesbian cabaret bar in the film's second half.

Nolot's film can be productively aligned with Tsai Ming-liang's *Goodbye, Dragon Inn,* which came out around the same time. The material qualities of Tsai's film resonate with those of Nolot's; *Goodbye, Dragon Inn* is similarly underwritten by a tension between boredom and immersion. The luminous, delicate, and ephemeral quality of screened images offer only a momentary reprieve from the existential heft otherwise characterizing Tsai's film. For both filmmakers, the turn-of-the-millennium cinema is colored with a particularly melancholy tinge. Auditoriums swell with cigarette smoke, which, as Lesley Stern has brilliantly argued, offers up both an index of and synecdoche for dead time.[34] But while both films illustrate how the obsolescence of the cinematic medium dovetails with the loss of certain sociosexual practices—for physical cruising becomes an analog practice in a digital age—an abiding concern with finitude is felt more palpably in Nolot's film given its more explicit reckoning with HIV/AIDS.

The paradox at the core of Nolot's film is that despite the creative means by which it seeks to undercut an economy of the spectacle, it nonetheless cultivates a latent cinephilia. An attentive viewer may well note *Porn Theatre*'s cryptic allusions to canonical postwar avant-garde cinema in an American context, not least through its choreography of on-screen bodies that work to forge a somewhat subterranean pathway to a broader corpus of queer film. For example, at the level of form and composition, the erotic tableau I discussed above resonates with a scene in Jack Smith's cult classic *Flaming Creatures* (1963) in which we witness an orgiastic concatenation of limbs amid group sex. In another scene, which takes place in the hemmed-in space of a bathroom, Nolot makes use of a mirror as a structural motif to present both the object of queer desire, a shirtless man who is getting into drag, as well as the gaze of an onlooking man who pleasures himself, thereby recalling a similar interplay of gazes that formally mirrors a scene in Andy Warhol's *My Hustler* (1965). As Nolot goes on to traffic reflexively in Warholian tropes, we can also sense his absorption of the influence of structuralist theories of film spectatorship. In one particularly protracted scene we are enjoined to watch one of the patrons as he watches the screen: the camera is perched behind the spectator, revealing only the back of his head. After a short while, the head of the *travesti* in yellow emerges from this spectator's lap, leading us to register (once again belatedly) that we were in fact bearing witness to an altogether different activity. Spectatorial eventlessness is displaced by erotic eventfulness. Not only does Nolot's perspectival sleight of hand—a quip that is richly suggestive of Warhol's *Blow Job* (1964)—ask us to consider the politics of the pornographic *hors-champ* (thus literalizing the spatial dynamic of Linda Williams's notion of "on/scenity"), but he also asks us to respond critically to the constant modulation of the film's affective register—the ebb and flow of titillation and boredom, immersion and distraction, affect and intellect. We would do well here to invoke a well-worn aphorism from Barthes's *The Pleasure of the Text:* "Boredom is not far from bliss: it is bliss seen from the shores of pleasure."[35] Offering his own (more *literal*) twist on this dictum, Nolot shows us that boredom might just be bliss seen from the row behind, a conceit that pithily encapsulates the relation between both texts I detailed above.

Two problems beset our attempts to grasp Barthes's slippery writing on the erotics of spectatorship. The first pertains to what critics have dubbed Barthes's "allergy" toward the cinematic medium. The second concerns how we might best interpret the suffusion of sexually saturated tropes that populate his prose, such as the polysemic term "erotic" that frequently exceeds the bounds of sexuality, narrowly conceived. By literalizing the metaphorical register of "Leaving the Movie Theatre," Nolot's insistently material staging of cinematic desire extends the spirit of Barthes's writing. As Philip Watts suggests, it is the assertion of the author's own body, rather than that of the disembodied spectator, that represents Barthes's most potent attempt to counteract the "universalizing gestures" of apparatus theory.[36]

Moreover, his framing of the essay as "a short speculative embodiment of his attempt to leave theory behind" is particularly instructive because it foregrounds the intractability of "theory" in a way that mirrors Nolot's own oblique positioning in relation to the Symbolic.[37] The import of "Leaving the Movie Theatre" lies not in Barthes's treatment of the image, then, but in his theorization of that which commonly recedes from view—the spaces of the cinema ("hall"), the material margins of the cinematic experience, the ephemeral and site-specific practices that the optical vacuum seeks to disavow by consigning it to the status of epiphenomena. In turn, *Porn Theatre* subjects its theoretical urtext to a similar process of displacement by making bad objects of both the viewing encounter and the theoretical frameworks that subtend and sustain it.

Philip Rosen disambiguates the French terms *appareil* and *dispositif,* which are often conflated by virtue of the theoretical currency of the English word *apparatus.* He suggests that rather than instantiating a crude determinism that would reduce the apparatus to its technological base (*appareil*), the cinematic apparatus ought to be understood within broader cultural and discursive parameters as "one nodal point of a social construction of knowledge, desire, pleasure, signifying adequacies."[38] When conceived within this expanded frame, Nolot's turn to the space of the theater can be understood to animate alternative histories of (para)cinephilia and to scrutinize with a more critical eye the political possibilities of social and sexual experimentation. Yet, as the increasingly melancholy tone of Barthes's writing on his experiences in these theaters suggests—a shift in mood that D. A. Miller and Dan Callwood note is consonant with the "elegiac note accompanying all of [his] late writing"—such spaces are often susceptible to disappearance.[39] Nolot's untimely *Porn Theatre* therefore erects a monument to a lost past. It is a poignant meditation on the obsolescence of media forms and relational practices, as well as the glimmer of their momentary revivification: a call to project them anew.

Entering the Apartment: *Before I Forget*

I noted in the introduction to this chapter that Jacques Nolot's cinema often brings to the fore those spaces, places, bodies, and things that commonly recede from view, but this position requires careful qualification. For while his films are undoubtedly anchored in a gay male context, Nolot still manages to cast an oblique gaze on this privileged milieu, given that his trilogy foregrounds queer forms of living that often go overlooked as France's gay culture (which is habitually infatuated by the spectacle of youth) so often cedes to younger generations. Nolot has been hailed for providing a "striking antidote to the sort of comforting imagery of older people, generally to be found elsewhere in cinema," and for positioning his work at a critical distance from, and out of step with, "an increasingly self-satisfied and self-ghettoizing Paris gay community fixated on youth and beauty."[40] But rather than attending to the representational omission of the aging queer in positive terms, his films also deign to show the indignities of later life by dwelling on the ethical, political, and sexual gray areas of life as gay men enter their sixties. Given that Jacques Nolot's cinema signifies against the "standardized imagery of metropolitan gay culture," Rees-Roberts positions the filmmaker's work *hors milieu*.[41] In the French gay vernacular, *hors milieu* (a spatial figure of speech meaning literally "out of the scene") names a departure from a legible and "hypervisible" Parisian gay scene whose symbolic epicenter we might presume to lie somewhere in a bar in the Marais. But when rendered into English, the term accrues added baggage as it resonates with notions of the "ob/scene," which brings us much closer to understanding Nolot's fraught position in queer circles and his vexed relation to contemporary French cinema more generally.

For Dennis Lim, Nolot's cinema is one "of carnal embarrassment and corporeal ruin."[42] Scenes of abjection surface throughout his films: the naked corpse of his mother—inescapably freighted with psychoanalytic baggage—is glimpsed by Agnès Godard's camera in *Hinterland;* postmasturbatory detritus coats the seats of his *Porn Theatre;* and his loose bowels and weak bladder burst any pretense toward propriety and decorum in *Before I Forget* (in one scene the protagonist aborts his plans to visit an old cruising haunt by the booths of a sex cinema in Montmartre because he shits himself). The cumulative effects of these examples routinely lead critics to describe Nolot's approach to sex, death, and the aging body as "unflinching"—a choice description that reveals just as much about these critics' attitudes and projections as it does the filmmaker in question. But so far critics have judiciously resisted the straightforward absorption of his work into the generic category of the New French Extremity, given that "the measured pace and energy of his experiments in self-exposure are calibrated by the limitations of his own ailing physicality."[43] Both abjected from a dominant strain of queer cinema in France that is focused on youth, and too muted to titillate fans of Extreme cinema, Nolot's scenes of sex and senescence have yet to find their place in the landscape of contemporary French cinema. The awkwardness of his position within the two contexts of France's gay culture and its cinematic zeitgeist tells us much about how these categories are normatively constituted and governed, and such processes of in/exclusion are importantly at stake in the final film in his trilogy, *Before I Forget,* which I consider here.

Above I noted that Nolot's cinema advances a biographical arc. But perhaps it is more accurate to note that this biography proceeds by way of folds. The trilogy's "chapters," which guide spectators forward in time, are invariably shaped by the recursions, diversions, and digressions of the protagonists' memories. Questions of space and place play a vital function in his cinema by allowing him to articulate moments of connection to these previous moments. James S. Williams notes that each installment of his work explores a different space.[44] He thus encourages us to notice within the narrative architecture of Nolot's cinematic triptych a formally pleasing—and pleasingly formalist—symmetry. But given that the ineluctable question of mortality occupies a central place in his cinematic vision, each film explores not only a different space but also a different death. For example, it is the death of Nolot's mother that demands his return to the southwestern village of his youth in *Hinterland,* a trip that leads to discomfiting, yet unremittingly sensual, scenes of familial and psychosexual reckoning. The loss of Nolot's adopted son Saïd forces the protagonist of *Porn Theatre* out of bed and toward the erotic consolations of the movie house. And the third film, *Before I Forget,* is shot in the wake of another fictional loss—namely that of Toutoune, the former client turned partner of the film's protagonist. This death leads the film's existentially unsettled lead—here incarnated as Pierre Pruez, a fifty-eight-year-old writer and ex-hustler—to turn his analytic lens inward. In this film, Pierre reckons with his quotidian existence, complicated his twenty-four-year battle with seropositivity, by situating everyday life against the future horizon of his own finitude. The austere portrait of Pierre's life archives "the minutiae of a life structured by frustrated creativity, unsatisfactory sex, and the life-saving medication that he is reluctant to take" (a reference to his tritherapy treatment).[45]

If we detect in *Porn Theatre* at least a glimmer of hope or a palpable sense of nostalgia, no such encomium to the past is to be found in *Before I Forget.* So, while the title of the film might suggest a summoning forth of life's affirmation, its focus tends decisively toward the moribund. This tone is set in the film's establishing shot in the Père Lachaise Cemetery, where two men (one of whom is Pierre) are framed with their back to the camera, marking the passing of a third, unidentified, character. The brief scene ends with a panning shot across the cemetery, and we move into the constricted space of the protagonist's apartment. The film goes on to unfold in a succession of domestic spaces.

Before I Forget is perhaps Nolot's most personal film. Its mode of address is largely introspective. He provides us with what we might call, to here adopt a French psychogeographic idiom, *un repli sur soi*—the inward folding of one's gaze and attention and a refusal of help, assistance, or sociality. Central to this move is the film's choice to expose to the gaze of the film's spectators Pierre's own apartment (which is to say, *un retour chez soi*). For while the semipublic setting of *Porn Theatre* served as a backdrop to animate the dynamism of Paris's cruising cultures and queer zones, Nolot's consignation to a small apartment here marks a period of social and sexual withdrawal. Unable to come due to the secondary effects of his medication, Nolot's alter ego, Pierre, confides to a friend that he can no longer fuck. He chooses instead to "sublimate" his erotic drive.

The film follows the daily travails of Pierre, who finds neither peace in isolation nor consolation in writing. The impasses and blockages of his everyday life (little desire to cruise; inability to write or sleep) play out at a glacial pace and in minute detail within the claustrophobic confines of his Parisian apartment. The narrative significance of everyday gestures and actions are amplified within these tightly packed four walls, revealing a stark and bleak vision of gay senescence that rarely finds its way to the silver screen. I focus here on the material environs of the film—the role of apartment spaces, objects, and property—to explore how Nolot's framing of these aspects of the mise-en-scène animate and amplify the questions of realism, finitude, and death that constitute a mainstay of his work. Toward the end of the chapter, I treat Nolot's film as an invitation to move beyond the four walls of the apartment, as it were, and to think about broader socioeconomic concerns with property ownership and processes of urban gentrification, which have constituted a bone of contention within gay and queer history in recent decades, both in France and farther afield. For while the film is hermetic, both in terms of the area of its limited spatial surroundings and the narrowness of its privileged social milieu, Nolot nonetheless invites us to consider discourses of possession and materiality—and their entanglements with class and race—in ways that resonates well beyond the film's immediate echo chamber.

A Journey across My Room

Much of this book considers cinema's privileged capacity to capture, frame, and mediate the *social* spaces of queer life—the bars, parks, and streetscapes that have historically acted as privileged loci of queer connection, sexual or otherwise. Yet while I have tapped two rich veins of spatial film theory—theoretical accounts of cinema's formal affinities with the built environment, on the one hand; and historical accounts of cinema's foundational entanglements with the spaces of the modern metropolis, on the other—it is worth acknowledging that these lines of inquiry tend to converge around questions of communal space and the public sphere. In *Spectacle of Property,* John David Rhodes makes a powerful case that a focus on domestic space "allows us to complicate some of the familiar accounts of those allegedly co-natal cousins, urban modernity and the cinema."[46] Rhodes's study, which I propose we read alongside Pamela Wojcik's *Apartment Plot,* ought to be understood as a collective attempt to address the oft-overlooked importance of domesticity on screen. Both Rhodes's and Wojcik's accounts of cinematic space impress on us the fact that the built environment—and more specifically its domestic confines—does not function simply as a passive backdrop on screen. Rather, these spaces subtly, but nonetheless actively, scaffold narrative possibility. For Wojcik, "space sets the parameters for the plot, themes, and ideology of not only individual films but also of genres," and she thereby encourages readers to recognize both a geographic and a narrative valence to the term "plot" that, as her title indeed suggests, acts as the conceptual linchpin of her argument.[47] Relatedly, Rhodes makes a compelling argument for how the domestic architectures yield their own narrative taxonomies, and how a focus on the house—ubiquitous yet crucially undertheorized in film studies (or perhaps undertheorized because ubiquitous)—allows us to cut across disparate generic boundaries and reorganize cinema's periodization according to principles of architectural commonality. Both works appeal to forms of spatial and interpretive redistribution; they ask us to consider how cinematic "backdrops" might emerge from the recessed space of narrative insignificance to assume center stage. Cinema's rendering of domestic space heightens our apprehension of the textures and rhythms of the everyday while illuminating the medium's capacity to poeticize or spectacularize those habitual spaces that might otherwise elude our attention.

"The house," writes Rhodes, "is where much of everyday life transpires. [It] shelters, structures, temporalizes, differentiates, makes private, and also publicizes this life."[48] Victoria Rosner similarly notes how a closer attention to the interior attunes us to "architectural dynamics of privacy and exposure, spatial hierarchies demarcating class, the locations and routines surrounding the care of the body, and the gendering of space."[49] By bringing domestic space into the conceptual fold of gender and embodiment, Rosner's statement anticipates the focus of my own approach to *Before I Forget.* For while Pierre's single occupancy of a sixth-floor Parisian apartment, and his retreat from sociality, might not initially tell us much about the gendered division of labor, his starkly transactional interaction with young hustlers invites a more thoroughgoing exploration of gender, sex, and race. Nolot also foregrounds "the care of the body" with both acuity and asperity in the film, given that the narrative is structured around his protagonist's reticence toward the adoption of a tritherapy treatment. But how might a closer reading of Pierre's immured existence allow us to expand on the themes Rosner and her contemporaries lay out above, and therefore bring thinking on cinema's domestic spaces into more meaningful contact with queer life?

Wojcik writes that "the apartment is key, of course, to the imaginary of single and queer life."[50] But the assumed self-evidence of the statement seems to foreclose the possibilities of its conceptual unpacking. In the field of film studies, it is perhaps Lee Wallace who has gone the furthest in theorizing the relationship between queerness and domestic space, with a particular focus on the apartment. Situating her intervention in contradistinction to many of the queer thinkers we have encountered in these pages thus far, she writes that "any number of scholars are now engaging in compiling a spatial history of homosexuality in the twentieth century that focuses on . . . oppositional strategies of homosexual occupancy and the semipublic sexual traditions they generate around such loci as the street, the bar, and the bathhouse."[51] Casting doubt on Barthes's abovementioned understanding of domestic space as a site of erotic foreclosure, she argues that an overwhelming focus on zones of public, and semipublic, sex largely occludes "the equally rich history of gay and lesbian domesticity."[52] If Wallace's strategic move away from scenes of publicity and toward the domestic is articulated in spatial terms, there is indeed a gendered corollary to this move. Though the terms "gay and lesbian" often cohabit the discursive space of her book, Wallace's study clearly figures a response to this conflation, and she ultimately invites us to divest our attention from paradigmatic accounts of (gay) public practices in order to attend to (lesbian) private spaces. Given my bleak summation of the place that gender relations occupy in *Porn Theatre,* it may come as little surprise that *Before I Forget* has little to say about same-sex relations among women. Nor, regrettably, do women figure substantively in this film at all. Yet Wallace's point on the overemphasis on the "generative loci" of gay semipublic sexual practice remains instructive here, even if only in a negative sense to lay bare another blind spot that Nolot *does* tackle: gay domesticity. Given the tight intertextual structure of Nolot's triptych, we are encouraged to understand the apartment space in *Before I Forget* in opposition to the site of the porn theater. Pierre has a complex and ambivalent relation to his apartment. On the one hand, it acts as a site of respite and seclusion; but on the other, he also experiences it as a space of torpor, lassitude, and profound anxiety. While much less sex takes place in the space of the apartment than in the theater, this shift in physical and thematic locus allows Nolot to reveal "off-scene" moments that his contemporaries would rarely put on display.

Above I suggested that Nolot's on-screen presence does little to shore up textual boundaries between diegetic space and the extratextual realm. Put simply, it is hard to ascertain in his cinema where the actor's biography ends and fiction begins. In a recent retrospective Nolot admits that "the peculiar path that my life has taken means that, unconsciously, my life has been informed by fiction, by autofiction."[53] The contiguity between the biographical reality and cinematic fiction also extends to our consideration of the film's primary setting: Nolot's own apartment. The film's setting is an unwitting index of the film's checkered mode of production. The decision to shoot in his flat was initially due to strict budgetary constraints. Nolot explains that the film was funded entirely by *avance sur recettes* (a modest up-front grant from the French government) and completed over the course of twenty-four days. But because circumstantial factors so habitually enfold themselves into the diegesis of his films, an initially economic decision might be retroactively understood as a means of furthering the filmmaker's aim to attain greater self-exposure. *Before I Forget* grants us unfettered access not only to Nolot's house but also the minutiae of its contents. The camera's focus on the filmmaker's personal effects, from his car and furnishings to his lubricant and the condoms on his bedroom dresser, operate as an inventory (or even a premature index?) of a life lived. The film's narrative seeks to take stock of antiquated or anachronistic forms of gay life before consigning them to the annals of social history, making the materiality of these objects ever more resonant.

From Lived Space to Dead Time

Set in the wake of his lover Toutoune's death, and following Pierre's contemplation of suicide, *Before I Forget* rests tenuously on the border between life and death. This underlying dynamic is once again foreshadowed by Nolot's meticulous crafting of cinematic space in the film's establishing scenes. Following the opening shots in the Père Lachaise Cemetery, we move indoors, where our eyes adjust to a scene of near darkness. Caught in the grip of insomnia, Pierre writhes in his bed before shuffling to the nearby bathroom to wretch into a basin. The obscurity of these images amplifies the auditory element of his distress. Pierre takes a pill before going back to bed. Unable to sleep, the naked protagonist goes to his kitchenette to prepare a *cafetière,* retires to his writing desk to smoke his first cigarette of the day, before returning, ritualistically, to pour another coffee. The camera captures the movements between the kitchen and study in a single shot from a fixed position at the threshold of an adjoining living room. The condensed space of the apartment—which Nolot habitually, though erroneously, demotes to the lowly status of a maid's room or *chambre de bonne*—intensifies our attention to how space is used.[54] This uninterrupted shot encourages us to take note of the apartment's layout as the protagonist's naked body is momentarily obstructed by a small corridor. Medium shots framing him against these sparse and bare surroundings reveal a sustained commitment to spatial realism, as well as an abiding interest in the otherwise unremarkable spatial practices of domestic life.

Before I Forget offers a poignant reminder that the registration of lived space is often underwritten by the lag of dead time. Addressing the film's cinematography, Nolot has spoken of his decision to reject the close-up, which he attributes in part to his aversion to the illusion of psychological depth. He goes on to note, "However, I would have wanted to include long takes, silences, nothings [*des riens*], though I had neither the time nor the money to film these."[55] In another conversation he notes of the filming process that "there was no room, we had to 'compose' space," and that "the experience was at once interesting and stressful."[56] Rather than circumscribing aesthetic creativity, the film's material constraints (its small set, tight budget, and even tighter time frame) only strengthened the resolve of Nolot's commitment to spatial realism. Critics have positioned his cinema within a broad and distinguished lineage of French filmmaking. Quandt has likened Nolot's work to that of Robert Bresson; Williams's frame of reference includes, inter alia, Chantal Akerman, Marguerite Duras, and Philippe Garrell, each of whom share Nolot's "ascetic focus on the body," "expansion of the possibilities of sound and silence," and "hollowing out of time as duration."[57] By situating his work within these constellations of art cinema, we can appreciate how his formal predisposition exhibits a small debt to the film theory of André Bazin. As Nolot explains, "I am seduced by the elegance of the long take, its ability to imbue both space and time in another dimension."[58] Such a predilection for durational aesthetics, when coupled with a tinge of the spiritual, feels familiarly Bazinian. While Bazin's theory of deep-space cinematography and the enigmatic *autre dimension* of the long take are crucial when considering Nolot's aesthetic choices, the way objects are captured in Nolot's film also points to another foundational aspect of his philosophy of film: the indexical bond between objects as they exist in the world and on screen.

The title of the film anticipates a state of future forgetting, which, when considered within the narrative frame and biographical arc of Nolot's triptych, refers less to a generalized condition of amnesia and more to questions of entropic desire, queer senescence, and ultimately mortality. The French phrase *avant que j'oublie* might therefore be considered the logical antecedent to Barthes's account of photography's *noeme* (or its essential condition) as its capacity to attest that *ça a été* (that has been), a deictic phrase figured in the future perfect tense.[59] In his discussion of the film's production, Nolot explains that "there have been certain emergencies in my life which have propelled me toward writing, and writing has subsequently brought me to images."[60] Bypassing Maurice Blanchot in his turn toward Barthes and Bazin, Nolot tarries with the question of death in distinctly visual terms. The film registers his presence (which is already figured as a future absence) through this tangible appeal to his material surroundings, rather than turning to the creative affordances of the written word.

On numerous occasions in the film, we come across elliptical sequences that gesture obliquely to the protagonist's wish for self-effacement. Toward the end we see Pierre (now firmly in the grip of his existential angst) perching out of a skylight window in his living room, looking down to the street below. Making a passing allusion to a near-identical scene in Vittorio De Sica's *Umberto D.* (1952), a blurry point-of-view shot is followed by a shot from the same angle, in which Pierre's body is absent, revealing a partial view outside the window onto the mansard roofs opposite. This static shot, which reveals the vacant domestic space that frames the exterior window view, is rendered even more conspicuously empty in light of the previous image. Throughout the film, Quandt notes, the camera "sometimes lingers a beat or two after actors have exited the frame."[61] We are therefore asked to read shots such as these in terms of the absence of a presence that might otherwise bring them to life. The apartment's empty frames are haunted by the dialectical tension between what Lefebvre calls "lived space" (*l'espace vécu*) and the notion of dead time (*le temps mort*). These shots, which often resemble real estate photographs, form a constant refrain throughout the film, thereby pointing to a logic of dispossession I will address below.

Consider the film's still life sequences. In one of relatively few scenes of stylized camera work, eight minutes into the film, there is a lateral panning shot that feels strongly reminiscent of Chantal Akerman's short film *La chambre* (1972). The camera glides in medium close-up as it pans the shelves of Nolot's office: a lamp shade; antique camera, cassette tapes, cigarette pipes, and other miscellaneous ornaments stacked on shelves; a hi-fi system; French books (identifiable by their characteristically minimalist covers in various states of off-white); a writing desk on which is haphazardly housed a box of pens, a pile of cash, a littering of draft manuscript paper, and a row of sixteen cigarettes propped, fence-like, at the table's outer boundary. More than a gratuitous *exercise de style,* the scene conveys the sense of emptiness that resonates across the film as a whole. Offering a cinematic twist on the art historical tradition of the *vanitas* painting, Nolot gestures toward long-standing affinities between inanimate objects and the figuration of death.[62] The row of upright cigarettes materializes both the passing and the parsing of narrative time that is chiefly at stake throughout the film. Here cigarettes represent, in physical form, dead narrative moments waiting to happen; they disclose to us the temporality of the film in advance of its expired duration. Within the film's system of objects, the cigarette's function is not only metronomic but also metonymic. It is a prop that acts as just another indexical object pointing "deictically," as Stern would put it, to the tension between life and death that structures the film's temporality as a whole.

Personal Effects

Tempting though it may be to situate Jacques Nolot's investment in material objects and domestic spaces against a broader backdrop of structural film (by casting our mind back to the interiors of Akerman's earlier films, and the broader experimental tradition into which her early work is routinely enfolded), this risks flattening the material circumstances and queer specificities of *Before I Forget*. In one sense, objects work as memento mori, granting Pierre a tangible link to his deceased lover, Toutoune. Yet his highly instrumental approach to objects in the film also sheds light on another dimension of his relationship with his partner: its material underside.

Before I Forget continues to mine the rich conceptual territory that Rainer Werner Fassbinder previously explored in *Fox and His Friends* (*Faustrecht der Freiheit,* 1975), a film in which the seeming financial ascendancy of its gay working-class protagonist is met by a precipitous decline. As we are told firsthand, Pierre met his much older and wealthier partner when he was in his early twenties, shortly after his move from a small town in the Southwest into the queer fold of Parisian high society. Yet while the two men would come to love each other later in life, their ties were initially transactional; the younger Pierre, that is, was unceremoniously demoted to the perfunctory "trick." After Toutoune's death, Pierre, who was not named in his partner's will, experienced significant financial distress and legal acrimony due to the lack of legal recognition of their relationship.

A scene in the Hôtel Drouot, an exclusive Parisian auction house, puts on display his partner's considerable estate for the film's spectators. Within this cabinet of curiosities, objects of note include works by Alberto Giacometti, Henri Matisse, and an Henri Michaux that Toutoune had verbally bequeathed to Pierre. The scene marks the point at which Pierre confronts the memories that accrete in and around the objects on display. He leaves the auction house before the bidding gets underway, after a run-in with the extended family of his deceased lover, which contains a bitter homophobic undercurrent. Though the film's central focus is

Pierre's existential anguish, his financial worries are also a significant part of the story. The price he pays for sex work, the sums he owes in taxes, and the ambivalent affective ties that his inheritance engenders all play a central role in *Before I Forget.* "Sums stipple dialogue," notes Quandt, who suggests that the film "could well be called *L'Argent*" given its preoccupation "with matters of inheritance and commerce."[63] Pierre's dicey finances also lead to his retrospective reappraisal of his earlier years spent as a hustler in and around the place Saint-Sulpice.

The penultimate scene shows him making a considerable effort to impart the lessons of his life to a younger gigolo, in a rare gesture of cross-generational solidarity. However, earlier on in the film, he is more interested in reflexively staging bad examples than he is in setting moral lessons. For example, the scene that precedes the trip to the auction house opens with Pierre stationed at his writing desk with a cigarette in hand before he receives a grocery delivery from a young man of Moroccan origin called Khalid. Pierre shows the man around the apartment, leading him to the spare room that houses his father's leather barber chair. (Curiously, this chair has an intertextual history of its own, having previously appeared in both André Téchiné's *La matiouette* from 1983 and in Nolot's *Hinterland* from 1997.) A childhood photograph of Toutoune sits on the shelf adjoining the mirror unit. Pierre invites the unassuming man to sit in the barber chair before fellating him in the frontal and detached fashion to which spectators of the film are now accustomed. They are positioned laterally to the camera's point of view to hide his cock. This dedramatized sex scene underscores the transactional nature of the encounter; sitting still, though submitting to Pierre's impulses, Khalid is reduced to the status of a prop, among other props, within the narrative and spatial economy of the film frame. The scene therefore curiously, though not unreflexively, replicates a logic of transactional sex that echoes the firsthand experiences of a younger Pierre that are recounted in detail throughout his film. Once again, the film's mise-en-scène and its material furnishings are far from ancillary; the prop (a word that, Rhodes reminds us, is short for property) plays a crucial role within the unfolding of the film's apartment plot.[64] The uneasy cohabitation of objects in this scene gets to the crux of the ethical import of *Before I Forget*—a film that, through its improbable combinations of bodies, objects, and bodies *as* objects, frames each element in front of the camera with the same detached gaze. Nolot thus raises pressing ethical questions about the value ascribed to persons and things within the ruthlessly hierarchized social context of the film. Ultimately, the sober gaze we grow accustomed to in *Before I Forget* allows us to apprehend the notion of materiality in two different, though clearly interrelated, senses. I am referring, first of all, to the film's investment in spatial realism, the registration of material stuff and the contours of lived space that the medium of film endeavors to undertake (even if this approach often has the effect of decentering Pierre as subject). And my second understanding of the term relates, more pointedly, to the materialistic obsession with money and material possessions, which is no doubt informed by the fallout of the protagonist's past life as a hustler and the tenuousness of his grasp on his financial and physical health in the present. But what might Nolot's film be telling us about the world that exists outside of Pierre's immured setting? How does it speak to questions of spatial justice in both the privileged milieu of Nolot's gay Paris and contemporary France more generally?

Just as we saw in *Porn Theatre,* Nolot's reflections on queer politics contain moments of superficial crudeness and critical perceptiveness in equal measure. His cinema both *reflects* and self-critically *reflects on* the

Figure 5. *Before I Forget* (Jacques Nolot, 2007). In his apartment, Pierre (Jacques Nolot) fellates his home assistant, Khalid, in his father's barbershop chair.

iniquities that underpin gay social spaces. On the one hand, the film's dialogues reveal what Rees-Roberts terms the "fault lines" surrounding race, ethnicity, and class in France's white gay community. The literal objectification of the Moroccan sex worker resonates with the more or less subtle interactions between Pierre and his wealthy boomer friends in conversations throughout the film. In an early scene, a friend brags about finding a Slavic trick who charges fifty euros (half the going rate), before describing the thrill of sleeping with a police officer who put a gun to his temple during intercourse. Pierre states wryly, "When I am seeking out sexual thrills, I go to the banlieue. That's where *real* fear is," neatly overlaying his own sexual geography onto a social map of greater Paris that is skewed by racial prejudice. (He continues glibly, "It's what [Pier Paolo] Pasolini used to do. But then again, Pasolini is dead.") On the other hand, Pierre's relation to sex work is deeply inflected by his personal biography. Unlike the other men of his generation, into whose privileged Parisian coterie he has now insinuated himself, he remains all too aware of the tenuousness of his own position within this sexual economy of value whose currency, as he notes to a younger gigolo, is either looks or money (the former of which depreciates with time).

To approach the film's sexual politics from a slightly different angle, such an ambivalence reflects a generational tension within urban gay communities that Sarah Schulman has explored with admirable clarity. In *The Gentrification of the Mind,* a study that articulates conceptual and historical through lines between the HIV/AIDS crisis and dynamics of gentrification that emerged in its wake, she notes that gay men occupy a "particularly interesting and complex" relation to the processes of gentrification that contribute to the widening of inequities in global cities.[65] The situation is complex, she argues, because "wealthy white gay men" who lived through the HIV/AIDS crisis have intimate historical knowledge of what it feels to be dispossessed, yet many of them continue to perpetrate these logics of displacement and dispossession against communities of color in the present moment. (In fact, Schulman's description of the "colonial attitudes toward communities of color" among white gay enclaves is already aptly illustrated in the examples above and will be pursued in greater depth in the following two chapters.)[66] Crucially, the social processes described here are not reducible to the material or demographic facets of gentrification; gentrification extends to the realms of ideology and cultural capital, as the "mind" in the book's title makes clear. Although Schulman's argument doesn't map neatly onto the narrative of Nolot's film, the juxtaposition brings to light some compelling parallels. For as I noted above, HIV/AIDS is a central subject matter in *Before I Forget,* both in terms of its foregrounding of early tritherapy treatments in the 1990s and Pierre's frequent evocation of forms of gay sociality in a pre-AIDS past. It builds an affective charge that attains a particular force for those spectators with intimate knowledge of the social context of the HIV/AIDS years and its ongoing aftermath as these themes come into proximity with the film's present-day dramatization of the financial distress caused by Pierre's loss of Toutoune, and its depiction of familial homophobia in the light of his partner's death. So by bringing the past to bear on the present in this film, Nolot invites the kind of "simultaneous thinking" that Schulman argues is key to making sense of the messiness of queer politics.[67] Simultaneous thinking, that is, complicates the simplistic narratives and blanket judgments of culpability that might otherwise provide us with easy, but empty, consolation.

While Nolot's cinema casts a backward glance toward his youth—whether through tales of cruising with Barthes in the place Saint-Sulpice, his excursions to the porn theater, or his reminiscing about the queer zones of the French capital that have all but disappeared—this always exists in tension with his depiction of younger queer communities and their own problems in the present. Despite its shortcomings, *Before I Forget* is not a film that risks forgetting this present; Nolot proposes a cross-generational through line that connects a fast-receding queer past to the new queer landscapes and spatial iniquities of our day.

Entering the Theater Anew

The abovementioned description of Nolot's overarching project as one that commits "his life to film" ought to be read as a formal attempt to index a life lived, to impersonally document its material inventory. As he makes expressly clear, the narrative spaces he puts on display comprise a complex admixture of real and fictional elements. His final film is clearly cut from the same narrative cloth as the two preceding sections of the intertextual triptych, yet the shifting names of the central protagonist

(Jacques, then Pierre) attest to the fungibility, fugitivity, and quasi fictionality of his characters. More of an index than an *aide-mémoire,* however, *Before I Forget* also traffics in proper names and precise geographic points of reference to limn the contours of a queer Paris the filmmaker knows intimately but is destined for obsolescence. Considering the baroque recursiveness of Nolot's cinematic space, then, it is perhaps fitting to end where the geographical arc of his filmmaking comes full circle.

The final scene shows Pierre moving beyond the privations of private property to engage with the subterranean world of cruising for the last time. This venture outside is initiated by his habitual trick, Marc, whom we encounter earlier on in the film. It opens with a car driving along the boulevard de Clichy before parking outside the Ciné Atlas, whose location is marked in neon lighting with a lurid red *x*. Marc helps his client out of the car, revealing Pierre in full drag. He wears a sleek black dress that clings to his figure, and his hair is long and brown. The camera then faces Pierre, who is appositely framed against the nocturnal rhythms of Pigalle of which he speaks so frequently. He takes a cigarette out of his handbag and sets it alight, as the portentous, stirring sound of a Gustav Mahler symphony creeps into the background. The bane of

Figure 6. *Before I Forget* (Jacques Nolot, 2007). Pierre (Jacques Nolot) dons an elegant black dress and lights a cigarette before entering a porn theater in Paris's red-light district.

every continuity editor's life, smoke unfurls in real life. Cigarettes are a temporal marker of the real's incursion into the fictional space of the diegesis. (There is, as the proverbial saying goes, no smoke without fire. Within Charles Sanders Peirce's semiotic schema, cigarette smoke—like photography—pertains to the category of the indexical sign). To this indexical image *en abyme* Nolot adds the shuffling of passersby whose noises are not masked by the extradiegetic soundtrack. While Pierre savors his cigarette, we witness two men walk by before noticing the filming and entering the frame—another intrusion into the hermetic space of the film's fiction. From one patron's apologetic nod of the head, we presume that the film's crew has alerted the two men to move on. Moments later Pierre, too, must leave the threshold of the entrance lobby, marking the passage from "real" to "reel" that was also at play in *Porn Theatre.* Moving away from the lobby's outdoor threshold, the camera yields to what Barthes calls the *lure* of cinema—the fantasmatic promise of its interior spaces. Escaping the background noise and the indignities of the world outside, Pierre sets foot in the theater. The camera angle shifts to offer us a view of his back, as he is engulfed in the darkness. "What does the dark of the cinema signify?" (346), wonders Barthes in "Leaving the Movie Theatre." As Pierre enters the theater anew in these final frames, Nolot holds this question enigmatically open.

3

QUARTIERS CHAUDS LOITERING, QUEER ZONES, AND BANLIEUE AESTHETICS

> By choosing to film in this town's hot spot, I wanted to understand the word "hot" in an erotic rather than violent sense.
>
> —Christophe Honoré

THE SOCIAL WORLD THAT JACQUES NOLOT puts on display in *Before I Forget* is an exclusionary vision of Paris. And the film's whiteness is articulated primarily through its treatment of nonwhite others and the role they play in structuring the gay social imaginary. As I suggested in the previous chapter, there are two noteworthy moments in which race surfaces conspicuously. First, in an early scene the Parisian banlieue is described as a space of both danger and racialized fantasy. To recall this moment from the film, Pierre explains to a friend, "When I am seeking out sexual thrills, I go to the banlieue. That's where *real* fear is. . . . It's what Pasolini used to do. But then again, Pasolini is dead." Nolot strikes an ambivalent note by placing these "risky" sexual escapades under the sign of Pier Paolo Pasolini. On the one hand, what links the Roman *borgate* whose textures we find richly documented in Pasolini's *Boys Alive* (1955) and the fantasmatic space of Nolot's banlieue is that these are working-class neighborhoods—areas that will act as the ground for both writer–filmmakers' sexual slumming. Yet we can also note how Nolot's citational strategy also enfolds himself within an intellectual tradition of gay cruising poetics. What is clear, however, is that within this curious operation of sublimation and desublimation, the exploration of social and sexual alterity is a one-way street. The banlieue subject hovers menacingly out of frame.

The second moment in which these dynamics are played out is in the domestic scene in which we encounter Khalid, a young Moroccan man who delivers Pierre's groceries, receives oral sex from him, and promptly leaves. This taciturn character occupies what Ann Marie Stoler, writing in the context of French literature, calls the "emptied space of 'the Arab.'"[1] Khalid also represents what Mehammed Amadeus Mack, Nick Rees-Roberts, and Maxime Cervulle refer to as the *garçon arabe,* a common character or trope in the gay cinematic or literary récit whose very name bespeaks the paternalistic and Orientalizing overtones that remain pervasive in this mode of cultural production.[2]

In both moments, the film gestures, albeit dismissively, to those spaces and subjects that are habitually consigned to the narrowest of representational leeways in French queer cinema. In this chapter I aim to broaden out a discussion of the social geographies of Paris and its suburbs and address the question of race that hovers in the background of Nolot's final film. I delve into these two motifs—the figure of the *garçon arabe* and the space of the banlieue—to explore the place of the racialized queer within the French cinematic landscape. I do so first by turning to Sébastien Lifshitz's *Open Bodies* (*Les corps ouverts,* 1999), a film that explores a queer *beur* youth and his experiences of Paris, and I then cross over to the Parisian banlieue in Christophe Honoré's *Man at Bath* (*Homme au bain,* 2010).

Race and sexuality are entwined in highly specific ways in French culture. In *Sexagon* (a study whose very title brings together ideas of sexuality and nationhood), Mack frames the banlieue as the front line in an ideological battle for contemporary debates about sexual liberalism and national belonging. And in *Homo exoticus: Race, classe et critique queer,* Rees-Roberts and Cervulle analyze a variety of cultural texts that bespeak the geopolitics of racialized eroticism in France, most notably the "postcolonial pornography" produced by adult media studios like Citébeur. If Mack's portmanteau of the sexagon braids together understandings of space and belonging, then Rees-Roberts and Cervulle's privileged object, Citébeur, echoes this formal logic in reverse: the *beur* (a French slang term for "Arab") represents the social subject who does not belong, in a zone of nonbelonging, the *cité* or housing project.

Nolot's framing of the banlieue as a locus of danger performs a lot of semiotic work that might not be immediately apparent to those unacquainted with political discourse in contemporary France. In essence, his evocation of this overdetermined space becomes a way of speaking about more intractable questions of race by another means. To understand these subtle rhetorical maneuvers, a comparative lens can prove instructive. In *Badlands of the Republic,* Mustafa Dikeç notes that in France the primary object of urban policy is "space," rather than the notion of "community" that we find discussed in British and American contexts.[3] The choice to avoid "community" as a key term is one that stems back to the founding idea(l) of the French Republic as "one and indivisible." Communit*ies*—when figured in the plural—represent a threat, a splintering, an erosion of this foundational principle of unity (and the related the notion of *communautarisme* names a form of identity politics that is to be avoided). The notion of "space," by contrast, has the benefit that it is infinitely parsable or divisible but always retains its status as a unitary whole. As such it does not entail the threat of separatism. Such appeals to the language of space also belie another kind of ideological framing. These semiotic maneuvers do not meaningfully change the fact that in France (as in the United States or Great Britain) socioeconomic and racial disparities persist as social issues. If the term "community" figures as a euphemistic way of naming and encompassing racial difference within Anglo-American contexts, then the signifying chain moves one step further in a French context that appeals to ideas of "space" rather than "community." A French Republican ambivalence toward frankly discussing race displaces these important questions and nudges them into the seemingly neutral domain of space. Though, as Nolot's film makes clear, merely the mention of the banlieue has a distinctly racial connotation, which I will explore below. Before I do this I want to linger in the center of Paris for a little longer to inhabit it from a very different perspective.

While this book is motivated by the contention that a space-based approach to cinema is productive, we ought to be cognizant of the shortcomings this method entails. For example, in *Spectacle of Property*—a book that explores cinema's enduring fascination with the space of the house—John David Rhodes reminds us that even the seemingly neutral choice of his book's object (the single-unit family dwelling) runs the risk of producing its own methodological "zoning law," whereby those (often racialized subjects) who have only a tenuous grasp on this privileged form of property fall outside its purview.[4] One way of avoiding such a pitfall in spatial analysis, I suggest, is to conceive of space less as a synonym for *a* place, site, or built environment, but rather as a realm of experience that comes into being through a mobile subject's spatial practices. As a way into exploring the lived spaces of queer and racialized bodies who exist in between spaces, I turn to Sébastien Lifshitz's *Open Bodies,* a film that reflects on the tenuous position of the queer Maghrebi subject in Paris. Departing from the organizing principles of the rest of this book, my focus here is less on any specific location and more on how racialized bodies navigate space.

Open Bodies, or The Right to Loiter

Open Bodies is the first part of a tryptic of early films that queer filmmaker Sébastien Lifshitz made with Yasmine Belmadi, a Franco-Algerian actor who grew up in the banlieue town of Aubervilliers and tragically died in a motorcycle accident in his early thirties. Across Belmadi's three performances, we find a crystallization of a particular kind of young queer *beur* subjectivity. His first role was as Rémi in *Open Bodies,* a final-year high school student fast approaching a series of crossroads in his life regarding his professional future, his identity, and the perceived incompatibility of his sexuality with his North African heritage. In Lifshitz's subsequent film, *Cold Lands* (*Les terres froides,* 1999), he embodies and reconfigures a long-established figure of the "difficult Arab boy" (a neocolonial and paternalistic motif with a long and persistent history in French literature).[5] Here Belmadi's character Djamel leaves greater Paris in search of his father in the Alps. If his troubling of the (white) family unit might be read as what Rees-Roberts and Cervulle call an "entryist" narrative (indeed, the figure of the Pasolinian angel was also explored in a 1999 film by François Ozon, *Sitcom*), then the dignity Lifshitz bestows on Djamel is decidedly *un*-Pasolinian insofar as his subjectivity is fully fleshed out. In Lifshitz's third film, *Wild Side* (2004)—whose central love triangle neatly embodies and metonymizes themes of sex work, ethnic difference, and racialized precarity—we are introduced to Belmadi's character, a hustler also called Djamel, as he solicits clients in Paris's Gare de

L'Est railway terminal. In the subsequent scene, Lifshitz introduces a sequence of intercalated shots that point to Djamel/Belmadi's upbringing (childhood photos) followed by high-angle shots of a tower block in Aubervilliers. Space plays a fundamental role in this triptych, given that each film explores how social and geographic locations either encourage or prohibit various forms of sexual expression. *Wild Side* charts the movement away from Paris and toward the desolate lands of northern France. There, the film's protagonist, a transgender sex worker named Stéphanie, and her two lovers reckon with questions of domestic space and rural tradition. Similar dynamics are also explored in *Cold Lands.* In the case of *Open Bodies,* what Rees-Roberts identifies as Lifshitz's overarching attention to questions of inhospitality in France at the turn of the twenty-first century is brought to bear on the city of Paris itself.

Open Bodies occupies an important place in the Lifshitz oeuvre. In 1998 the short film garnered the prix Jean Vigo, a prize dedicated to uncovering emerging talent in French auteur cinema. It follows Rémi, a seventeen-year-old *beur* teen, over the course of a few days. He lives with his ailing father and his sister in northeastern Paris while completing his final year of high school and working part-time in a grocery store. He answers an ad to be in a film, directed by an older man named Marc, but is given few details about what this will entail. While there appears to be some sort of sexual relationship between Rémi and Marc, the precise nature of this relation remains illegible.

The film presents a young man at the cusp of adulthood. It explores Rémi's everyday existence, focusing on the moments of emptiness, drift, vacancy, transit, loitering, and—toward the end of the film—cruising, which give texture to his daily routine. Here we find an early iteration of a theme Lifshitz would go on to explore further in *Wild Side:* the existential reckoning of the queer subject who is in the process of losing their parents, and with this, loosening the binds of paternal prohibition.[6] But lest we assume that his queerness will come into direct conflict with his origins, thereby staging a clash of cultural values, Lifshitz resists pitting sexuality against religion or ethnicity. He is much more interested in uncovering the gray areas, queer zones, and spaces of political ambivalence that open up if we simply follow Rémi's daily movements.

The film opens with a shot of Rémi standing on a bridge, overlooking the rail tracks of the Gare du Nord transit station. He sings a song that combines Tamazight (a language spoken in North Algeria) with French. This coalescing of cultures is also echoed in the geographical location of this scene. We are in the environs of the Goutte d'Or, a district of northeastern Paris tucked behind the Gare du Nord, whose character bares the impress of the Maghrebi communities that have lived there over the past half century. Lifshitz's presentation of a distinctly postcolonial Paris is also echoed in a scene toward the end of the film that combines diverse visual and auditory elements to similar effect. Here we follow Rémi meandering through the streets of Belleville late at night, listening to his Walkman. (The soundscape is dominated by an improvisation played on the oud, a stringed instrument of Arabic origin.) Lifshitz cuts to a point-of-view shot that reveals a glowing Eiffel Tower in the distance that, coupled with the motif of the headphones, we might adduce, seeks to reproduce the phenomenological coordinates of Rémi's experience of city space. His experience feels temporarily coextensive with our own. If "headphones invite complicated questions about the relation of bodies to world, and how our bodies extend into space or retreat from it," as Kyle Stevens writes, then these questions obtain an important political valence in *Open Bodies* given the film's exploration of the differential distribution of, and access to, space in the French capital.[7]

Following the opening scene, Lifshitz sets out some of the coordinates of Rémi's life in a nonchronological fashion. We watch Rémi tuck his ailing father in bed; we cut to a scene of him and his partner, Marc, in a café on the verge of a breakup; we cut abruptly to a scene of Rémi fingering the nipple of a woman and kissing her in bed. The speed with which Lifshitz moves undermines the ostensible purpose of establishing scenes—far from shoring up a sense of epistemic certitude, they suggest the film's governing tone will be one of tentativeness and indecision. On one level, the film details Rémi's movement through the spaces of Paris and its fraught, contradictory set of ideological coordinates: from the religious space of the home, to the Republican site of the school, to the city's subcultural and queer zones (underground raves, sex shops, and cruising grounds). Yet to pass too quickly to a description of these spaces is to miss the film's interest in how Rémi lingers, and loiters, at their thresholds. It is to this process of loitering that I dedicate my attention. For while it would be tempting to move to the subject of cruising that constitutes a recurrent motif in this book, I linger with the notion of loitering because it allows us to better appreciate Rémi's spatial practices and, by extension, how racialized queers inhabit urban space.

While "loitering" might be understood as a cognate to the two spatial practices I have discussed so far in this book—*flânerie* and cruising—this term (and its French equivalents, *trainer* and *roder*) contains subtle nuances that are worth considering. Loitering leads us in a different direction from *flânerie* because it is the preserve of the idle wandering subject who, for various reasons, is not predisposed to consume the delights of the city in the liberal, luxurious, and deliberative manner that characterizes the *flâneur.* The figure of the loiterer, moreover, offers us an important point of reference insofar as he sits between the erotic disinterest of the *flâneur* and the sexual single-mindedness of the gay cruiser.

To be clear, I am not the first person to mention the notion of loitering in a discussion of this film. Joe Hardwick draws on the term to describe the film's digressive, aleatory, circuitous formal structure as well as Rémi's spatial practices.[8] His understanding of loitering is drawn from Ross Chambers's *Loiterature,* a book that describes a corpus of texts whose shared "emphasis is on digression and which feature principal characters who loiter, wander, stroll, tour or cruise without a specific destination in mind."[9] For Hardwick, the notion of loitering resonates with two aspects of Lifshitz's film. First, the film's scrambled narrative exemplifies what Chambers calls the "time-out" quality of loiterly writing: "Its failure to detach itself completely from a linearity from which it departs only to return in due course, is as characteristic a feature as its digressivity and errancy."[10] Second, Hardwick describes Rémi as "loiterly figure" who is "under pressure to shore up his future identity in different ways, for it is not only in terms of age that Rémi is seen as a figure that mediates between different contexts."[11] While a discussion of secondary scholarship on *Open Bodies* might feel like retreading old ground (or loitering in the byways of somebody else's argument, as it were), I draw attention to this critical framework because I believe Hardwick's appeal to Chambers misses a *trick.* Or rather, he narrowly misses an encounter with Roland Barthes. Both "Barthes, the intellectual" who penned the preface to Renaud Camus's *Tricks* (and who, like Chambers, understands the loiterly practice of cruising as not only a subject to be depicted, but also a formal structure and mode of reception), and the "off-duty Barthes" whose firsthand experiences of loitering and cruising in Paris and North Africa we came to learn of only in his posthumously published work.

In a chapter from *Loiterature* titled "Pointless Stories, Storyless Points," Chambers offers an appraisal of two essays by Barthes in which the theorist describes the fragmentary, digressive, and recursive rhythms of his cruising encounters. In "Incidents," Barthes offers diaristic reflections of his time in Morocco that lays bare his sexual preferences for Maghrebi "boys" and is replete with Orientalizing clichés. In "Soirées de Paris" (a text I mentioned briefly in chapter 2), Barthes strikes a more desultory tone, describing his unconsummated sexual encounters with hustlers in Paris some ten years later. Reading these two texts in tandem, Chambers wonders, "If the *stress* on commoditization in 'Soirées de Paris' functions as a sign of the sexual cruiser's forgetting of his (nevertheless readable) colonial identity, does the corresponding *de-emphasis* of commoditization in 'Incidents' indicate . . . *another* way of forgetting 'coloniality,' one that corresponds structurally to the sexual tourist's desire to naturalize his relation to the (commoditized, colonized) cultural other?"[12]

By reading Barthes's narratives contrapuntally—which entails holding in tension the vast geographic distance between Paris and the Maghreb, as well as the colonial continuum between these spaces—Chambers sees the generative friction between the two posthumous texts as emblematic of something "of which gay male theory and historical research has been, I think symptomatically, relatively oblivious, namely the incidences that might connect the emergence in the West over the last century or so of a gay male sexual identity with the historical apogee of colonial empires, like the British and the French, that conceived of themselves as modern."[13] In Chambers's exegesis of these two essays, they emerge as symptoms of a specifically gay mode of postcolonial amnesia, an "illusion of the (homo)sexual cruiser who forgets the identities that make [Barthes], say, white, middle class, and wealthy, and is thus able to relate on 'equal' terms with, say, working-class or racially 'other' men."[14] Ironically, this same amnesia is unwittingly reproduced in Hardwick's own invocation of *Loiterature* to discuss a film that centers the queer Maghrebi subject yet fails to interrogate how the experience of cruising in the French capital so often bears the ineluctable residue of colonial relations.

In *Homo exoticus,* Rees-Roberts and Cervulle place Barthes within a wider constellation of French gay authors whose récits share a number of common traits: these texts, which often discuss cruising and sexual tourism in the Maghreb, routinely fetishize younger *beur* subjects, and the "enunciators" of such texts "remain the same: white gay men."[15] What is therefore particularly striking about Lifshitz's film is how it is both conscious of this tendency (notably through Rémi's entanglement with the older figure of Marc, and with a cameo from Lifshitz himself) but maintains a committed focus on how Rémi's movements through space might take us away from the Barthesian paradigm of the white gay subject. Through its attuned to other economies of loitering, cruising, and inhabiting public space, *Open Bodies* brings to light a *differential* sexual and spatial economy—one in which attention, risk, and precarity come to be organized along lines of race and class.

In his work in Black queer studies, La Marr Jurelle Bruce argues for a reappraisal of the practice of loitering. While loitering, as per its dictionary definitions, is to "remain in an area for no obvious reason" and to "linger aimlessly or as if aimless," Bruce argues that this "appearance of aimlessness might conceal a truth of deliberation, strategy, and care."[16] Loitering, when reconceptualized as a "willful, ethical, critical, radical inertia," can form part of an arsenal of tactics used by queer people of color to resist the disciplinary forces that keep them in place.[17] Understood as a practice of resistance or opacity, loitering poses a challenge to normative ideas of spatial dwelling. To loiter, moreover, is not only to linger in and with an immanent present but to tarry with the past. The queer racialized loiterer does not conspire with post-racial platitudes and dominant discourse insisting we ought to "'get over' or move past" a past characterized by more flagrant forms of racial and spatial segregation.[18] Bruce explains that the act or charge of loitering more readily attaches to racialized bodies, which shows how access to space is organized along racial lines. "Loitering," he continues, "queers and signifies upon the legal category of 'vagrancy.'"[19] In conscripting such a loiterer to my own cause (a reading of the precarious emplacement of the queer subject in Paris), it is not my intention to level differences between France and an American context, nor to evacuate from Bruce's powerful critique its cultural specificity.[20] Rather, I insist on this term insofar as it offers a useful foil to the oft-romanticized and overdetermined figures of the *flâneur* and the *cruiser.*

The place that minor practices of loitering, wandering, digression, and divagation occupy in relation to canonical French spatial theory has been briefly addressed in the work of Sarah Cervenak. In *Wandering: Philosophical Performances of Racial and Sexual Freedom,* she pushes against the coupling of spatial practices and speech acts, or walking and writing, that is paradigmatically articulated in Michel de Certeau's essay "Walking in the City." De Certeau's formulation of "walking as a space of enunciation," she notes, both "implies a shared quality of discursive availability" and "rests on the presumption of the walker as agent."[21] How, Cervenak asks, are these presuppositions about agency and legibility complicated or cast into doubt when the wandering subject in question is not a racially unmarked *flâneur,* but a subject whose "acting out(s) are always already surveilled"?[22] I wager that Lifshitz's film is cognizant of and attentive to such strategies of surveillance. Rémi is often careful not to reveal too much through his minimal speech and tentative movements. The question of his corporeal "legibility" is also explored in relation to his sexuality. In an early scene, Rémi undertakes a screen test

Figure 7. *Open Bodies* (Sébastien Lifshitz, 1998). Having entered a sex shop in central Paris, Rémi (Yasmine Belmadi) surveys his new surroundings. The dimly lit corridor will lead him to an underground dark room.

for his filmmaker/lover, Marc. Seeking to catch him off guard, Marc has set up a camera. It is only midway through the scene that he reveals Rémi is being filmed. In a later scene, which is also drawn from these screen tests, Rémi inquires about the subject of these films. The ever-evasive Marc asks if he would be willing to play *un mec marginale* (a marginal man). Upon further probing, the term "marginal" refers to not only Rémi's ethnicity but also his queerness.

There is a moment in the film when Rémi's loitering gradually abuts onto the more eroticized practice of cruising. Immediately before the scene in question, Rémi is in an economics lesson but decides to skip the rest of class. In a fragment of the classroom discussion, we hear his teacher extolling the virtues of "learning to decrypt the information you are given every day," given that "it is important for you, as citizens, to understand your environments." Rémi's discovery of the queer zones of Paris in the following scene will extend his education in the reading of space. We follow Rémi as he takes the subway and wanders through the streets of northern Paris. Once again, the evocative, extradiegetic soundscape of the oud inflects these multicultural streetscapes with the not-so-subtle signifiers of "Eastern" alterity. Lifshitz cuts to a shot from inside a sex shop, the since-closed Club 88, on the rue Saint-Denis. (It is worth noting that this street was historically home to one of the most famous red-light districts in the heart of Paris. Nowadays, sex shops stand side by side with Arab-owned businesses catering both to tourists and the passing footfall from the nearby transport hub of Châtelet–Les Halles.) The ensuing sequence guides us through a labyrinthine pornotopia: a traveling shot reveals a wall-to-wall selection of erotic VHS tapes. Further into the sex shop we see a wall of television screens framed by a backlight, followed by a close-up on dildos, silicone fists, and other sexual paraphernalia. The camera tracks Rémi's body as he wanders, semisurreptitiously, through the shop and up the stairs to an adjoining sex club. We continue to watch him from behind: his body basks in the glow of a dim, electric blue light as he walks through a maze of video cabins. A flurry of pornographic images, produced by "zapping" through channels in the booths, acts as a connective tissue between this corridor space and the subsequent shot, in which we see Rémi enter a porn theater. As with Nolot's film by that name, the screened images are partially obscured by the bodies that circle in front of the screen. The contours of their silhouettes warp the plane of the projected image. Rémi moves deeper into the depths of the building, into a cruising zone dimly lit with dramatic red and blue lights that produce high contrasts and deep shadows. There he encounters a man, played by Lifshitz himself, with whom he will have his first cruising encounter. We cut to the two men walking out onto the rue Saint-Denis and parting ways. Each layer of this sexual and spatial initiation brings Rémi closer to the consummation of his carnal desires—the scene moves from VHS tapes to their private exhibition in video booths, from public exhibitionism to cruising and its eventual consummation. And with this gradual movement from mediatization of sex to its corporeal fulfillment, we also witness Rémi's own spatial practices gradually shifting in nature, from the tentativeness of the loiterer to the sexual frankness of cruising—and with it a new "understanding of [Rémi's] environments."

The Occlusion of Bisexual Space

Open Bodies, and the critical readings it has generated, provides an object lesson in the problems of conceiving bisexuality on screen. In a formalist reading, Todd Reeser draws attention to its nonlinear narrative, elaborating a theory of the "queer cut" to describe how it is "impossible to transition from heterosexuality to homosexuality in any kind of linear way."[23] Here he focuses on the transition between two early scenes: the lover's quarrel between Rémi and Marc, followed abruptly by a close-up of a woman's breast, which Rémi fondles in a different space and time. For Reeser, this "sudden move from potentially homoerotic to female body allegorizes the lack of a linear coming-out process and the queerness of anti-linear temporality."[24] While a "coming-out process" is invoked only apophastically here, Reeser's reading is predicated on a definitive move, however temporally convoluted it may be, from one sexual object choice to another. However, a key term that remains absent from his reading is bisexuality. By way of closing, I briefly consider what it might mean to read the film's depiction of a sexual awakening not simply as an affirmation of Rémi's homosexual awakening, but also as a move from monosexuality (or a primary orientation toward one sexual object choice) to bisexuality.

Bisexuality is often treated as an epistemologically slippery concept, frequently attracting the charge of bad faith. And for Rémi, "bad faith" reverberates not only in a strictly existentialist sense (of not being true to oneself) but also in religious terms—although both understandings are, of course, interrelated. While queer studies has become increasingly attuned to the entanglements of race and sexuality, the more localized nexus of race and bisexuality has not received as sustained a consideration. I argue that the figure of Rémi in *Open Bodies* animates some of the specific tensions that emerge at this intersection. Within a Freudian schema, bisexuality has a particular *temporal* dimension; Freud's notion of an "originary bisexuality" is a state that subjects are expected to grow out of as they mature into a stable and legible (which is to say *monosexual*) identity. On this point, Merl Storr explains how bisexuality complicates Freudian doxa of an "originary psychical disposition from which the child evolves, passing through the Oedipal crisis and the rigours of repression to develop into either heterosexuality or homosexuality."[25] (The seventeen-year-old Rémi, who is on the cusp of adulthood and turns down the opportunity to name his sexuality on at least two occasions, embodies some of these tensions.) Marlon Ross has argued that Western discourses of sexual modernity, evolving in lockstep with colonial logics, are crucial to understanding the geopolitics of sexuality in an expanded field wherein the notion of "development" that subtly informs this temporal logic is crucial.[26]

In the sexological and anthropological imaginary, then, the teleological language of "development" is intimately entwined with racist and colonial logics; or as Clare Hemmings puts it, "bisexuality, as potential or behaviour, thus becomes associated with primitive societies, while homosexual or heterosexual monosexuality becomes a marker of modern civilisation."[27] In Lifshitz's film, Rémi feels the weight of this bind palpably. His unwillingness to name himself as queer according to dominant monosexist understandings is read as a sign of epistemological evasiveness and cultural or religious constraint. The difficult articulation of Rémi's bisexuality adds a further knot to what is already a double bind (or what French commentator Franck Chaumont calls *la double peine*, the double punishment) of being both queer and a racial minority. When understood from this perspective, Rémi's furtive movements through the complex and overdetermined ideological coordinates of Parisian space—

movements I characterize as a kind of loitering—ought not to be read as a sign of idleness. Rather, it figures an attempt to resist the imperatives of sexual self-nomination and the fixing of his subject position. While the protagonist of Lifshitz's film inhabits a marginal position in relation to Parisian space, these dynamics grow increasingly difficult for those queer of color characters who cross over the boulevard Périphérique and enter the zone of the banlieue. It is to this ideologically contested space we now turn.

Banlieue Aesthetics in *Man at Bath*

The banlieue names those urban spaces that exist between the formal limits of a given city and the peri-urban spaces on the outskirts of a metropolitan area. In the case of the greater Parisian region, it refers to all that falls on the other side of the boulevard Périphérique. Though it would be tempting to translate *banlieue* into English as "suburbs," this equivalence would be misleading. "Suburbs" suggests connotations of affluences, leafiness, and single-unit dwellings, whereas the banlieue has become synonymous with high-rise housing projects, social deprivation, and the failures of the Republican project of integration. As it has become pro forma to note, the term *banlieue* refers to space of banishment (*un lieu de ban*), naming a long tradition of relegating the urban poor beyond the boundaries of the city and precluding access to political power and cultural life. The evolution of today's Parisian banlieue can be traced across several key moments in the past century and a half. During the project of Hausmannization in the mid- to late nineteenth century, "dangerous" classes and social undesirables were pushed to the outer edges of the city. As a result, the previously porous boundary between Paris's center and its peripheries started to shore up. The postwar period saw the emergence of shanty towns in northern Paris that lodged immigrants from France's colonies who had been brought over to provide cheap labor for the nation's rebuilding efforts. During a thirty-year period of postwar prosperity known as Les Trente Glorieuses, large housing projects (*les grands ensembles*) were created in the banlieues to cater to middle-income households. Many of these populations moved on to better housing stock, such as single-unit dwellings (*la banlieue pavillionaire*), while immigrant populations moved into the cheaper high-rise buildings. The outer ring road created in 1958 thus acquired its prophylactic status retrospectively. By the late 1970s, a confluence of factors, including the oil crisis that marked the end of this period of prosperity, led to the scaling back of state funding for these housing estates. From the 1980s onward, these environments grew increasingly degraded and became a site of intense political contestation.

If the banlieue constitutes one of the primary "sites of a struggle for meaning" in contemporary France, as Carrie Tarr notes, then what is at stake in these contests?[28] Isabelle McNeill argues that these spaces are "haunted by a colonial history that media and state discourse has often obscured, a disavowal that testifies to the ongoing 'fracture coloniale' [colonial fracture] in France."[29] In *Badlands of the Republic* Mustafa Dikeç similarly understands the banlieue as a discursive fulcrum point, a site of ideological contestation, and a metonym that evokes the lack of social integration in France. The time at which the banlieue started to gain its negative representation (the early 1970s) coincided with the moment that Henri Lefebvre's political theory of spatial reordering was starting to gain traction in France. Indeed, the banlieue provides an object lesson for Lefebvre's argument that how we describe and "conceive" of spaces discursively has material effects on spatial policy.

Echoing Lefebvre's broader argument against commonsense understandings about a presumed neutrality of how space is ordered, James F. Austin notes that "the banlieue is not . . . a spatial accident or fatality, but is rather generated as a spatial function of some larger system." For Austin, the banlieue serves as an index of "the role of the state in supporting the capitalist system in producing, through violence and political power, a separate, dominated space of repression and constraint; worrisome groups (the 'dangerous classes'), e.g. workers, are pushed to the periphery, while the center becomes a rarefied concentration of wealth, political power, and decision making."[30] Pushing this line of thinking a little further, Dikeç offers a timely reminder that "urban policy [is] a particular regime of representation that consolidates a certain spatial order through descriptive names, spatial designations, categorisations, definitions, mappings and statistics. In this sense, it is a place-making practice that spatially defines areas to be treated, associates problems with them, generates a certain discourse, and proposes solutions accordingly."[31]

Where do concerns with sexuality figure within the ideologically freighted terrain of the banlieue? We would do well to recall the claims, collectively advanced by Mack and Eric Fassin, that the vilification of France's nonwhite populations has taken new forms over recent decades, primarily through a renewed focus on gender and sexuality. Situating this line of argument alongside that of Dikeç, I argue, brings into view a curious triangulation of themes: in contemporary France, questions of race have been rearticulated both as concerns with urban spatial management (Dikeç) as well as questions of sexual citizenship and democracy (Mack and Fassin). There exist striking parallels between these two conceptual moves, both of which speak to an uneasiness with trafficking overtly in racial signifiers by turning to other concerns, whether spatial or sexual. As Mack goes on to argue, the banlieue has become the primary national site in which the intersections of race and sexuality are staged, developed, and contested.

Media panics about the state of the banlieue have been a common refrain in the French press since the 1990s and grew most pronounced in response to the infamous riots of 2005. Yet around 2009, this incendiary rhetoric took a new form as media outlets and cultural commentators focused their attention on the plight of the *queer* populations residing in France's banlieues. A steady stream of interventions elaborated a vision of the banlieue as a hotbed of homophobia and misogyny. As Fassin notes, 2009 alone saw the publication of two books that aimed to shed light on the grim realities of queer life in the banlieue: Franck Chaumont's *Homo-ghetto: Gays et lesbiennes dans les cités,* a putatively sociological study encompassing testimonies of six gay and lesbian subjects living in the banlieue (figures he dubs "the clandestines of the Republic"); and Brahit Naït-Balk's *Un homo dans la cité: La descente aux enfers puis la libération d'un homosexuel de culture maghrébine,* a first-person account of a Franco-Moroccan man growing up gay in the housing projects of Aulnay-sous-Bois.[32] Such interventions would also take different forms such as documentaries: Naït-Balk, for example, would go on to feature prominently in Mario Morelli's *Banlieue Gay* (2010), one of a number of documentaries on this topic whose governing tone and affective key is invariably characterized by miserabilism.

Although we should neither deny nor downplay the existence of misogyny and homophobia in the banlieue, it is important to lend a critical eye toward how these terms are framed. Our task, Fassin notes, is "to describe [the phenomenon of banlieue homophobia] without reinforcing it, by avoiding the traps of a rhetoric that, in opposing 'them' and 'us,' forces the former to define themselves in opposition to the latter, as if reaching to the clear conscience of a sexual democracy (which is not devoid of racism) where that expectation is most often imposed only on the other."[33] It is also important to question the political ends to which autobiographical récits are mobilized, given that these texts are more interested in stigmatizing minority ethnic populations than drawing attention to racialized stigma queer banlieue youth often receive from white sexual partners. What is left untroubled by the rapid proliferation of texts that traffic in "impressionistic examples" of queers who come out as "good sexual citizens" by leaving "once and for all the darkness and telos of *la banlieue*" is precisely the hegemonic whiteness of French queer culture itself.[34]

Fouad Zeraoui—whom we briefly encountered in this book through his on-screen role as a patron in Jacques Nolot's *Porn Theatre*—offers a crucial corrective to dominant discourses on the dearth of queer life in the banlieue in a tense exchange with Franck Chaumont.[35] While Chaumont describes the banlieue gay subjects who exist on the down-low as "schizophrenic," Zeraoui's approach to the closet, and questions of queer self-nomination in general, is more sensitive, situated, and pragmatic. (Or "reparative" rather than "paranoid," to redeploy two of the key terms of the closet's preeminent theorist, Eve Kosofsky Sedgwick.) Where Chaumont suggests that the gravitation of queers from the banlieue toward the city center is desirable (an indicator of free choice), Zeraoui questions whether this is necessarily a good thing. Moreover, whereas Chaumont's (white) liberal conception of sexual freedom finds its geographic home in central Paris, and the Marais in particular, Zeraoui finds within these elite spaces a powerful sense of conformity, as they "revolve around a few gay men with the same look, they represent the paucity of intellectual debate and cultural production," disabusing us of the seductive myth of liberal choice.[36] Much like Rémi, the *beur* protagonist of *Open Bodies* whose intuitive response to the pressures to become legible to a white gay monoculture is to refuse this very imperative, Zeraoui also valorizes the subtle strategies of resistance employed by queers of color and banlieue subjects. For these individuals, opacity ought not to be understood as a sign of bad faith or evasiveness, as Chaumont's paranoid reading would have it, but rather a powerful strategy of resistance to the overdetermined logic of the closet and the imperative of hypervisibility.

The commonplace (mis)conceptions associated with the banlieue that we find replicated across *Homo-ghetto*'s impressionistic portrait of urban subcultures are both nourished and amplified by the cinema. In *Une histoire des banlieues françaises,* Erwan Ruty argues that cinema is the primary cultural vehicle for representations of the banlieue. From the 1990s onward, a so-called *cinéma de banlieue* came to name a particular genre of popular French filmmaking, which reached its cultural apex with the release of Mathieu Kassovitz's 1995 film *Hate* (*La haine*). Explorations of same-sex intimacy in the banlieue, however, are much harder to come by outside of the realms of sensationalist TV exposés or, indeed, adult media. Apropos the latter category, the banlieue often emerges as a privileged backdrop for postcolonial pornography, a term Rees-Roberts and Cervulle use to refer to low-budget production studios such as Citébeur that traffic in scenes of racialized and hypervirile sexual performances unfolding in the "supposedly sexy underworld of poor, peripheral housing estates."[37]

To animate my discussion of the queer banlieue I close this chapter by turning to Christophe Honoré's *Man at Bath,* a film that complicates these general—and *generic*—tendencies. On one level, this is a formally experimental film made by a director who has been described as a queer auteur and "grandchild" of the French New Wave, and it features film star Chiara Mastroianni, whose presence returns us to an erstwhile golden age of art cinema. (The child of French actress Catherine Deneuve and Italian actor Marcello Mastroianni, she effectively embodies the meeting point of two illustrious national traditions in European art cinema.) But at another level, Honoré draws from the sphere of adult media by casting in the film's leading role François Sagat, a white but Arab-coded actor who came to prominence in the gay pornographic imaginary via his performances as Azzedine for the aforementioned Citébeur studio. I suggest that Honoré's daring and promiscuous intermingling of cinematic traditions and cultural registers in this film offers a way out of the miserabilism that so inflected representations of the queer banlieue at the moment of its release. Yet by bringing questions of aesthetics, style, and cultural capital to the forefront of its consideration of banlieue representation, Honoré's film stages a kind of catachresis that amplifies, rather than quells, iniquities in queer culture.

I want to take up a formula that Mack advances in *Sexagon,* only to revise it and redeploy it to new ends. The first chapter of his book opens with the bold hypothesis that "the banlieue has a gender." By this, he refers to the idea of virility that characterizes subcultural expression in the banlieue. This culture of virility, which is indexed in clothing, gesture, language, and affective disposition, is habitually constructed by the French media as an "ethnicized sexual antimodernity" and dismissed by critics such as Chaumont who "neglect the contemporary socioeconomic factors that frequently bond the expression of virility to working-class communities and minority groups."[38] That this virility is not tethered to an understanding of masculinity, and exceeds stable gender categories, inflects it with queer potentiality. Mack excavates from a rich body of banlieue cultural texts scenes and moments of disidentification (or resistance to a [white] gay monoculture). The banlieue, therefore, becomes a "laboratory" for sexual and gendered expression. These urban peripheries emerge at the cutting edge of France's queer culture, rather than as its backwaters.[39] But while his work brilliantly excavates moments of queerness within canonical banlieue films (such as the eroticization of police brutality in an ostensibly hetero text like Jean Paul Ricquet's *My City's Gonna Crack / Ma 6-T va crack-er* [1997] or the queering of women's bodies in Céline Sciamma's *Girlhood / Bande de filles* [2014]), what largely falls outside the purview of this analysis is an attention to the *generic* norms of the *cinéma de banlieue.* Put another way, I suggest that the banlieue has not only a *gender* but a *genre,* and moreover that the queerness of Honoré's *Man at Bath* inheres not only in its presentation of diverse, plural, fleshed-out, and socially viable gay characters in the banlieue (important though these representational concerns are) but also in its subversion of the generic and aesthetic tropes we associate with banlieue cinema. However, as we will also see, such generic and aesthetic subversions are not de facto liberatory.

Quartiers chauds

The opening of the film presents a gay couple's relationship on the rocks. François Sagat plays Emmanuel, the live-in lover of Omar (played by Omar Ben Sellem), a hipster filmmaker with a 1970s moustache. The pair live together in a flat in a Gennevilliers tower block that serves as the film's primary setting. Omar is about to depart for a trip to New York to promote a film with Chiara Mastroianni. Prior to leaving, he is brutally fucked by Emmanuel in a manner that recalls the virile tropes and macho gestures for which Sagat's porn persona is renowned. Omar tells him to clear out of his apartment before his return. Honoré's film presents two parallel narratives that are built around a series of sexual encounters. In Gennevilliers we follow the loiterly and aimless existence of Emmanuel, who has little money on which to survive. He meets up with a range of sexual partners, from art aficionado Robin (played by Dennis Cooper) who resides in the flat above and pays to see him naked; Rabah, a *beur* high schooler who follows him around the neighboring streets and tries to seduce him; and another mustachioed hipster whom Emmanuel encounters while cruising the wasteland below the tower block. In the second strand of the film, which Honoré describes as "a Jonas Mekas–type diary," we follow Omar's video camera as it tracks Mastroianni around New York City to promote a film. Here he will pick up a Dustin, a Canadian film student.[40] The film ends with Omar returning to an empty apartment.

Man at Bath received mixed reviews, with some critics describing it as a spatially disorienting film and others reproaching it for its single-minded orientation toward sex—or *le cul,* to invoke the more apposite French term that refers both to sex in general and Sagat's posterior in particular. Honoré's rough-hewn film shuttles its spectators back and forth across the transatlantic divide that separates the two lovers. This jet lag effect is amplified by the constant switching between crisp digital cinematography and blurry handheld footage. In one sense, the film's form (its patchiness, susceptibility to meandering, and inability to tie up narrative loose ends) might be said to allegorize the couple's strained relationship. However, this reading risks overlooking or obscuring some of the circumstantial and material conditions of the film's production. If, as David E. James writes, every film "internalizes the conditions of its production," making "itself an allegory of them," then in *Man at Bath* this "encoding" of the film's embattled mode of production is etched into its very textures from its very first scene.[41] To offer some context, *Man at Bath* was made with the financial backing of the Théâtre de Gennevilliers, whose annual filmmaking fund Honoré had secured for 2010. (Previous recipients of this award include Bertrand Bonello and Jean-Paul Civeyrac.) The modest funding gave him carte blanche to produce a short film, with the stipulation that the resultant work would be filmed in and respond to the municipal area of Gennevilliers, a working-class banlieue town northwest of Paris. The project, however, was not given the green light by all the associated stakeholders and filming rights were not granted to Honoré by local authorities in Le Luth, the so-called *quartier sensible* (difficult area) in which much of the film unfolds. As a result of this prohibition, the outdoor images of the housing estate that we see in the film's opening were filmed on the fly by a handheld camera. The film begins with a shot of an iron fence in the foreground, a concrete lot, some storage facilities, and a huge housing estate in the background. The scene is accompanied by an ambient soundscape of revving motorcycles and some distant commotion. The shaky camera pans leftward to reveal another building, followed by a glimpse of Omar, who is holding the camera as he tries to light his cigarette. A third shot, now taken from inside the housing block, focuses on a man walking amid the parking lot below, before zooming out to show a panorama of the *cité*. The prohibition on filming these images of Le Luth imbues the opening shots with an air of clandestinity. The shaky footage of the projects recalls another genre of commonly circulated moving images of the banlieue, the numerous exposés that vie for attention on French evening television and are largely composed of hidden camera footage documenting daily altercations and legal infractions.

In the film's press release, Honoré explains his preconceived ideas about the banlieue: "I always found it hard to think about the Parisian banlieue as anything other than a province where Paris was at once accessible but untouchable."[42] He continues, "I had this facile idea that a province so close to Paris—at arm's length, but nonetheless ignored—could not produce dreams but only frustrations; a logic that signals humiliation and defeat. A place that evokes *vengeance rather than desire.*"[43] At first glance, his authorial statement might be read as a commitment to redressing common misrepresentations of the banlieue of the kind I mentioned above. (In fact, he goes on to envisage the film's setting as a "utopian frame in which desires can circulate without fear.") Yet in the final sentence, which sets up an opposition between vengeance and desire, Honoré unwittingly introduces a new problem into the discourse that accompanies the film. In effect, these putatively oppositional terms cannot be so neatly separated in this film, given that gay desire remains intimately entangled with dynamics of force and conflict, vengeance and virility. Because the tension between these drives constitutes the film's central problematic, *Man at Bath* ought to be understood as staging a broader tension in queer discourse between a logic of positive representation and a logic of transgression. This tension surfaces obliquely in Honoré's discussion of the film: "By choosing the area that had been designated the 'hottest' in town (Le Luth, whose officials in local government—for this very reason—did not authorize our shooting), I wanted to take this word 'hot' in its erotic, rather than violent, sense." I would contend, however, that the double valence of *quartier chaud*—which can be understood as a crime hot spot and also a space of (erotic) "hotness"—cannot be so neatly disambiguated given that representations of the banlieue we find in the films produced by Sagat's own former studio, Citébeur, vividly and problematically suggests hotness itself to emanate from the frictions in France's social fabric (or as Rees-Roberts describes it, the studio's "neat . . . package[ing] of a complex array of explosive dynamics").[44]

Figure 8. *Man at Bath* (Christophe Honoré, 2010). Emmanuel (François Sagat) loiters outside his housing project in Gennevilliers shortly before cruising his lover's look-a-like (Sebastian D'Azeglio).

What emerges from Emmanuel's sexual exploits in the Gennevilliers component of the film is a vision of sexual diversity. Here Honoré puts on view a "banlieue in counterpoint to the mainstream media as a relative paradise of spontaneous sexual opportunity and unchallenged homophilia."[45] This vision also resonates with Zeraoui's earlier account of the banlieue as one of the last bastions of sexual resistance to the dominant norm embodied by the space of the Marais. Yet the film is not so straightforwardly beholden to a logic of positive representation. Honoré's presentation of a wide range of sexual typologies—from the racialized thug (*caillera*s) to the twink schoolboy, from the mustachioed hipster to the aging art collector—reveals his abiding interest in the sexual and sociopolitical frictions that exist among them. Through his exploration of gay types who each evince a different relation to the space of the banlieue, the film reflects on the logic of gentrification of which Zeraoui (who was writing at the same moment) was also well aware. Omar is part of a transient population of queers and artists for whom the banlieue towns near Paris mark only a stepping stone toward some more promising horizon. Moreover, to further signal the recent emergence of the hipster type in the banlieue as part of a broader logic of gentrification, Emmanuel will cruise Omar's doppelgänger—credited simply as *l'homme à la moustache*—and invite him into his apartment, where he covers his face in yellow duct tape (perhaps an oblique reference to the masked icon of the hookup app Grindr), obscuring all but his moustache. Fuckable, fungible, a dime a dozen—Honoré's framing of the hipster in the banlieue ironically reverses the often-racialized logic of sexual "types" (i.e., the commerce in bodies) we find in much gay erotic cinema.

The Aesthetics of Banlieue Cinema

What I have so far been describing here is the rich *sociological* tapestry of the film. But it would be a mistake to reduce the film's political and aesthetic import to these terms. In "Re-presenting the Urban Periphery," a *Cinéaste* article that offers an evenhanded summation of banlieue cinema, Will Higbee characterizes the dominant mode of this genre as a "realist esthetic that employ[s] the alienating architecture of the housing estates to reflect the exclusion felt by the[se] films' youthful protagonists."[46] A similar emphasis on realism, and attendant notions of sociological transparency, characterizes Carrie Tarr's *Reframing Difference,* which focuses on two often overlapping products of French minor cinema from the 1990s onward: *beur* filmmaking and the *cinéma de banlieue.*[47] Too often, however, scholars and critics who focus on the banlieue reduce this space to its sociological import, thereby foreclosing the possibility of a consideration of the formal, aesthetic, and generic potentiality of these film texts. Honoré, whose film represents a queer outlier in the *cinéma de banlieue,* seems to actively anticipate the work's future conditions of reception and engages the aesthetic in highly original ways in a bid for us to treat the subject differently.

One of the primary conceptual throughlines in *Man at Bath* is the film's interest in the male form. Honoré explains that while his earlier films had become increasingly preoccupied with language, this film registered a conscious effort to go back to one of the primary objects with which cinema also traffics: the body. The body of Sagat, which stands at the center of the work and frames its promotional materials, is a rich text, replete with signification. His impressive musculature not only indicates the weight he pumps but carries a lot of (sociological) baggage. Sagat's form pushes the thuggish *cailleras* stereotype to its limit, forming an unlikely arc between a brutish macho virility and kitsch fascination. Thrown into this mix of corporeal signifiers, of course, is also the question of ethnicity. The crescent that crests along his back seems to place his body under the sign of Islam, but his tattoo is a red herring. He claims no Arab heritage and is of white Slovak ancestry, despite the racial cosplay we encounter across his pornographic back catalog.[48] Many of the forces that animate discourses of the queer banlieue—Arabness, masculinity, virility—find themselves metonymically inscribed onto, or ascribed to, his hypertrophied body. The aesthetic critique of his body, and by extension the *space* with which this body type is associated, thus forms a crucial part of the film's geographic commentary.

Following the film's opening shots, which move us from the space outside the housing project and into the apartment, Emmanuel's lover Omar puts down his handheld camera and wanders into his bathroom. His voyeuristic gaze aligns with that of the camera. A point-of-view shot presents the spectacle of Emmanuel's body as he emerges from his bath and dries himself with a towel. The camera's gaze fixes on his body, focusing at first on his calves before gradually tilting upward to reveal his ass, his muscular back, and his signature shaved head and tattooed scalp. On the one hand, the visual cathexis of Sagat's body parts in this scene recalls the scopic regime of pornography. (Indeed, a shot–reverse shot sequence reveals Omar to be gazing lasciviously at Emmanuel's ass). Yet the film's spectators are invited to see within these images the contours of another man's body—one that circulates in a very different cultural register.

While Honoré knew little about the shooting location prior to making the film, he associated with Gennevilliers an artist who resided there in the mid- to late nineteenth century: "Gennevilliers inevitably evokes the name of the artist Gustave Caillebotte, who lived there for many years. Then this painting comes to mind, *Homme au Bain*"—which would end up providing both the name and aesthetic coordinates for the film.[49] Taking the image of a "virile" naked man in his Gennevilliers apartment as a guiding motif, he sought to create "a narrative at the start of the 21st century in response to this Man in the Bathroom from the end of the 19th."[50] But what exactly do the formal resonances, and the historic dissonances, between these two superimposed images reveal?

First, if we set Caillebotte's painting within the frame of its art historical reception, we note that much of the transgressive charge of *Man at His Bath* (*Homme au bain,* 1884), which depicts a naked man by a zinc bathtub drying himself with a gray towel, derives from its flouting of art historical conventions. The painting marks the male nude's incursion into a space of aesthetic representation (the domestic interior) typically reserved for women. But given that this genre of nude painting often depicted sex workers, there is also something apposite about Honoré's reenactment of this scene by a character who, we later learn, is also a part-time hustler. Sex work, in effect, sutures the present-day body to its historical antecedents.

But what is most significant in Honoré's art historical allusion is the way the male form is made to embody a certain idea of the banlieue. If Caillebotte's painting acts as an associative shorthand for a nineteenth-century idea of Gennevilliers in the mind of Honoré, then the queer filmmaker's reimagining of this scene, which draws on Emmanuel's striking physicality, takes this embodied logic in a different direction. When placed alongside its nineteenth-century source image, we learn that the present-day Gennevilliers and the body that comes to metonymize it share two essential features: both have become "built up" and their menacing reputations are both racially coded.

There is indeed another scene that bears the impress of art history and related notions of aesthetic judgment. Following the dramatic departure of Omar, who leaves his lover with neither food nor money, Emmanuel goes upstairs to the apartment of Robin (played by Dennis Cooper). He hastily undresses and starts to pose for the art critic, who sits in an armchair. Robin's apartment, replete with mid-century furniture and modernist art, feels like a relic from a bygone age: a superannuated vision of a way of life seemingly at odds with what we would imagine finding in the block's interiors. It is therefore not surprising that Emmanuel, who embodies a banlieue aesthetics down to the level of his corporeal form, strikes us as out of place in Robin's rarefied aesthetic frame. This art collector comments, "You're kinda like a sculpture. You know I like art. I mean, you look like someone who has carved something out of someone you thought was too simple, too raw. But would I buy you like I bought this other art? No, 'cause you're bad art. You're kitsch." Robin's words—like those of Cooper, the queer writer who gives voice to them—are measured, cold (like a scalpel), cut to the measure of a distinctly Sadean variant of desire. (Indeed, Leo Bersani remarks in his essay "Is There a Gay Art?" that Dennis Cooper's writing enacts a "cold and brutal ripping open of bodies as a means of knowing the other," and this ruthless detachment is clearly channeled by the writer/actor here.)[51] On this occasion, though, the obviousness of Sagat's corporeal offering obviates Robin's desire. For this true Kantian aesthete, the appetitive and beautiful, the hot and cold, are very much kept apart. The only way the cash-strapped Emmanuel can be paid, Robin explains, is by beating up and brutalizing a young twink named Rabah, who has become the new object of Robin's lust. In the scene, the Sadean figure of Robin thus returns us to the distinctly Pasolinian framework with which I started this chapter—one where the racialized banlieue queer is reduced to his capacity to play the thug to cater to the whims of the white wealthy aesthete. (Honoré in fact asked François Sagat to watch Pasolini's *Salò, or the 120 Days of Sodom / Salò o le 120 giornate di Sodoma* [1975] to help establish some of the aesthetic and erotic coordinates for the film.)

But what *Man at Bath* explores once it breaks out of Robin's apartment and its narrow aesthetic frame is an homage to the banlieue, one that looks beyond the received opinions of Robin the aesthete or the dicey sexual proclivities of Nolot's protagonist Pierre. Honoré goes on to explore the vibrancy of the *cité*'s sexual offering and the relationship between queer men (mostly men of color) on their own terms. Yet while Mack contends that the film strikes an "optimistic tone, as far as sexual opportunity and affective contentment are concerned," such a ringing endorsement of the film's sexual politics should nonetheless be attenuated.[52] In an interview conducted with Julien Nahmias the filmmaker explains his motivations for the film: "I was very attracted to the idea of going to Gennevilliers to film, and to bring a body like François Sagat's, who, for the little thugs in the area who spend their time at the gym, was the ideal guy, exactly what they wanted to become. It amuses me very much to think that these people start dreaming of becoming something like a porn-star bottom from homo porn, clearly unaware! In a way, it's a bit of perversity on my part."[53] On the one hand, we find powerful echoes of the argument Mack sets out above: namely, that there is a latent homoerotic potentiality in "excessive" (read: racially coded) displays of banlieue virility. But on the other hand, we can also detect in Honoré's statement a logic of epistemological entrapment ("these people" who are "clearly unaware") that risks reinforcing rather than destigmatizing the valence that "homo porn" and the figure of a penetrated "bottom" acquire in the banlieue. If *Man at Bath* reveals the spaces of the banlieue as queerer than we might otherwise have imagined, then it is perhaps instructive to ask to whom this "we" refers.[54]

4

A QUEER WINDOW ONTO THE WORLD?

VINCENT DIEUTRE'S DOCUMENTARY FRAMES

> The anchoring of gay cruising in the heart of Paris eliminates temporal gaps, while at the same time acting as a marker of identity and a trace of history.
>
> —Bruno Proth

TO PROGRESS TO THE CONCERNS of the present chapter it is once again necessary to cast a backward glance toward a previous one. Early on in *Before I Forget,* Jacques Nolot's alter ego Pierre is stationed in his car following a meeting with his lawyer. He pauses to smoke a cigarette before heading to Pigalle. The narrative (in)action in this scene gives way momentarily to the sound of a gravelly male voice broadcast over the car radio speaker. The topic of the on-air monologue is *la bêtise* (stupidity). The voice proceeds to recite a steady stream of aphorisms that runs thus: "Stupidity reduces the world to an 'I,' the other to the same, and difference to identity. It acknowledges original thought without really ever encountering it. It is the opposite of the exceptional, the ally of the ordinary, and the antithesis of the singular."[1] The portentous passage we listen to was penned by French philosopher François Zourabichvili, who takes as his theoretical point of departure Gilles Deleuze's meditation on the same subject in *Difference and Repetition* (1968).[2] Yet without this provenance, or indeed any other contextual indices ready to hand, we are encouraged to interpret the passage as a treatise against solipsism or hubris—themes that invariably align with Nolot's wry and introspective outlook as a writer, filmmaker, and autofictive subject. The text goes on to discuss self/other relations via a range of scopic analogies. Stupidity, we are told, "represents the part of us that, treating the other as if they were a concave or convex mirror, traverses the world in search of his likeness or his alter ego, his shadow or reflection." The deep voice that delivers this philosophical tract belongs to none other than Vincent Dieutre, the documentary filmmaker I take as my focus in this chapter.

Just as Nolot's intrusion into the cinematic universe of Claire Denis gave us a brief glimpse of his interests as a filmmaker, so, too, Dieutre's intervention in the narrative space of Nolot's film allows us to discern his own interests and approach to filmmaking. First, Dieutre's presence is summoned in auditory (rather than visual) form, pointing proleptically to the central role the acousmatic voice-over plays in his cinema.[3] Second, the philosophical fragment Dieutre recites raises themes that resonate with particular force in his work; ethical questions about self/other relations, and the tension between sameness and difference, are engaged with particular acuity in Dieutre's filmmaking, which rests at the increasingly porous border between autofiction and documentary.[4] And third, the text's foregrounding of travel and self-exploration anticipates the psychogeographic themes that are afforded a privileged place in his oeuvre, as we will see.

Between Men

If keen-eyed readers detect a presumptuousness in the translation of the text above, which renders the possessive adjective *son* in the masculine form (i.e., his), I do so deliberately to convey the idea that in the cinema of Vincent Dieutre any exploration of the limits or extensibility of the self is filtered through a specifically gay male model of relationality. Similarly to the intellectual project of Leo Bersani, who appears in his documentary *Tenebrae Lessons* (*Leçons de ténèbres,* 1999), the filmmaker's exploration of the tension between otherness and sameness, difference and identity, is read primarily through the lens of male homosexuality. Or as Emma Wilson writes, a "tangibl[e] focus on and champion[ing] of the specifics of male homosexuality, or 'homoness' to borrow Bersani's term" is evident across his body of film.[5] For Dieutre, the subjective apprehension of space remains entangled with questions of sexual sociability. Thus to extend the conceptual through line of this book, cruising will continue to provide a seductive metaphor to think through questions of cinematic space in his work.

The fertile connections between gay cruising and spectatorship are made explicit in an essay Dieutre penned in 2007 titled "'Et plus si affinités . . .': Le trick comme figure de la modernité au cinema" for a project conducted under the auspices of Jacques Aumont at the Cinémathèque française. Here, the filmmaker–theorist turns to Renaud Camus's infamous 1979 diary of sexual exploits, *Tricks,* to explore the erotic motif that lends the text its title.[6] The Camusian "trick" (or "hookup" in present-day parlance) is defined by Dieutre as "an immediate, nontransactional, consenting sexual encounter between two unknown subjects which, in principle at least, is without consequence."[7] The term, whose sexual and textual valences so fascinated Barthes, is deployed to describe his own relation to spectatorship and filmmaking practice. Operating in a manner akin to *la drague* (cruising), which became Barthes's choice metaphor when theorizing the cathexis of the reader–text relation in *The Pleasure of the Text,* the "trick" names a way of describing how certain cinematic techniques (e.g., elliptical editing, fragmentary montage) key to the arsenal of "modernist" filmmaking practices might queerly reorient the spectatorial experience.[8] Dieutre's writing on cinematic spectatorship encourages us to read between the lines to discern a fuller spectrum of erotic relations between bodies on screen: "Through my training as a spectator, I came to grasp intuitively how certain films hinted to the potentialities of this element [the 'trick'], and that it constituted a figure of modernity (or postmodernity) that broke with the typical amative discourse we find in literary or cinematic narratives in particular."[9] Echoing the vernacular criticism of Boyd McDonald (whose landmark text on queer film spectatorship, *Cruising the Movies* [1985], proposed an idiosyncratic approach to Code-era cinema to extract moments of homoerotic and queer pleasure from otherwise "straight" texts), Dieutre traces the "trick" across a body of cinema, inviting his cospectators to read for acts and relational forms that lie outside mainstream cinema's chastened moral economy and to linger with the sexually suggestive gaps, lapses, and ellipses to which the heteronormative gaze is all too often impervious.[10] His cinematic practice figures a formal attempt to give commensurate form to the subjective experience of dwelling in, and cruising through, the spaces of the European city. He asks how we might best capture in distinctly cinematic terms what Henning Bech terms the "special blend of closeness and distance, crowd and flickering, surface and gaze, freedom and danger" found in the modern city.[11]

The modern city continues to act as the privileged representational ground for Vincent Dieutre's cinema, and by extension this chapter. Given that Dieutre's work has largely eluded scholarly discussion, I start by offering a detailed introduction to his work. The three texts I go on to discuss offer a sense of the formal and thematic dimensions of his film, and each raises important documentary questions about how the world comes to be framed. The first of these is *Bonne Nouvelle,* a medium-length film that offers a series of visual and auditory snapshots of the eponymous Parisian neighborhood. Here, largely static shots of city space are overlaid with the filmmaker's voice-over. Implicitly evoking the Baudelairean motif of the *tableau parisien* (albeit in a way that supplants the poet's choice figure of the *flâneur* for that of the gay cruiser), Dieutre presents his audience with a series of diary entries, or vignettes, that serve to animate and populate the Parisian arrondissement in which he lives.

The second part of the chapter effects a move from the poetic tableau to that of the painter. I focus on the filmmaker's *Tenebrae Lessons,* a film that acts both as an autobiographical travelogue across Europe and an exploration of the fertile intersections among cinema, the art gallery, and urban space. The film unravels two narrative strands: the first is a documentary exploration of the artwork of the Caravaggisti, and the second is a personal meditation on cruising, loss, and gay desire. Through his careful crafting of voice-over narration, deployment of the close-up, and use of paratactical editing, Dieutre posits a series of visual and narrative equivalences between the film's cultural registers and narrative strands that grow increasingly entwined.

The final section of the chapter looks away from the painted frame and toward a window's aperture. In *Jaurès* (2012), Dieutre's camera films the eponymous Parisian neighborhood from the vantage point of his ex-lover's apartment window. Themes of intimacy, love, and sexual identity are superimposed onto Dieutre's exploration of the street scene below, thereby raising questions about how the construction of documentary space might negotiate the relationship between public and private spheres. By staging a set of encounters that moves us, in turn, from the urban tableau, to the painted canvas, to documentary cinema's "window onto the world," the thread of spatial inquiry that runs throughout this chapter is concerned with *how* Dieutre's films teach us to look. What are the possibilities and pitfalls of using gayness as the primary prism through which to view the world? Is a cinematic vision predicated on "homoness" antithetical to documentary cinema's constitutive fascination with alterity? Such questions, I argue, surface throughout the filmmaker's oeuvre.

Framing Vincent Dieutre's Cinema

Vincent Dieutre's work has enjoyed considerable success on the art cinema and documentary film circuits. Given the autobiographical thrust of his work, some details about his personal and professional trajectory are indispensable. Dieutre grew up in Rouen in the 1960s and studied art history at the University of Paris, followed by a practical film course at the prestigious IDHEC (Institut des hautes études cinématographiques, now known as the Fémis) in the mid-1980s. Upon graduation he was awarded a grant by the Villa Médicis, which afforded him both the time and means to travel to Rome and New York as a practicing filmmaker. The period in question, however, was marked by the filmmaker's increasing dependency on heroin and coincided with the early days of the HIV/AIDS epidemic. Both topics would be granted an assured place in his first film. Released in 1995 to largely critical acclaim, *Desolate Rome* (*Rome désolée*) presented Dieutre's formative sojourns in and around the Italian capital while also tackling from a largely autobiographical perspective the vicissitudes of his drug addiction and the enduring effects of AIDS, which had claimed the life of his former partner. Following several releases in the late 1990s and early 2000s, Dieutre started to forge a distinctive body of filmmaking that enmeshed autobiographical inquiry with explorations of urban space.

Dieutre's cinema represents a "sustained interrogation of what it means to be a gay man in the Europe of the early twenty-first century."[12] While his earliest films took as their focus the urban spaces of Paris and Rome, he has since ventured further afield, both geographically and thematically, to consider Europe's increasingly contested Mediterranean frontiers. This can be seen in his later films such as *Jaurès* and *Orlando Ferito* (2015), both of which tackle geopolitical questions of border-crossing and migration. Alongside his work as a practicing filmmaker, he has taught in universities and written extensively about cinema; he was a founding editor of the influential French film journal *La lettre du cinéma* and continues to play an important role in a community of "minor" French filmmakers involved with the *pointligneplan* collective and assembled under the banner of *le tiers cinéma* (a third cinema).

Dieutre's work is poised at the crossroads of three burgeoning movements in French cinema: experimental documentary, autofiction, and queer film. His list of artistic influences is notably expansive. Though he draws heavily on a recognizable canon of art cinema (notably Jean-Luc Godard, Marguerite Duras, and Jonas Mekas), he is not exclusively beholden to the cinematic medium. His films glean and scavenge from histories of art, sculpture, architecture, and literature, combining high art and subcultural objects with willful irreverence. Pulsing across his formally experimental practice is what I term an intermedial promiscuity—an interest in both putting art forms into conversation and collapsing the boundaries between discrete art forms and media *dispositifs*. Given the heterogeneity of Dieutre's practice, what assures his body of work a sense of coherence? For Tom Cuthbertson, his particular "brand of filmic autobiography entails a distinctly spatial emphasis."[13] Laurent Guido seems to concur with this assessment, noting that his "body of work offers a wide-ranging reflection on the state of Western culture by means of a series of travel narratives."[14] The titles of his films clearly attest to the central role afforded to place in his work. Some take their names from Parisian districts and Métro stations (*Bonne Nouvelle* and *Jaurès*), while others look to European cities (*Letters from Berlin / Lettres de Berlin,* 1988; *Desolate Rome / Rome désolée*; *Bologna centrale,* 2003) as the filmmaker explores his past. Some of Dieutre's lesser-known films take ideas of space and place into more conceptual territory, exploring movements across time and space and the navigation of historical archives; these include *My Winter Journey* (*Mon voyage d'hiver,* 2003), a road trip through the German hinterland under the sign of Franz Schubert, and *Journey through Post-History* (*Viaggio nella dopo-storia,* 2015), a film that charts the waning of one of Dieutre's relationships and the concomitant reaffirmation of the filmmaker's love for Roberto Rossellini's Naples. As Jean Pierre Carrier explains, Dieutre's spectators can expect to travel "to German and Italy, from Rome to Berlin. But also to Buenos Aires. And certainly to Paris."[15] Across this expansive cinematic cartography, they can expect to encounter common sights, sites, and motifs including "static shots of crossroads, or tracking shots slowly stretching the length of roads. Images that are most often nocturnal. Narrow alleys that are poorly lit. And an abundance of rain."[16]

While Dieutre's approach to cinematic space recalls the work of Patrick Keiller or William E. Jones, the filmmaker acknowledges a clear debt to two francophone filmmakers in particular: Chantal Akerman and Frédéric Mitterrand. He has previously suggested that it was a screening of Akerman's *Jeanne Dielman, 23, quai du Commerce, 1080 Bruxelles* (1975) as an impressionable teenager that alerted him to film's capacity to transform the rhythms of quotidian life into visual poetry. Two of his formal signatures—the use of acousmatic voice-overs and slow horizontal panning shots—are strongly reminiscent of Akerman's *News from Home* (1976), in which she adopts an epistolary mode of address to consider questions of exilic subjectivity when she, too, spent a formative period in New York in her twenties. Structural resonances can equally be found in their later works: Akerman's *Down There* (*La-bàs,* 2006) and Dieutre's *Jaurès* are both filmed from the aperture of an apartment window, and both offer explicit meditations on the psychological themes of interiority and exteriority and the delineation of public and private spheres. Yet while Akerman long remained reticent about the absorption of her work into a broader corpus of queer cinema—a position that critics have attributed to a French resistance to identitarian labels and/or an auteurist exceptionalism—Dieutre readily assumes such a label.

Dieutre's other significant forebear, Frédéric Mitterrand, is a little-known experimental filmmaker whose 1980s films contain a more explicit gay valence.[17] In *From Somalia with Love* (*Lettres d'amour en Somalie,* 1982), Mitterrand explores the first-person *journal intime* of its gay protagonist through the prism of travel, yoking together anthropological exploration and psychogeographic inquiry in a manner that clearly prefigures Dieutre's interest in the travelogue. In an analysis of *From Somalia,* which might also describe Dieutre's work, Roger Odin argues that

Mitterrand's filmmaking calls into question typical delineations between form and content, and between subjective and objective modes of address: "These long takes—which are obsessively fixed and obstinate in their wish to give us little or nothing to see—are not necessarily images of objects or places. Rather, they are images of mental, or even sentimental, spaces."[18] Treading a narrow path between realist modes of documentary filmmaking (that insist on documenting the exteriority of worldly appearances, of capturing the singularity or ipseity of a historically given "then" and "there") and subjective approaches (in which the contours of the exterior world are inflected and modulated by mood, subjectivity, affect, or emotion), Odin identifies a middle ground that Dieutre similarly occupies. As with his cinematic precursors, Dieutre's visual investment in empty, exterior spaces frequently serves as a counterpoint to the intimate and even introspective dimension of the spoken word. There is an implicitly thematic charge to the spatialization of voice and image across Dieutre's work; the position from which he speaks is crucially important.

This brings me to an important film-theoretical concern in this chapter. In her sustained body of scholarship dedicated to generically hybrid forms of modes such as the essayistic film and the subjective documentary, Laura Rascaroli argues that we ought to center our attention on the interplay between word and image to understand the accrual of meaning in documentary film. In a discussion of the "vococentricity" of essay filmmaking in *How the Essay Film Thinks* (2017), she suggests that while much ink has been spilled on the (social) *positionality* of a documentary's enunciating subject, we perhaps ought to heed greater attention to the *spatiality* of the spoken voice in documentary—its spatio-temporal positioning on top of, and its relation to, cinema's visual track.[19] The question of the voice has, of course, been thoroughly parsed in film theory, from the seminal accounts of Michel Chion, Pascal Bonitzer, and Mary Ann Doane to recent work focusing on the field of documentary in particular. Rascaroli warns against a tendency to reinforce the overdetermined position of the voice in documentary and naturalize its status as the primary locus of meaning-making. If such a consideration calls for a dialectical relationship between words and images on screen, then Dieutre's work is eminently suited to this task.[20] His films are often split between a largely impersonal image track (recording, for example, stretching landscapes, street scenes, or architectural details) and a voice-over that suffuses these images with personal stories and imbues these spaces with emotional resonance (producing "sentimental spaces" as Odin describes it). His work also provides an apt reminder that cinematic space is not reducible to the field of vision. Rather, as we will see, it entails an auditory dimension.

"Une microhistoire de drague et de drogue"

By way of a point of entry, let us first turn to *Bonne Nouvelle,* for it is here that we can find a fair encapsulation of Dieutre's formal techniques and thematic preoccupations, as well as encountering the spaces of his everyday life. The film presents a series of urban portraits of the eponymous neighborhood of Bonne Nouvelle, which straddles the second and tenth arrondissements of Paris and has been Dieutre's home over twenty years. In a pithy summary of the film, Vincent Ostria calls it "an exploration of [Dieutre's] neighborhood of the tenth arrondissement that is interspersed with micro-histories of drug use and cruising."[21]

The actual district of Bonne Nouvelle might accurately be described as one of historical and economic contradiction, with extremes existing in close proximity. In the narrow alleys between Grands Boulevards and Bourse (the apex of Haussmannian Paris and the city's former financial heart, respectively) we find the former textile workshops of Le Sentier that, as Dieutre reminds us, continue to operate as spaces of clandestine labor. Long-established Turkish and North African communities live on streets and squares whose names hark back to Napoleonic expeditions: rue d'Aboukir, rue du Nil, place du Caire. And while the district is perhaps best-known for architectural splendors such as the Grand Rex, an arts venue housed in a sumptuous former movie palace, or what the film's narrator describes as the "majestic arch" of the Porte Saint-Denis, Dieutre also touches on the social and historical complexities that belie the neighborhood's ostentatious facades. *Bonne Nouvelle* summons via voice-over narration a demimonde of precarious subjects for whom the auspicious connotations of the district's name—"Good News" in English—seem to ring especially hollow.

There exists, of course, a long tradition of essay films that turn to the streets of Paris to mount their particular brands of ideological critique, from Agnès Varda's feminist project *The So-Called Caryatids* (*Les dites cariatides,* 1984), which interprets the stone-carvings adorning Parisian buildings as expressions of patriarchitecture (to borrow Victor Burgin's terms) to Jean Rouch's *Chronicle of a Summer* (*Chronique d'un été,* 1961), a cinema verité project that documents the streets and the people of Paris, mining them as sociological data points to be captured and stored for posterity. The ambition of *Bonne Nouvelle* appears more modest by comparison. Dieutre's subjective engagement with his neighborhood figures an effort to deconstruct (or rather delaminate) a shiny picture postcard view of Paris. The series of urban cinematic snapshots (or *clichés* in French) the film presents attempts, ultimately, to resist cliché. The film's image track is composed of a sequence of largely static shots that present various corners of the area. Using voice-over narration, these are transformed into spaces that bear the traces and residue of life while also being haunted by historical absences and evocations of lost loved ones. Much like the filmmaker's own infallible memory, the liminal spaces the film puts on display are both structured by gaps and subject to the ruinous vicissitudes of time.

The opening of the film presents an epigraph against a black background, which declares that "the metropolis materializes not only the integral loss of community, but at the same time the infinite possibility of its recovery." This aphoristic quotation is torn from the pages of *Tiqqun,* a short-lived journal published by a critical–theoretical collective active in the Paris of the late 1990s. Though the intellectual heritage of *Tiqqun* stems rather self-consciously from the Situationist project, the overarching sentiment that guides Dieutre's film can be traced further back in time. Mutely summoning the specters of Charles Baudelaire (for whom cities elicit a contradictory sense of excitement, anxiety, and anomie, among the other affects that animate the "modern" condition) and Walter Benjamin (for whom city spaces oscillate constantly between states of ruin and renewal), the filmmaker portrays the social spaces of his own metropolis as fertile and fleeting in equal measure. In an ode to Baudelaire's "Tableaux parisiens," a series of poems that mounted a subtle critique of urban modernity, *Bonne Nouvelle* is structured as a web of urban fragments or a record of fleeting sense impressions that, when cobbled together, offer an intimate chronicle of everyday life in the neighborhood.[22] Over the course of the film, the voice-over introduces us to a string of characters: Youssef, the Turkish lover Dieutre meets on Tuesdays (*l'amant turc du mardi*); Wajberg, a young cocaine trafficker he encounters outside a café; Farid, a hairdresser whose touch the filmmaker longs for; and a nameless figure sleeping in the doorway of Dieutre's apartment block who is unceremoniously named "the dead man in the stairway" (*le mort de l'escalier*). Because the characters Dieutre describes across the string of vignettes are never present on screen, his voice-over description takes on the added task of populating the empty spaces the film displays visually.

We open with a view of a streetscape at the intersection of the boulevard de Bonne Nouvelle and rue Poissonnière. A circular panning shot surveys the street in near obscurity; the lurid reds and yellows of bright neon lights contrast with the deep blue of the sky at dusk. While the sound of passing traffic initially goes unrelieved, the scene is subsequently overlaid with the sound of a string concerto before the title credits appear. In a gesture that will come to be atypical of the film (which is otherwise largely made up of street-level shots), Dieutre cuts abruptly to grainy images of gay pornography on VHS (a close-up of anal penetration) though the baroque music remains. From somber streetscapes and string soundscapes to bootlegged footage of bareback sex, the opening sequence's processes of montage and juxtaposition invite us to consider spatiality and sexuality in tandem. Throughout the film, the spaces of the neighborhood are presented through the prism of the filmmaker's erotic life. Somewhat fittingly, the subsequent image presents an unmade bed in medium close-up. Behind the duvet, the bed is lined with tired cushions embroidered with recognizable scenes of Paris. A hand enters the frame from the top left to retrieve Dieutre's diary. We subsequently learn that the entries will shift back and forth between the nearby streets and the filmmaker's bedsheets.

The first chapter opens with visual footage that records unsuspecting passersby on the boulevard Bonne Nouvelle while a voice-over recounts the filmmaker's diary entry. One day, when walking along an adjoining street, Dieutre recognizes a man, named Youssef, whom he first encountered in the nearby Rex Club but who on this occasion fails to reciprocate his erotic gaze: "Accustomed to such fits of desire, which routinely punctuate my strolls along the boulevard, I turn around to check if he is still there." Upon his realization that the man is now following him, he launches into a phenomenologically rich description of the ensuing experience: "All of a sudden, time thickens . . . life acquires added density." He goes on to describe in granular detail the gestural dynamics between both men: the interplay of furtive gazes exchanged, the subtleties of body language, the choreography of gestures and glances set to the metronome of Dieutre's quickening heartbeat. As Youssef slips through the door of the filmmaker's apartment building, he initiates the start of a string of sexual encounters that would continue with regularity for several months. Discretion played a key role in their short-lived relationship: "Youssef became my Turkish lover on Tuesdays, he was punctual and powerful. Never did he divulge his address or telephone number (and nor did he get mine). Ultimately, I inferred that he hung around the place du Caire, he was an undeclared worker in one of the Sentier workshops, and my curiosity stopped there."

There are clear echoes here of the detached simplicity, or the dryness (*sécheresse*) as Dieutre puts it, we find in Renaud Camus's *Tricks.*[23] (And as with Camus's text, Dieutre's references to the ethnicity of his sexual partners are far from inconsequential. At key moments in the récit, markers of race or ethnic difference serve as a reductive shorthand for certain sexual typologies.) As the film continues to candidly explore queer sexuality, cultural difference, and urban marginality through the lens of Dieutre's first-person perspective, two tendencies become increasingly pronounced. First, he unself-critically extends his documentary exploration of the district's multicultural character to Bonne Nouvelle's sexual offering, a strategy that does little to interrogate the power dynamics undergirding these sexual liaisons. Second, the film's focus on a string of chance encounters (sexual or otherwise) with clandestine subjects such as drug addicts, homeless persons, and undeclared workers seeks to arrogate to the filmmaker himself this same status of marginality, raising important questions about the ethical limits of one's affinity with, or appropriation of, this particular district's "character." When read against the grain—which is to say, against the grain of Dieutre's own voice—*Bonne Nouvelle* unwittingly raises important questions about the tenuous place of gay sexuality within this broader constellation of social themes and the positionality of the filmmaker within these communal spaces.

The interplay between auditory and visual space plays a key role in this film. While *Bonne Nouvelle* "anchors itself in the flux of the real, in streets that are either buzzing or empty, in building doorways, in the passageways of covered markets, garment workshops, grocery shops or Pakistani barbers," these visual images do not straightforwardly align with the spaces that come to the fore via voice-over narration.[24] When confronted with the film's two disjunctive registers, spectators are invited to partake in what the filmmaker terms *un travail de reconstruction*—a "labor" of reconciling the two spatial narratives.[25] To return to the first scene, for example, which combines images of the Boulevard de Bonne Nouvelle's pedestrian footfall with Dieutre's account of serendipitous afternoon cruising, spectators are asked to associate these two narratives. In amidst the city's corporeal traffic, we scan the on-screen image in search of the gestures, gazes, and interactions of which Dieutre speaks, straining to identify signs that typically fall below the threshold of visibility. In a later "chapter" of the film, titled "Le Métro" (The Subway), Dieutre attends to another specifically urban form of public intimacy. Here he speaks of the erotic frisson of a stranger's body as it presses against him in a densely packed train carriage. Couched in the evocative prose that we have by now come to expect of him, the filmmaker's monologue describes a passenger's "musky, exotic, delicious scent" (a description that exudes more than a whiff of Orientalism), before wondering whether the stranger's incursion into his intimate space represents an unintended effect of the spatial constraints of the carriage, or if the gesture might be read as a conscious sexual advance. The image that corresponds to this scene remains fixed on the stairwell leading to the station's entrance. Although this visual signifier relates, all too obviously, to the subterranean setting of the scene's description, the gap between these two spaces ends up underscoring the conspicuous absence of bodies on screen. The tendency to couple verbal descriptions of erotic bodies with visual depictions of empty spaces is one that can be traced across Dieutre's cinema (and it is often mobilized, as we will see shortly, to conjure the specter of AIDS-related loss). As Cuthbertson notes, he frequently "holds out the initial promise of bodily presence and intimacy only to immediately withdraw it."[26]

The image track of *Bonne Nouvelle* alternates between street scenes, densely populated by pedestrians, and depopulated shots of alleys, backstreets, and dimly lit passageways. At one point, we gaze for an extended period at a wall plastered with the remnants of bill posters. The material accretion of multiple layers aptly serves as an index of time's passing, which in turn alerts us to the palimpsestic quality of the city. Dieutre's presentation of urban spaces in various states of ruination tallies with Gilles Deleuze's description of the *espace quelconque* (any-space-whatever), a notion developed over the course of *Cinema 1: The Movement-Image.*[27] Deleuze describes the *espace quelconque* as neither an abstraction nor a space that exists within a spatiotemporal vacuum. Rather, it denotes "a perfectly singular space, which has merely lost the homogeneity, that is, the principle of its metric relations or the connection of its own parts."[28] The image track of the film might best be described as an assemblage of shots that present "the undifferentiated fabric of the city," as Deleuze puts it.[29] While the extended shots of billboards, shop windows, courtyards, and alleyways denote a space that is unmistakably Parisian, they often lack the identifying details necessary to tether them to any given street or location. Dieutre's privileging of empty spaces helps to create, within the broader textual and spatial economy of the film, a composite or "rhizomatic" space in which "link ages can be made in an infinite number of ways."[30] At various points in the film, the voice-over track alternates between Dieutre's distinctive voice and that of a woman (his friend Eva Truffaut, whom we will encounter later). On other occasions, we notice how the voice-over script slips, deictically, from the first- to the third-person singular. The cumulative effect of the film's decontextualized images, its shifting mode of address, and various other forms of verbal/visual asymmetry is to loosen up the work's spatiotemporal coordinates in a specific way, and one that Deleuze himself had anticipated. For Deleuze, the *espace quelconque* reenvisages cinema's empty spaces as loci of possibility: "What in fact manifests the instability, the heterogeneity, the absence of link of such a space, is a richness in potentials or singularities which are, as it were, prior conditions of all actualization, all determination."[31] Correspondingly, Dieutre's film proposes a reconceptualization of marginal, interstitial urban settings as fertile spaces that are open to future (sexual) encounters. But here lies the problem of the film's spatial logic: by presenting an undifferentiated vision of urban space as open to sexualization and showing the frictionless ease of access that comes with this, such a vision tells us more about Dieutre's own positionality than it does about the social hierarchies that underpin these experiences of urban marginality.

Cruising Galleries and Curating Encounters

Elsewhere in his writing Gilles Deleuze reminds us that "the archive, the audiovisual is disjunctive. So it is not surprising that the most complete examples of the disjunction between seeing and speaking are to be found in the cinema."[32] While he has in mind the work of Duras, Jean-Marie Straub, and Danièle Huillet, among others, whose work hinges on a critical tension between voice and place, this sentiment finds a particularly concrete expression in Dieutre's feature-length film, *Tenebrae Lessons*. Much as *Bonne Nouvelle* constitutes a subjective documentary that weaves together an exploration of Parisian city spaces and the filmmaker's sexual chronicles, daily experiences, and memories, *Tenebrae Lessons* also pursues two alternating narrative strands. Here, Dieutre turns to the art gallery as a spatial locus and thematic focus to consider how queer sexualities and art-historical discourses entwine. To approach this film through the prism of space demands both that we consider the conceptual spaces that gay cinema's invocation of gallery spaces and museums opens up and that we brush up against queer art history.

Although at first glance we may well wonder whether there is much common ground between the two elements of Dieutre's film—gay cruising and art galleries—his exploration of the nexus between homosexuality and museum spaces is not without precedent. To cite just two prior examples from the history of French queer cinema—one in the rarefied realm of the *film d'art*, the other in the aesthetically disreputable domain of pornography—we might mention the work of Lionel Soukaz and Jean-Daniel Cadinot. *The Homosexual Century* (*Race d'Ep!*, 1979), a documentary project conceived by Soukaz and queer theorist avant la lettre Guy Hocquenghem, proposes an idiosyncratic account of the entangled histories of queer sexuality and photography since the late nineteenth century. The film, which Greg Youmans describes as "an image track to Michel Foucault's discourse-based history of sexuality," undertakes the ambitious and provocative task of excavating a transhistorical genealogy of queer visual culture.[33] It is significant here that the film centers on the artist's studio (rather than the sexologist's clinic) as the starting point for its survey of homosexuality's discursive elaboration. Using cinematic techniques of montage and superposition to underline formal correspondences between the eroticized male bodies that appear on screen and those plucked from the art-historical canon, Soukaz's experimental film offers a queer twist on Aby Warberg's ambition to elaborate a gestural archive of poses as they appear across the history of Western art.

An altogether more literal staging of cruising the art gallery can be found in Jean-Pierre Cadinot's *Musée Hom* (1994), a pornographic film whose minimal narrative is structured around a string of gay fantasies unfolding in a fictive museum. Spectators pore over sculptures of male nudes; heavy-handed guards discipline the more overeager visitors; historical artifacts find a second life as sex toys. In a hyperbolic but no less instructive way, *Musée Hom* points to the overlooked relationship between sex and spectatorship in a potentially homoerotic milieu. For while we are perhaps not accustomed to thinking about them together, the museum space and the cruising ground share a surprising amount in common: both are spaces of aesthetic selection and evaluation activated by publics with shared (erotic or aesthetic) investments; curatorial choices of how to display or disclose govern how spectating bodies are organized in space; and while art museums and cruising grounds are organized primarily by an ocularcentric logic, this often comes into tension with other forms of sensory apprehension (e.g., an invitation to, or prohibition of, touch).

Such connections have also been drawn out in contemporary art theory. Simon Ofield has written about cruising as a metaphor for erotically invested approaches to archival exploration. In an essay that draws playfully on Barthes, he speaks, in terms that are especially germane to the present discussion, of homosexuality as "a kind of spatial practice, intimately informed by browsing, sometimes searching, perhaps cruising" for sexual, textual, and visual objects.[34] Fiona Anderson similarly invokes cruising to name the process in which artistic canons are reimagined and reactivated according to otherwise occluded logics of nonnormative desire. Cruising, she writes, "suggests a furtive mode of undertaking artistic research and practice, of looking eagerly through photographic documentation and archival ephemera, or looking closely for ideas or motivation in the words and images of others."[35] Between Cadinot's refreshingly literal presentation of gallery cruising and the more figurative accounts proposed by art historians, there exists an entire spectrum of modes of attachment that Dieutre will explore in *Tenebrae Lessons.*

Another theorist to invoke cruising as a mode of doing and relating to art history is Adrian Rifkin, whose wide-ranging interventions in the fields of French and art history bring us closer to the cultural and intellectual terrain on which Dieutre's film operates. Consider, for example, Rifkin's role in a colloquium titled "Let's Queer Art History!" organized by Patricia Falguières during her short curatorial residency at the Centre Pompidou in Paris. The event sought to redress a missed encounter between the teaching and curation of art history in France on the one hand, and queer theory on the other. Invoking the thought of Jacques Rancière in his lecture–performance, Rifkin articulated a call for approaches to art history that might prompt an alternative, and willfully anachronistic, "distribution of the sensible."[36] Reading against the grain of art history's periodizing impulse, which is often predicated on a tacit, untroubled conception of the universal, his intervention resonated with what we might retroactively term queer theory's archival turn. Privileging affective engagement over an adherence to chronology, Rifkin spoke of an ethical necessity to elaborate, in the register of the first person, "histories of arts which are interwoven with our own experiences." This is precisely the impulse that motivates Dieutre's film.

By making a sideways move from the domain of art criticism to film aesthetics, we might provisionally note how this appeal to plural histor*ies* already anchors us firmly in a rich tradition of French experimental cinema. Jean-Luc Godard's metacinematic behemoth *Histoire(s) du cinéma* (1989–98), for example, represents just one filmic artifact to bring to the fore the cinematic medium's propensity toward archival bricolage and temporal reconfiguration. Here, the polysemy of the French word *histoire*—denoting both "story" and "history"—cuts between the individual and the collective, while the parenthetic pluralization of Godard's title constitutes a further opening that might encompass multiple (hi)stories. Dieutre's *Tenebrae Lessons* further expands this gesture. Released in the year following the final episode of Godard's *Histoire(s)*, it cruises the archives of Western visual culture to propose alternative spatial, temporal, and curatorial praxes. Enmeshing queer autobiography and art-historical engagement, the film fleshes out many of the art-theoretical ambitions mentioned above.

Art history is not only the subject explored in *Tenebrae Lessons*. Rather, Dieutre's investment in art history furnishes its spectators with

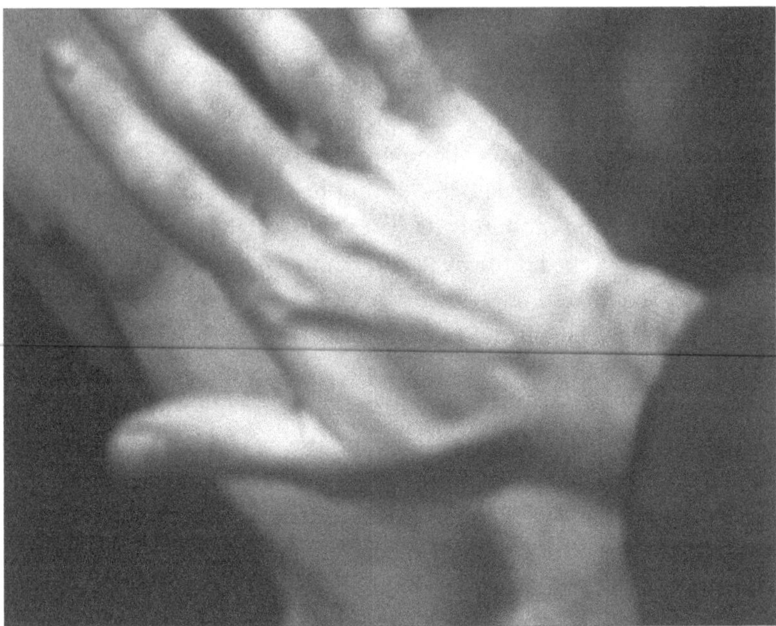

Figure 9. *Tenebrae Lessons* (Vincent Dieutre, 1999). A tactile close-up presents the filmmaker's hand as it extends to caress the torso of Christ in Caravaggio's painting *Christ at the Column.*

a critical lexicon and a set of conceptual tools to help think about how the film formally negotiates the relationship between word and image. The first term I want to insist on here is "curation." Notoriously difficult to fix from a temporal standpoint, cinematic curation implies a relation of posterity to a body of on-screen images; it is considered as a supplementary, explicative layer, bringing out the preexisting contours of an art object. Yet in the context of queer visual studies, thinkers as diverse as J. Jack Halberstam, Ann Cvetkovich, and José Esteban Muñoz have advanced understandings of curation as a set of generative practices that reassemble visual material to identify countervailing genealogies and forge queer futures. Moreover, by exploring the overlaps between art-historical commentary and autobiographical enquiry, Dieutre also leans into the idea of *self*-curation, or the mediatization of intimate experience.

Tenebrae Lessons is a fragmentary film that combines a range of cinematic media such as digital video, Super 8, and 35 mm film. Both complementing and complicating this multitextured aesthetic, Dieutre intercalates multiple narrative levels. The film simultaneously presents a narrative about a protracted breakup with his ailing partner Tadeusz who, various periphrastic cues lead us to suspect, is suffering from HIV/AIDS-related illness; a journey from the Netherlands (Utrecht) through to Italy (Naples, then Rome); and an "unconventional" art documentary on Caravaggist painting where we will have the chance to encounter the queer theorist, and consummate theorist of cruising, Leo Bersani—albeit under the aegis of his art-historical credentials.[37]

While the peripatetic film moves constantly between locations, two sites are afforded a central role: the cruising ground and the museum. Over the course of the travelogue, Dieutre effectively charts the reverse trajectory of the Caravaggisti, whose influence moved gradually from Italy to northern Europe. Given that the spatiotemporal logic of the film goes against the historical framework in which its documentary component is ostensibly invested, we have to look elsewhere to understand its governing principles. Previous accounts of the film emphasize how its divergent narrative strands are brought into dialogue through close attention to the sensuous dimensions of baroque painting. Throughout the film, the tonal ambivalence of chiaroscuro lighting is called on to intimate both pleasure and pain, providing Dieutre with the affective register to explore the themes of love and loss that propel its narrative. There is also a mimetic function at play: as Cuthbertson explains, Caravaggio's engulfing and "fleshy chiaroscuro provides Dieutre with the visual idiom for presenting his own bodies."[38] The filmmaker also makes extended use of a cinematic *tableau vivant* to stage scenes with his sexual partners, thus confounding clear-cut distinctions between different bodies, discrete art forms, narrative layers, past and present. While the film has previously been analyzed through the generic and cinematographic lens of the "cinema of sensation," foregrounding the affective and material plenum of its diegesis, such an investment in a logic of visual immersion runs the risk of flattening its structural complexity.[39] For, as I argued above, Dieutre's cinema pivots on the dialectical tension between disjunctive words and images; reducible neither to what we see nor hear, his use of acousmatic voices and eidetic evocations of past encounters bespeak altogether queerer configurations of presence and absence, time and space.

A key term that hovers around previous discussions of the film is "ekphrasis." Marlène Monteiro suggests, but leaves largely undeveloped, the idea that an exploration of the rhetorical figure of ekphrasis (itself an early form of curation) might yield fresh insights into the film.[40] Pursuing this line of inquiry, I suggest that the ekphrastic commentary that runs throughout *Tenebrae Lessons* serves both a temporal function (that of enmeshing the past and present) and an erotic function (that of binding together a corpus of homoerotic art and the bodies of sexual partners). To pursue this line of argument, though, it is necessary to take a detour via Dieutre's unwieldy body of writing on film.

In his 2003 essay "Un abécédaire pour un tiers-cinéma," in which he proposes a manifesto for experimental filmmaking at the dawn of digital video, Dieutre dedicates much space to a discussion about the porous boundaries between media. "In literature, the plastic arts, and even dance," he writes, "autobiography surfaces in many forms." While the written word has for a long time been considered the privileged medium of autobiographical inquiry, "autobiography is now also principally at stake in the *tiers cinéma.*" In a particularly dense passage studded with the names of his cinematic forebears (presumably in a bid to spell out the aesthetic coordinates of his project and secure its credentials), he stakes out his vision for a "third cinema" by reflecting on its origins and its possible future: "Necessarily literary in its earlier iterations ([Marguerite] Duras, [Frédéric] Mitterrand, [Hervé] Guibert), a first-person cinema [*cinéma du je*], led by the digital video rebellion, is starting to invade the public sphere, and risks becoming a genre ('my father is a transvestite') [*mon père est un travesti*]."[41] What might initially strike us as the most perplexing element of this passage is perhaps also the most pertinent. Dieutre's parenthetic comment on the hybrid origins of the *tiers cinéma* is articulated via an unusual metaphor of queer filiation. Exploiting the polyvalence of the word *genre* (a semiotically slippery French word that encompasses both "genre" and "gender"), Dieutre's pun subverts a rigid delineation of the arts, based on purity and medium specificity, to gesture toward the creative affordances of intermedia. Within his statement we find an analogy between queerness and transversal arts practice that resonates with, but importantly reconfigures, a well-established trope in ekphrastic discourse: the logic of the paragon, or antagonism between the "sister arts."

In the simplest terms, ekphrasis names a rhetorical device which seeks to represent visual objects verbally or in written form. Going beyond the mere practice of description, however, the ekphrastic impulse exerts pressure on the rhetorical capacities of language to evoke images eidetically. This rhetorical device—a particular mode of "speaking out" (combining *ek,* go beyond, and *phrazô,* explain or show)—aims to traverse media registers, reterritorializing visual images in the realm of imagination via the medium of language. Recently, the term has shed its classical origins and migrated into the domain of film theory. For example, in her account of the audiovisual asymmetry in Jean-Luc Godard's oeuvre, Ágnes Pethő uses it to name the space of cinematic signification that exists between word and image.[42] Given that another definition of ekphrasis might be to harness "the power of words to direct imagining," it might also be aligned with the techniques that filmmakers often deploy to create what Sarah Cooper terms "imagined images."[43]

While ekphrasis constitutes a hallmark of experimental cinema—from Duras to Straub and Huillet, to cite Deleuze's earlier examples—I draw attention to the queer specificities of Dieutre's deployment of this figure in his cinema. Brian Glavey writes that "the relationship between word and images often becomes a means of negotiating some of the most basic features of our interaction with the world and its inhabitants."[44] Such a relationship, he argues, is actively inflected by the politics of desire and difference, as well as broad social hierarchies pertaining, for instance, to gender. Complicating the gendered metaphor of the "sister arts"—a trope that W. J. T. Mitchell suggests typifies the social biases subtending interart relations in the Western aesthetic tradition—Glavey centers his focus on sexuality as a crucial vector of analysis.[45] Through a detailed exploration of the curatorial strategies of queer artists and writers, he contends that "ekphrasis is in many ways the queer art par excellence, in part because it explicitly pursues its examination of errors and eros in relation to the question of art itself."[46] While queer theory and ekphrastic praxis seem like "unlikely bedfellows," their affinities and resonances come to the fore when addressing minor modes of aesthetic appreciation. On the one hand, "the story of modern sexuality necessarily revolves around the relation between what can be seen and what can be said," whereas "ekphrasis is not simply about seeing; it is also about showing and sharing."[47] A queer ekphrastic practice—one that is also alert to the possibilities of *mis*describing or recathecting its object—might therefore be dedicated to exploring an "unpredictable spectrum of relationality, multiplying ways of desiring, identifying with, attaching to, loving, imitating, envying, and sometimes ignoring works of art."[48] Glavey offers a number of insights that find their expression in Dieutre's practice and resonate powerfully across his oeuvre. He notes that ekphrasis is a mode of expression inherently suspicious of generic categories; it is often used to explore states of anachrony and asynchrony; and, perhaps most pertinent to our current concerns, it is a discursive technique and exegetic mode that is particularly susceptible to homoerotic cathexis.

As with Dieutre's earlier films, sophisticated processes of audiovisual layering shape the film's aesthetic form. The vast body of images in *Tenebrae Lessons*, gleaned from Dieutre's southward trip throughout Europe, range from fluid, phenomenological detailing to sober, measured architectural forms. Spectators variously move between unsteady close-ups that linger on bodies, gestures, and the rhythms of daily life to static shots of empty streetscapes and urban infrastructure. The multiple cinematic formats Dieutre toggles between imbue the cinematography with added texture. Again, this process of layering also extends to the auditory realm. The filmed footage is set against the ambient noises of the filmmaker's environs: amplified sounds emanating from car radios, church bells, traffic, and voices coalesce in a dense sonic collage that gives way, intermittently, to the acousmatic pull and the "writerly timbre" of the filmmaker's voice.[49] And once again, too, there is an intentionality to the film's disorienting movement between images, sounds, and narrative layers.

As I noted above, the overarching form of the film is that of a travelogue, one that retraces an artistic, affective, and erotic cartography of Europe. Early in the film—during the first chapter, which takes place in the Netherlands—a short passage recalls Duras's experimental short film *Aurélia Steiner (Melbourne)* (1979) in its form and structure. The camera moves along the banks of a canal, continuously recording long stretches. Over these images of the city, we hear Dieutre's gravelly voice-over and an extradiegetic soundscape of reverberating drips. In an unusual confluence of spatial movement and narrated subject matter, the boat's motion and the voice-over's topic both point toward ideas of cruising.

The moving images map the expanses of the canal, varying in light exposure. As the image alternates between the dark arches and the dawn-lit quay, Dieutre describes an anonymous encounter with a sexual partner in a nearby sauna that culminates in a scene of fisting. The twin registers of the visual and verbal, image and voice, enter into an oddly suggestive partnership here; the cavities of bodies and the infrastructure of the canal are explored *ana*logically, offering a peculiar inversion of what Emma Wilson has elsewhere termed "a new geography of the body" in which bodies are "stretched out . . . like territories to be mapped."[50] Dieutre deploys a technique that is also used to great effect in *Bonne Nouvelle:* his voice overlays images of empty spaces and scenes, and the urban geographies we encounter in these travelogues come to be informed by the bodies that once occupied them. Dieutre's summoning of the erotic is not visualized, but rather situated at the interstices of image, sound, and discourse. While this approach might solicit more open-ended forms of cinematic stimulation (the poetic description of sex, the pull of the narrator's voice, and the lapping of the water all contribute variously to the passage's evocative sensory sway), the lag between description and depiction imbues his film with a palpable sense of absence and pathos. In its reflection on cultures of public sex in the wake of the HIV/AIDS crisis, the film's figuration of sexual possibility is often met by its negation.

Dieutre's play with processes of subtraction and substitution becomes even more pronounced in a later scene, which moves seamlessly between the spaces of the city and those of the art gallery. At one point, the screen space is filled with a graffitied brick wall in a nondescript back alley. (Lacking both narrative coordinates and a point of geographic anchorage, the scene's setting recalls the urban *espaces quelconque* discussed above). The voice-over proceeds to describe what seems to be a sexual encounter between men that took place at that precise locale. Smell and touch are foregrounded in Dieutre's narration, which commences in medias res: "He is there, tense and shivering, and he can feel, near his tired face, the drunken scent of the two men's breath." In his finely wrought voice-over prose he exploits the affective ambiguities bound up in the unvisualized relations he describes as taking place between men; sex is only hinted at in these deictic recollections. However, as the on-screen image of the brick wall cuts abruptly to the Caravaggist painter Dirck van Baburen's *Jesus Crowned with Thorns* (1623), the aforementioned voice-over description is subsequently reunderstood as an ekphrastic account of the painting. The editing therefore reinflects the significance of both mental and visual images in relation to one another, remediating them in a very different affective and aesthetic context.

Exploiting the subtextual ambiguities of Dieutre's previous description (itself oscillating between intimacy and domination, pleasure and pain), techniques of parataxis are used to forge a new set of relations between men (both those depicted in the painting and those recalled aurally) as well as highlighting the homoerotic contours of the iconographic frame of reference. The film's fragmentary and nonlinear form invites its spectators to respond to its body of images in light of verbal cues. By simultaneously collapsing temporal distinctions and confounding affective ties, scenes such as these produce a dissonance that echoes the dynamics Elizabeth Freeman identifies in *Time Binds:* "The very inaccessibility of other times to touch guarantees a binding that cannot be reduced to the literal, the physical—yet cannot be thought elsewise than with the erotic at the center."[51]

Such sensuous entanglements of past and present course throughout *Tenebrae Lessons.* Consider the film's opening sequence in a museum gallery, which prefigures its multiple narrative and thematic strands: Dieutre's hand slowly extends as if to caress the shoulder and torso of a painted figure. Through the use of extreme close-up and a softened lens, the distinction between figure and ground dissolves. These prehensile movements gesture toward the peculiarly diaphanous boundaries between media, between autofiction and documentary, and between the contemporary and the historical he will continue to probe over the course of the film. If cinematic iterations of the baroque exhibit "a fundamentally correlative aesthetic that entangles one body with another," as Saige Walton writes, this film reveals such acts of "incorporation" to be erotically charged.[52] Dieutre brings the affective and erotic dimensions of Caravaggism into dialogue with his own ever-shifting situation—whether sexual, emotional, or geographical. "Through the craft of editing and cinematographic arrangement," he states, "I hope for a little bit of Caravaggio to enter into the [film's] nightclub [scene] and vice versa." We can similarly read the imbrication of the film's historically diverse visual registers—from pornography to art history as well as the various gradations in between—as a further instance of archival cruising, a navigation between "high" and "low" cultural registers, divergent media formats, and the temporal axes of past and present that is (to adopt the neologism central to Mieke Bal's study of the neobaroque) "preposterous."[53] Dieutre has spoken in knowingly suggestive terms about the "interpenetrating" registers of *Tenebrae Lessons*. In this film, "the experience of love" and "the aesthetic experience of the tableau" mutually inflect each other. The opening scene's enmeshing of body and painting illustrates not only Dieutre's point but also exemplifies what Glavey has termed the queerness of "near-identification," a form of aesthetic attachment that "resemble[s] an ersatz object relation by which the self strives to construct a world it can bear to live in."[54]

Entering the Frame

Toward the end of the film, when the viewer has grown accustomed to the rhythms of Dieutre's voice-over, it becomes evident that he describes artistic "encounters" (references to "Caravaggio, Honthorst, Caracciolo, Ribera . . .") in the same way that he enumerates past sexual partners ("André, Alain, Antoine, Antonio . . ."). The near-identical scansion of his voice as he recounts these lists yokes together the film's personal and art-historical relations. Once his ex-partner Tadeusz has left the picture, he finds himself alone in the streets of Rome. Here the film's loose narrative and geographic trajectory reaches its denouement, and the filmmaker takes this as an opportune moment to fantasize about consummating these links.[55] He addresses himself in the second person, noting that "Tadeusz is already far away. You are now able to cross over into the image, to finally breach the threshold of the canvas." As we move from images of the filmmaker to a sequence of embedded tableaux, his voice-over is rich in vivid description. His words emphasize the fragmentary detailing of painted bodies, placing particular emphasis on composition, namely light and form: "the shoulders, the shadows on shoulders, bodies arrested in their movements, the stifled cry of pain, of pleasure [*jouissance*], the sensual offering of the muscles, the somber splendor of the faces."

In the final sequence, desired and desiring bodies assume the center of the film's intermedial frame. Yet while the heady combination of eros (Dieutre's highly cathected visual pleasure) and pathos (his existential malaise) once again reshape the film's body of images, we ought not lose sight of the filmmaker's erotic and mimetic pull toward these images in the first place. As the film reaches its end, its curatorial strategy is thus caught in the very bind that Mitchell has identified, one in which "the question of desire is inseparable from the problem of the image [and] the two concepts [are] caught in a mutually generative circuit, desire generating images and images generating desire."[56] (That the recursive Möbian dynamics of Dieutre's desire bears a structural resonance with the visual pleasures of baroque painting is far from incidental). As Dieutre moves between the art gallery and the cruising grounds of the city, his curatorial strategies seek to entwine word and image, self and world, past and present, in ways that will ultimately render them porous. While the film has attracted criticism by some scholars such as Nick Rees-Roberts, who calls into question the equivalences it draws across its two registers—a culture of public sex on the one hand and a canon of high Western art on the other—to my mind this misses the bidirectionality of Dieutre's cinematic endeavors.[57] Not only does Dieutre "cruise" the archives of art history, but, in a reverse gesture, he is also interested in "curating" gay subcultural spaces and practices, drawing out their shared aesthetic contours while judiciously avoiding the twin pitfalls of sanitization and sublimation.

In his essay "Painting and Cinema," André Bazin offers a comparative account of how both painting and film articulate the spatial totalities they seek to represent. In the case of both media, the frame is of central importance. The painted picture, Bazin suggests, "frames" a world, producing a spatial plane and a textual totality that is both self-sufficient and enclosed.[58] From the picture's outer frame, our gaze is guided inward—or centripetally, as Bazin puts it—in a gesture of introspection. While the cinematic image is demarcated by a similar outer limit, its own logic is centrifugal. Bazin notes that the cinematic frame brings into view only a "portion of reality," a part that affirms the existence of a wider profilmic world with which the framed image is spatiotemporally contiguous. The ontological questions he raises about how we should account for that which does not inhabit the immediate field of vision continue to animate film theory after its classical period. Numerous thinkers from Jean-Louis Comolli to Stanley Cavell have summoned Bazin's thinking while seeking to theorize or taxonomize the relation between on- and off-screen space.[59] Proposing a working definition of off-screen space (*le hors-champ*), Jacques Aumont describes it as "the collection of elements . . . that, while not visible in the visual field, are nonetheless attached to this field in the spectator's imaginary."[60] However, this term is perhaps most readily associated with Pascal Bonitzer, for whom the tension between presence and absence is key to understanding the fundamentally dialectical nature of cinematic space. Writing in terms that call to mind Chion's account of the seductive and elusive pull of the *acousmêtre,* Bonitzer argues that "the cinematic image is haunted by what is not in it."[61] Our reading of the cinematic image, following Bonitzer, must necessarily cast its eye beyond the profilmic picture plane, accounting for all that lingers just beyond the threshold of frame. Such a "haunting" attains a particular valence in the cinema of Vincent Dieutre, which, as I have suggested, explores dialectical interplay between presence and absence to grapple with the ephemerality of urban encounters, processes of archival revisitation, and the theme of queer loss. In his 2012 film *Jaurès,* the final film I consider in this chapter, the relationship between on- and off-screen space is strikingly configured to explore the dynamics of love and loss, disclosure and discretion.

Ethics at the Intersection: *Jaurès*

Released some twelve years after *Bonne Nouvelle,* Dieutre's documentary *Jaurès* returns to the French capital to offer another exploration of a Parisian neighborhood. The film, which is essentially a mise en abyme of cinematic footage, follows two interlocutors (Dieutre and his friend Eva Truffaut, who are both sitting in a film studio) as they discuss the moving images the filmmaker had shot from the vantage point of an apartment window three years prior. Central to the affective charge of this metadiegetic footage is the knowledge that the apartment belonged to his former lover Simon, with whom he subsequently broke up. This sense of loss imbues the footage of the urban space with a melancholy tinge. Simon's longed-for presence is conveyed indirectly in numerous ways: he is the subject of conversational exchanges between Dieutre and Truffaut; his presence is registered the sonic *hors-champ*; and, on a few rare occasions, Simon's form can be glimpsed indirectly by way of the shadows and reflections projected onto the balcony window.

The film centers on the urban vista we see outside the apartment window—the northwestern tip of the neighborhood of Jaurès. In an interview accompanying the film's release, Dieutre describes the window's view as akin to the stage of a theater (*son petit théâtre*), implicitly positioning himself and Truffaut as spectators. They both gaze at the urban diorama in front of them as if it were an extension of their own immediate spatiotemporal situation. Over the course of the film's immersive long takes, which take us through the winter of 2009, they discuss the district's intersecting flows, its noises and rhythms, as well as the social strata that the Métro overpass so neatly cuts through.

In an obvious sense, the material in *Jaurès*, which resembles CCTV footage, reflects an understanding of the filmic medium as an archival agent, one capable of recording the flux and contingency of the world below. Our attention alternates between the facades of buildings, the overground subway line, a bustling streetscape animated by traffic and pedestrians, the northern edge of the Canal Saint-Martin, and an encampment of Afghan refugees who dwell on the quayside below. In press

Figure 10. *Jaurès* (Vincent Dieutre, 2013). A panoramic vista of the Jaurès intersection in northeastern Paris at dawn. Overground we see a subway car, at street level we see traffic, and below ground on the canal we see an Afghan refugee encampment.

interviews Dieutre has sought to inscribe his film into a lineage of hyperrealist engagements with Paris that stems back to Georges Perec's experimental writing exercise *An Attempt at Exhausting a Parisian Place,* which sought to capture in obsessive detail the minutiae of everyday life from the author's seat at a café at the place Saint-Sulpice.[62] But it would be a mistake to reduce Dieutre's film to its documentary function or to reduce his artistic ambition to a formal exercise à la Perec. Layered over the visual track of *Jaurès* is what Dieutre calls the film's auditory track (*plan sonore*). The voice-over conversations alternate between an ekphrastic commentary on the minutiae of the urban life below and an intimate description of the circumstances in which the film's footage was recorded. It is here we learn that the moving images were captured from a lover's balcony window shortly before an acrimonious breakup. With not so much as a photograph of Simon, the footage accrues deep personal significance. As with Dieutre's previous films, *Jaurès* paradoxically evokes the presence of a lost love through Simon's visual absence, given that we are never privy to the *hors-champ* of the apartment interior itself. Over the course of the film's conversation, the reflections of Dieutre and Truffaut grow increasingly entwined with their discussions of the world outside—most significantly the Afghan migrants who go about their daily rituals. The window aperture therefore functions as a hinge

Figure 11. *Jaurès* (Vincent Dieutre, 2013). The filmmaker is in a dimly lit recording studio. He and his friend Eva Truffaut look out toward the urban footage he captured in Jaurès and offer voice-over narration.

connecting the private sphere inside the apartment to the public space outside. Dieutre uses the corresponding boundaries between cinematic elements (on- and off-screen space, landscape, and soundscape) to negotiate competing themes of sexuality, migration, and, at the point of their intersection, the more abstract notion of "placelessness."

Writing on the film's autobiographical mode, Cuthbertson argues that *Jaurès* points outward rather than succumbing to introspection: "The limits of [Dieutre's] individual experience are gradually expanded outwards and rendered more porous," prompting us to "consider the place an individual occupies in a surrounding social and built environment."[63] In her documentary treatment of the filmmaker, Fleur Albert takes a similar view on the film's spatial configuration, which, she suggests, metonymizes his broader approach to a documentary filmmaking mode that exists in the space between the personal sphere of autobiography and the public realm of political documentary, or *entre la chambre et le monde* (between the room and the world).[64] Drawing attention to the film's documentary function, I suggest that a spatial analysis (broadly conceived to encompass its geophysical, cinematic, or symbolic facets) helps us to shed light on a number of recurring questions raised in and by his filmmaking. How should documentary filmmaking tackle sexual visibility and discretion? And should sexuality ever serve as the primary optic through which a filmmaker approaches questions of urban marginality? Moving between the space of the film studio, the window aperture, and the urban intersection of Jaurès down below, I advance a critical account of how Dieutre instrumentalizes these multiple facets of cinematic space to explore the film's themes.

Apartment Keys, Canal Quays: Competing Narratives of Dispossession

The establishing scene of *Jaurès* foregrounds the film studio, which is both the site of editing/voice-over production and the spectatorial encounter. The epistemological conditions of the documentary are made visible (by displaying the filmmaking apparatus) and audible (by way of the filmmaker's self-reflexive mode of address). In medium close-up, the metadiegetic image presents a view of the windows of the apartment block on the opposite end of the canal. As the camera zooms out, the footage reveals, by way of a mise en abyme, that these images were shot from, and framed through, the window of Simon's apartment. (That these windows bear the stubborn staining of watermarks represents yet another layer of mediation.) This is followed by a high-angle long shot that presents the quayside below. Acting as a proxy for us—this film's cospectators—Truffaut breaks the habitual silences of the footage by anchoring us in space and time: "Là on est où?" (Where are we looking here?). Dieutre explains that they are in Simon's apartment. With a little further probing, he explains that he first encountered Simon in the backroom of an insalubrious gay club (*une boîte un peu crade*). After a few repeated encounters over subsequent weeks, the two men decided they might be more comfortable in Simon's apartment. They would meet up regularly—up to three times a week, sometimes even for the weekend. Despite growing closer, we are told that Simon's ambivalence toward queer self-definition foreclosed the possibility of a lasting relationship. Framing the enclosure of the apartment as the space of Simon's sexual nondisclosure, Dieutre explains that he was never given a key to the flat. His words prompt us to bring together the film's concurrent themes and spaces (sexuality, the closet, domestic architecture, the space of cinematic visibility). The subsequent shot introduces a further theme that will invariably complicate these concerns and thicken the film's narrative: migration.

The image cuts to another pocket of urban space below, this time by the canal. Truffaut asks about the faint flickers of fire that burn in the dark. Dieutre explains that the fire belonged to a group of Afghan migrants dwelling in a makeshift encampment down below. This group of men represents part of a larger community of Afghan migrants whose presence in northeastern Paris was notable at the time. Eking out a precarious existence in and among the parks, canal quays, and Métro underpasses around the Gare du Nord and the Gare de l'Est, these migrants were caught in the crossfire of a political dispute between local community activists (among them Dieutre's ex-partner Simon, who did legal advocacy work and offered pro bono advice) and President Nicolas Sarkozy's hostile right-wing government. In 2010, shortly after the filming of this footage, the group would be forcibly evicted on the orders of Interior Minister Brice Hortefeux and Immigration Minister Éric Besson. In addition to archiving Simon's temporary presence in Dieutre's life, the film also memorializes the daily routines of the men below. In a summary of the film, Dieutre effects a kind of prosopopeic slippage between these two elements: "Avec un camp de réfugiées qui se disparaît, et une histoire d'amour qui se clôt, ce film est déjà sur la perte" (Between the group of refugees that disappear, and a love story that is on the rocks, *Jaurès* is a film that is already on the verge of loss).[65]

As the film continues to pursue the dynamic relationship between the apartment space above and the world laid out below, Dieutre's voice-over starts, cautiously at first, to advance implicit parallels between his own situation vis-à-vis Simon and the lived experiences of the refugees below. At various points in the documentary, he makes spatial and symbolic appeals to the theme of "dispossession," positing a questionable equivalence between both worlds. At a key juncture in the film, he asks, "Être le clandestine dans une vie amoureuse, comment est-ce qu'on s'arrange de ça?" (How is one supposed to deal with being the clandestine figure in a relationship?). Over the course of these conversational exchanges, the film maps a triangulation of relations between Dieutre, positioned comfortably in his studio; Simon, symbolically aligned with the private space of the apartment; and the migrants, who live precariously on the quay below. These three elements of the narrative are subsequently tessellated, their overlapping relations combined in various ways. Speaking of the increasing strain placed on his relationship with Simon, Dieutre notes, "C'était là où nos deux mondes communiquaient" (I experienced Jaurès as a threshold, the place where our two worlds conjoined). Regarding Simon's involvement with the refugees, Dieutre suggests that his voluntary work served to assuage deep-seated anxieties about his identity. (Or, less euphemistically, his sexuality: Toby Ashraf notes that "although Simon's life seems full of contradictions and unsolved questions, his care for the refugees . . . becomes a tangible and specific component in his otherwise mysterious biography.")[66] Finally, this leaves the third and most contentious side of the triangle: Dieutre's vicarious identification with refugees.

The exploration of this web of relations is articulated not only at the level of the voice-over, but also through choices of editing and image sequencing. The camera lens is not static. Some shots center on the migrants, whereas others capture contingent details elsewhere, such as the apartments opposite, the pigeons nesting on the balcony, and children as they return home at the end of the school day. Given that the footage also exposes us to a range of sounds emanating from the interior of the apartment (muffled conversations, a microwave, the recurrent motif of a ritornello played on Simon's piano), the perceptual and conversational coordinates of the film are constantly shifting. Visual and auditory details—nocturnal fires on the quay, the spectral shadow of Simon—often steer the course of the conversation, narrowing the distance between sound and image. Just as we saw above in the first scene of *Bonne Nouvelle,* where images of unsuspecting passers were overlaid with descriptive accounts of gay cruising, Dieutre's techniques of audiovisual collage serve to juxtapose disparate themes and subjects. In essence, while it might be tempting to read Dieutre's palimpsestic and formally inventive approach to the rendering urban space as receptive to fortuitous encounters, open to unexpected resonances, and attentive to lateral links and rhizomatic connections, these readings run the risk of masking the political hierarchies that underpin these relations. In a sense, *Jaurès* represents the culmination of a formal logic that was already at play in his earlier films.

Mapping the Margins

Largely sympathetic readings of the film have been advanced by a range of critics. Dieutre's movement beyond individual experience and his concomitant gesture outward toward the world are of primary importance to Tom Cuthbertson: "Through a fertile spatial logic, Dieutre constructs a filmic poetics based on showing and hiding that allows him to explore the definitional mechanisms that influence both public and private lives."[67] While he voices some of the potential ethical shortcomings of *Jaurès*—namely "that, in attempting to link [Dieutre's] experience to that of the Afghans, he uses destitution solely as the site of art and as the surface on which a projected self is reflected"—this line of critique falters when he goes on to exonerate the filmmaker. Drawing on Hal Foster's writing on the cultural politics of alterity, Cuthbertson argues that the documentary's end (a consciousness-raising effort intended to foreground the plight of Paris's Afghan migrants) justifies the narrative's means (Dieutre's conflation of experience and his vicarious investment in the suffering of others.) "Although problematic," he states pragmatically, "over-identification is surely better in such cases than dis-identification."[68] Marc Siegel similarly appeals to the film's spatial logic to understand its politics. He interprets the filmmaker's gaze "outside of the window" as an invitation to move beyond the ossified terrain of queer cinema (one characterized exclusively by questions of gender and sexuality, focused on a "hermetic view of the gay couple") and toward other more geopolitically pressing concerns.[69] By "forc[ing] us to view queerness against the background of a larger social and political world," Siegel argues, "[*Jaurès*] proposes a queer internationalism that has to be practiced locally."[70] The film's most ardent praise comes from Comolli, who preemptively insulates the film from the charge of voyeurism on the grounds that Dieutre judiciously "multiplied and maintained the signs of distance with [the Afghans subjects] he filmed and whose images he projects."[71] To reproach Dieutre for voyeurism, Comolli continues, "would be to fly in the face of the entire formal system of the film, which is predicated on absence (of his lover's body, of the filmed Afghan bodies kept too distant to fully enter into the film)."[72] What is striking in each of these redemptive accounts of the film is their common appeal to its spatial configuration. Somewhat ironically, Dieutre's mise en abyme film text yields examples of film criticism that end up mirroring the stated intention of the filmmaker. Might there be a way of looking outside the film's window differently? How might we bring into view another spatial logic that is less complicit with its creator's stated ambitions?

Let us return to the film's central image. Above, I noted that the window view onto *Jaurès* constitutes the film's subject rather than its setting. The CCTV-like positioning of Dieutre's camera registers the diurnal rhythms of one of Paris's busiest intersections. The crossroads of rue La Fayette, boulevard de la Villette, and avenue Jean Jaurès are presented at street level. And if we focus on the vertical axis, the image contains the meeting point of the overhead Métro line, the canal, and the quay. At once a geographic crossroad and a societal cross section, the architecture materializes the more metaphorical themes of contact, exposure, and social marginality that are chiefly at stake in the film. Once again, Dieutre's invocation of gay sexuality as the primary prism through which to make sense of this view risks flattening other forms of difference, assimilating them into the filmmaker's autobiographical frame of reference. Thus, to advance a counterreading to the spatial interpretations of the film outlined above, we might suggest that, given that the political, symbolic, and narrative valence of the film is so crucially predicated on the image of an urban intersection, this only renders Dieutre's lack of an *intersectional* optic more noticeable.

A multifaceted term that has circulated widely and has witnessed many permutations since Kimberlé Crenshaw's initial coinage in 1989, "intersectionality" names an approach to the "mapping" of marginal identities that resists figuring forms of difference (such as sexuality, race, and nationhood) in oppositional terms, but rather treats social particulars as co-constitutive facets of identity formation that position bodies differentially in social, cultural, and political space.[73] Given this term's welcome migration out of the academic social sciences and into a broader activist vernacular, we would do well to recall the image of urban traffic Crenshaw described when first elucidating the term. Indeed, Patricia Hill Collins has recently highlighted the metaphorical dimension of intersectionality and its capacity "to invoke the tangible, spatial relations of everyday life."[74] While theories of intersectionality are often used to analyze the experiences of individuals or social groups (e.g., to grapple with the particularities of people of color within the broader banner of "queer"), the term has also seen considerable uptake in critical geography and spatial theory. Thinking about sociospatial relations from an intersectional optic alerts us to the shortcomings of how, when undertaking an analysis of a shared public space, an exclusive focus on one prism of experience (e.g., sexuality) runs the risk of occluding other considerations (e.g., race, ethnicity, geopolitical positionality)—which, in turn, leads to the reification of representational iniquities and fails to account for the variegation, complexity, and contradictions of urban life.

As I showed above, Dieutre's cinema tends to subsume racial, national, or ethnic differences into a more general category of "marginality." Once shorn of its racial specificities, this position is more easily assimilated into the filmmaker's own frame of experience. In *Jaurès* the filmmaker's attempt to spatially and narrative "map" marginal experiences places too great an emphasis on his own subjective frame of reference. The voice-over often overreaches and oversteps, marking an incursion into the world outside rather than maintaining an ethical distance between himself and the film's other documentary subjects. In a brief but compelling appraisal of the film that brings into view the hierarchical relations, rather than the lateral connections, between sexual and geopolitical alterity, James S. Williams suggests *Jaurès* articulates a prominent fault line in French discourses on sexuality. Drawing attention to the film's formal imbalances, he wonders, "Why is it that contemporary French queer cinema, when engaging with racially and ethnically different migrants, often ends up projecting and framing them rhetorically in oppositional binary terms as the abject 'other' of French society?"[75] Although a comprehensive answer to this question would regrettably exceed the scope of the present book, we would do well to keep in mind Williams's gesture toward the French specificity of the text. In her comparative account of the affordances of intersectional thought in cultural geography, Marianne Blidon notes that if "using intersectionality has been done using sociological categories (gender, class, and race), geographers can offer other reading grids to think through relationships of domination and the experiences they produce, especially in terms of subjectivation."[76] She continues, "Although this approach is already widely developed in some European or English-speaking countries . . . this is still not the case in France," not least because, she goes on to explain, the politics of identity remain a point of contention within French discourse due to its perceived threat to social cohesion and Republican values. If we shift our attention from the geographic to the cinematic sphere, Rees-Roberts similarly diagnoses a "pervading 'French' unease with the space allotted to alien identity politics," which, he argues, has historically foreclosed the analysis of sexuality and migration in tandem.[77] Although it would be misleading to map the filmmaker's politics straightforwardly onto the overarching values of French Republicanism, I suggest that there exists a blind spot within French discourses on identity and difference, as well a long-established French literary and cultural tradition of romanticizing the status of "marginal" identities—and that these two (often contradictory) impulses find their expression in the form and narratives of Dieutre's cinema.

By way of conclusion, I want to tease out some of the conceptual through lines that run across Dieutre's thematically varied body of work. Here I have sought to argue that Dieutre's formal and autobiographical explorations are catalyzed by an overarching interest in space, place, and travel. But I have also shown how specific modes of framing, both physical (e.g., picture frames, screens, windows) and abstract (e.g., voice-over description, curatorial repositioning), can be used to rethink spatial, temporal, and self/other relations. While these techniques hold great promise, they also entail significant risks. For example, while there is something undoubtedly arresting about Dieutre's sensual description of the men we will never see (and less still hear) in *Bonne Nouvelle,* his overbearing use of voice-over description runs the risk of rendering others mute. And while the foregrounding of the editing apparatus in *Jaurès* seems to draw attention to the documentary's transparency and self-reflexivity, this obscures the more critical spatial logic hiding in plain sight. Reading his work against the grain alerts us to the shortcomings of "curating" a view from a singular perspective. Less of an unmediated "window onto the world," and an altogether more partial mode of framing the social sphere, Dieutre's filmmaking animates both the speculative promises and the ethical pitfalls of letting one's queer investments take center stage. In her highly perceptive study *Selfless Cinema? Ethics and French Documentary,* Sarah Cooper avers that "what is lacking in current debates is an exploration of how documentary may resist the reflective mechanism that would refer one back to oneself or one's own world."[78] Both mirroring the quotation with which this chapter opened ("Stupidity reduces the world to an 'I', the other to the same, and difference to identity") and holding up a mirror to Dieutre's autobiographical mechanisms, Cooper's words alert us to the formal, ethical, and political issues at stake in how we frame queer documentary space.

5

SEX BEYOND THE CITY
ALAIN GUIRAUDIE'S RURAL EROTICS

> I'm utterly bored of these forms of urban cinema stuck within four walls. I want horizons, I want a cinema where we can see far.
>
> —Alain Guiraudie

HAILING FROM SOUTHWESTERN FRANCE, Alain Guiraudie is a filmmaker and writer whose ambitious body of work has done much to reshape the terrain of French queer cinema over the last two decades. Initially tipped for success by Jean-Luc Godard following the release of his 2001 film *That Old Dream That Moves* (*Ce vieux rêve qui bouge*), Guiraudie went on to gain widespread acclaim with his 2013 feature *Stranger by the Lake* (*L'inconnu du lac*), a brooding thriller exploring the vicissitudes of lakeside cruising in a picturesque corner of Provence. Although Guiraudie is by now a well-established figure on the contemporary French filmmaking scene, Vincent Dieutre's description of the filmmaker emphasizes how his cinema has taken root at a considerable distance from the French cinematic establishment: "Far away from the hard core of Paris, Guiraudie, along with his band of actor friends, continues to operate a 'small film company' [*son petit commerce de cinéma*] in the region surrounding Toulouse."[1] Revealing a sneaking regard for the decentering energies of Guiraudie's cinema, he goes on to note how Guiraudie "partakes in the erosion of Parisian power, inviting cinema to exhibit itself elsewhere."[2] This chapter is concerned with the ways this move away from the city opens new aesthetic possibilities for queer cinema. By focusing on the postindustrial and rural settings we find in

Guiraudie's films—abandoned factories, bucolic forests, and tranquil lakes—I consider how these cinematic settings might enliven and complicate the discussions of cruising, duration, and spectatorial attention that have so far been at stake in this book.

From his earliest short film, *Straight Ahead until Morning* (*Tout droit jusqu'au matin,* 1994), to his more recent feature, *Staying Vertical* (*Rester vertical,* 2016), the titles of Guiraudie's films reveal a clear preoccupation with questions of space, orientation, and geometry. Critics have increasingly come to appreciate this through line in his cinema, and the broad variety of responses to his work attest to the malleability of "space" as a heuristic or critical lens. Previous explorations of cinematic space in his work have extended in many directions to address topics as varied as form and cinematography, sociocultural and geographical context, and questions of genre. In *Queer Cinema in the World,* Karl Schoonover and Rosalind Galt discuss how Guiraudie's predilection for depth of field and his "riveting long takes" map onto, and also queerly revivify, the terrain of Bazinian realism as well as its recent reincarnation under the auspices of contemporary slow cinema.[3] And in sharp contradistinction to the global remit of their project, Frédéric Majour turns his focus to the regional specificities of Guiraudie's cinematic universe; he shows how the filmmaker's early works tended to take place in his native region of Aveyron, before branching out across a wider range of Occitan territories, and then across the South of France more generally.[4] In his own account of the role that space and place play at the level of screenwriting, Guiraudie notes that "when I write, I have in mind a mix of specific and diffuse locations, spaces that exist and those that are fantasmatic."[5] Offering varied responses to this artistic statement, critics have explored the various ways his intricately crafted diegetic spaces traverse various generic boundaries. Just as his filmmaking attempts to intercalate these different spatial registers, the freewheeling, rhizomatic insistence of his cinema correlates physical movement with thematic shifts; as those familiar with his body of work can attest, it is not uncommon for Guiraudie to move from social realism, then to fantasy, and on to horror within the textual plane of the same film.

To offer a loose but unifying approach to my own exploration of his cinema, I'm interested in how his formal experimentation with space is suggestively bound to questions of gender and sexuality, and how his oeuvre gives form and texture to the wonderfully contradictory that we might associate with the rural: from wildness and seduction through to boredom. Moving from a reading of the factory setting in *That Old Dream That Moves* (hereafter *That Old Dream*) to a discussion of the affectively charged rural milieu on display in *Stranger by the Lake,* this chapter explores how Guiraudie's use of setting, location, and mise-en-scène open up a field of ideological and theoretical coordinates that can be productively engaged in conversation with recent debates in film and queer theory. His stripped-back film *That Old Dream,* shot in a steel factory destined for imminent closure, engages questions of labor and value that rub up against a lot of recent discussion about slow cinema, while his formally arresting exploration of the ontological continuum of bodies, beings, and landscapes in *Stranger by the Lake* enjoins us to complicate the discourses on queer ecology that continue apace in the environmental humanities.

While there is something timely about the preoccupations of his films, Guiraudie's vision remains out of joint with many of the precepts of contemporary queer studies. For example, a notable shortcoming in previous accounts of the relationship between queerness and rurality is their frequent reliance on the city as a conceptual yardstick. Offering a corrective to this tendency, Scott Herring draws a distinction between a "reactionary antiurbanism" (which, in either its positive or negative form, is ultimately still reliant on the urban as a foil) and a "critical antiurbanism" that, refusing these very terms of reference, would "torque" antiurbanism and its signifiers "into a tactic" to be wielded by the nonurban-identified queer.[6] Herring's notion of a rural counterstylistics, which I explore in greater detail below, finds much common ground with Guiraudie's filmmaking. Like Herring, Guiraudie has little truck with discourses of positive representation and almost no interest in recuperative efforts to "fill in" representational gaps. His genuinely novel, unsentimental, and often even troubling vision of rural life resists these corrective gestures. He bucks the trend of increasing numbers of French writers and filmmakers instrumentalizing nonmetropolitan settings within the narrative arcs of their bildungsromans, which are invariably propelled by sexual awakening and social ascension. His cinema's careful calibration of space, form, and duration seems to pull off an alchemical trick; the boredom we associate with sleepy town squares in provincial backwaters, barren spaces of postindustrial entropy, and lakesides and forests conspicuously untouched by modern technology, is transformed into spaces of erotic potentiality.

Thinking Space with Guiraudie

The implicit tropology that extends across the titles of his films—from *Straight Ahead until Morning* to *Staying Vertical*—has often influenced the way critics have engaged with his work. Just as his films mine linear metaphors for their symbolic import, so a range of commentators (from the curatorial collective Cruising Pavilion to the architectural theorist Nathan Friedman and through to French geographer Jean-Marc Fournier) have undertaken their own processes of plotting and mapping to account for how space operates in his cinema.[7] Guiraudie's protagonists are often social outsiders in various states of errancy and fugitivity, drift and abandon. For instance, *Straight Ahead until Morning* (hereafter *Straight Ahead*) follows a somnambulant vandal who daubs red paint across the walls of an Aveyronnais town center late at night, while narrowly escaping the resident nightwatchman. Frédéric Jaeger detects in this early film a psychogeographic thread that will resurface across his work: "Disperse or drift, break the roles or fall into line, search or wait—many of these questions that will later become so important can already be found in the beautifully concise *Straight Ahead*."[8] Guiraudie's *Staying Vertical*, whose aleatory structure proves similarly resistant to synopsis, follows the itinerant path of a bisexual writer named Léo who goes on the run when he finds himself in charge of a newborn baby. In both films, social marginality and spatial errancy are figured in opposition to ideas of rectitude, propriety, and the law—or in French, *le droit*. The earlier film is largely concerned with the policing of nocturnal space, while the latter stages a tension between lateral models of queer relationality and the prohibitive force of the *nom du père*.

Whether vertical, horizontal, oblique, curved, or sinuous, Majour notes, "lines are everywhere in Guiraudie."[9] Given this frequent invocation of lines and curves—often correlated to notions of straightness and obliquity—it is tempting to read the spatial valence of his work as somehow gesturing to the etymological roots of the word "queer," which Eve Kosofsky Sedgwick famously traced back to the Proto-Indo-European *twerkw* (twist), whose spatial implications, as we saw in chapter 1, constitute a privileged motif in queer spatial theory. My own account of sexuality and space in his cinema, however, unfolds differently. I largely resist the temptation to bring Guiraudie's cinema into line (as it were) with this theoretical paradigm, however fortuitous the metaphorical resonances may first appear, because such an approach risks privileging and naturalizing the English language on which the thought of Sedgwick and Sara Ahmed is contingently grounded. Of greater importance, I argue, are questions of national, linguistic, and regional identity.

While "language, regionality, voice, and tone" are key to Guiraudie's filmmaking, as Nick Rees-Roberts notes, these subtleties are easily lost in translation.[10] To demonstrate the importance of these concerns, we might turn to the first of his two novels, *Now the Night Begins* (2014), which explores the relationship between a middle-aged man, Gilles, and a nonagenarian called Pépé, who becomes the unlikely object of Gilles's desire.[11] One of the novel's most striking stylistic particularities is Pépé's linguistic oscillation between French and Occitan when he communicates with Gilles. Far from indicating Pépé's cognitive decline, these slippages reveal how different languages, dialects, and settings serve different purposes for Guiraudie, and it is significant here that the latter tongue signifies nostalgia. In a psychoanalytic reading of the novel, Enda McCaffrey deduces that Occitan is "evocative of another time, place, and state (of mind)" for Guiraudie given that the language surfaces at particularly affectively charged moments in the narrative.[12]

When we situate him within the broader constellations of French queer culture, Guiraudie is far from the only writer or filmmaker to be drawn in by the sensual particularities that circulate and radiate across the French Southwest. His regional affinities find much common ground with those of Roland Barthes, whose essay "The Light of the Southwest" (1977) offers lyrical, embodied, and psychogeographic descriptions of this region where he grew up. Barthes notes that "the Southwest" as signifier names many things at once: an imprecise geographic designation (a third of France), a "lived trajectory," and the intimate milieu in which he was raised.[13] He goes on to perform a semiology of the region that oscillates, in a quasi-Proustian manner, between evocative generalities and autobiographical particulars. Taking this very essay as his point of departure, Philippe Dubois has made the case that the Southwest figures as a privileged topos in the French queer imaginary: one that was kindled in Barthes's writing before extending outward into the cinema of André Téchiné and François Ozon. Dubois's suggestion that the "particular topography" of the region "seems to privilege the circulation of desire, [and] encourages the staging [*mise-en-scène*] of desire" resonates strongly with Guiraudie's sensual body of cinema.[14] For the Aveyronnais filmmaker, the fertile terrain of the Southwest provides an affectively charged locus for what Dubois calls the "transversal circulation of desire." Additionally, he exploits the Arcadian fantasies and urban anxieties relating to the perceived "backwardness" of his rural settings to set in motion a *transgenerational* circulation of desire.

Situating Alain Guiraudie

It is first worth revisiting the filmmaker's autobiography given that his upbringing and early exposure to politics and ecology informed his filmmaking in numerous ways. Born in the small town of Villefranche-sur-Rouergue, in Aveyron in 1964, Alain Guiraudie grew up in a rural working-class environment. His political awakening came in his adolescence, which unfolded against the backdrop of the decade-long *lutte du Larzac* (fight for the Larzac). Guiraudie was involved in the ecological struggle against President Georges Pompidou's proposed extension of a military base onto the Larzac plateau in southwestern France. This struggle has since become a metonymic shorthand for the proenvironmental and anticapitalistic politics on the French Left more generally. While at university in Montpellier in the mid-1980s, he joined the Parti communiste français, and following his studies he took on employment in several odd jobs including a stint as a nightwatchman. This job not only inspired his earliest films but also granted him the necessary time to pursue various other artistic pursuits.

Much like Jacques Nolot, Guiraudie wrote a series of "failed" novels before moving into cinema. A cinematic autodidact who considered enrolling in the prestigious Fémis in Paris but who ultimately eschewed the French capital, he started making films in the early 1990s. His first short films, *Heroes Are Immortal* (*Les héros sont immortels,* 1990) and *Straight Ahead*, were shot on 16 mm and funded with the aid of modest state subsidies. Both films, which Jaeger describes as "pilot studies," are thinly veiled autobiographical set pieces that paint drab nocturnal portraits of the milieu in which the young filmmaker grew up.[15] While *Straight Ahead* draws on his past life as a nightwatchman, *Heros Are Immortal*—a formal study in "killing time"—seeks to convey the ennui of rural life as a teenager. The latter film is set in the market square of a sleepy village in the dead of night; across its several nocturnal vignettes, we watch two young men (one of whom is Guiraudie) wait for a third man who, in predictably Beckettian fashion, never arrives. Already in these early films, which were as formally restrained as they were financially constrained, Guiraudie anchored himself in close-knit spaces of homosociality to explore the quiet humdrum existence of rural men. Faced with little in terms of narrative action, our attention is invariably drawn to the proximity of these idle bodies—waiting, loitering, lingering. Here we see him start to develop, in an admittedly crude and embryonic form, the formal preoccupation with cinematic slowness and a thematic interest in rural boredom that characterizes his body of work as a whole. Viewed with the retrospective knowledge of his later interest in cruising, little separates these characters from the bodies we encounter in his more recent work. Indeed, these pilot studies contained the kernel for both his first medium-length film, a brief foray into the life and death of a steel factory that was lauded by Godard following its Cannes premier, as well as his relatively late breakthrough in 2013 with *Stranger by the Lake.*

The question of how we might situate Guiraudie's cinema needs to be answered in two interrelated ways. In a straightforward sense, the locations of his films are firmly anchored geographically in the world in which he grew up: they move from Villefranche, to the landscapes of Aveyron, to the Tarn, and farther afield to Provence. But these geographic choices also ought to be understood as a strategic statement on where his work sits in relation to a broader body of French queer cinema. The social and sexual milieus explored across his body of work throw into sharp relief more visible, and actively theorized, modes of urban queerness. As Dane Komljen and James Lattimer write, "It's interesting to think about the spaces in his films in terms of France itself, because the places he chooses to film exclude the major centers, notably Paris."[16] Steadfastly resisting the gravitational pull of Paris, which remains the primary locus of French gay culture, Guiraudie chooses instead to negotiate questions of desire in the rural and postindustrial spaces of the South. Before we go on to pursue an exploration of the spatial dynamics of Guiraudie's cinema, it is necessary to touch on the (often antagonistic) relationship between queerness and rurality in theory and culture to foreground the broader conceptual interventions that he offers.

Sex beyond the City

In preceding chapters of this book, the subjects, settings, and modes of spatial apprehension that were under discussion enjoyed a privileged relation to the city. While I have argued that cruising offers a compelling adjunct to the notion of *flânerie* (which, despite its nineteenth-century origins, remains a metaphorical touchstone for articulating the interrelationships among cinema, space, and the experience of modernity), it is nonetheless important to recognize that the conceptual ground on which such discourses rest is, first and foremost, urban. One of the most common assumptions to underpin theoretical accounts of cruising is the received opinion that this sexual practice occurs almost exclusively between men in the spaces of the city. A backward glance toward the work of Henning Bech, John Paul Ricco, and Mark Turner indicates that the affective pull or lure of the cruising encounter is linked, implicitly but intractably, to an understanding of the fleetingness and contingency of city life. The question therefore remains as to whether cinematic explorations of same-sex encounters outside of urban spaces require different formal idioms and alternative calibrations of space, time, and attention.

The relation between sexuality, modernity, and city life has been articulated most forcefully in the work of Henning Bech. In *When Met Meet,* a quasi-sociological exploration of the conditions of modern homosociality, he asserts boldly that "the city is the social world proper of the homosexual, his life space," before later going on to write that "the city is invariably and ubiquitously, inherently and inevitably, fundamentally and thoroughly sexualized; and that modern sexuality is essentially urban."[17] Putting to one side the belabored style used to reinforce the axiomatic status of the latter statement, his thinking contains two orders of conflation. Not only is homosexuality figured in the masculine, but when these statements are read syllogistically it becomes clear that the city is used to elide male homosexuality and "modernity"—an argumentative gesture that, as many feminist critics of the visual arts have argued, ultimately has the effect of reifying dominant relations among sex, gender, and the city. As we saw in chapter 1, queer theory's foundational suspicion toward the blind spots and normative assumptions of other fields of inquiry has been put to productive use to refine, or even call into question, the biases of other disciplines, such as geography. By critically examining the norms and assumptions that postmodern geographers left unexamined and heeding the call to widen the remit of human geography, queer theorists and geographers have turned their focus to geographical and representational margins to put under duress master narratives such as those typified by Bech. In his contribution to *Decentring Sexualities,* for instance, a work with the express aim to uncover "socio-spatial hierarchies and dynamics in representations and constructions of sexuality," David Bell notes how queer studies has frequently defaulted to a metropolitan frame of reference—a tendency with potentially deleterious effects to queer subjects residing in nonurban and rural spaces.[18]

The impulse to decenter queer geographies can also be traced across the work of J. Jack Halberstam, from *In a Queer Time and Place,* which offers a corrective to the "metronormativity" that underpins discourses on queer spatiality, to *Wild Things,* in which the author invests the figure of "wildness" with significant queer potential. In the earlier text, he suggests that the decentering energies of queer theory, as well as its implicit valorization of the minor, marginal, and nonhegemonic, presents scholars of sexuality and space with "the opportunity for a developed understanding of the local, the nonmetropolitan . . . and the situated."[19] This broad idea finds a more speculative expression in his exploration of wildness, which shares with queerness a predisposition for the thwarting and disordering of organizing principles: "Wildness takes the antiidentitarian refusal embedded in queer theory and connects it to other sites of productive confusion, taxonomic limits, and boundary collapse."[20] Such a suspension of identity categories, he suggests, kindles intimacies with other forms of life, thereby enacting more horizontally distributed forms of relationality.

The project of looking for queerness beyond the city unfolds in a slightly different direction in the work of Scott Herring. For while he shares with Halberstam a commitment to the dethroning of metropolitan thinking, his work attains a more radical and polemical tenor. In

Another Country: Queer Anti-Urbanism, Herring argues that current interests in "queer-based non-metropolitanism" ought to be forcefully reinflected with a more contestatory, negative thrust, or "a queer-laden anti-urbanism."[21] Yet rather than taking aim at the field of human geography, he positions queer culture's own biases as his primary target. Against a backdrop of gay urbanism, which is at once "cartographic and performative, psychic and social, imaginary and all-too-materialized," he details "how ruralized queers have negotiated the urbane metropolitan stylistics that govern—and normalize—them with counter stylistics of their own."[22] Instead of simply redressing the perceived omissions of existing discourse (an essentially recuperative move), he seeks to uncover how "rurality—at once a geographic entity and a performative space that has often been shunned, mocked, and discarded by the metropolitan minded—can be a supreme site of queer critique."[23] By keeping in mind the tension between recuperation (conservation) and rupture (threat) that underpins these discourses, we can see the emergence of a significant fault line between positive and negative forms of nonurban and ecological representation. Taking these coordinates as a starting point, I suggest both that Herring's call to move beyond a myopic focus on the city as the primary locus of queer representation finds its cinematic corollary in Guiraudie's cinema, and, moreover, that there is an important political valence to this move.

The ethical stakes of Guiraudie's project of queer decentering are made explicit in previous accounts of the filmmaker. If Rees-Roberts names "metropolitan condescension" among the primary biases in contemporary French queer cinema, then Roy Grundmann and David Pendleton write that he "showcas[es] the . . . dignity and imagination [of rural subjects] rather than condescending to them, as one might expect in an era of global urbanist bias."[24] In a 2006 interview, revealingly titled "J'ai envie de refaire la France" (I want to remap France), Guiraudie pauses to consider the relation between the thematic territory and geographical situation of his cinema. He states that "though we might imagine that New York and Paris are better placed than a village in Aveyron in terms of their ability to speak to universal concerns," like sex and desire, "such a view is false."[25] He continues, "I started to make films at a time when cinema no longer looked to the countryside, when films unfolded within the four walls of the petit bourgeois

Parisian interior. My first works were motivated, in part, by a reaction to this naturalist Parisian cinema. I had a desire to shoot in the country, in a working-class setting."[26]

By connecting his geographic investment in the provinces of the Southwest to questions of working-class identity, it becomes apparent that the demarcation of Guiraudie's cinematic territory represents a sociopolitical parti pris. Here he is explicit about his investments. He has previously positioned himself as an activist of the countryside and spoken about the need to affirm a working-class queer identity that he dubs *la prolo-pride.* Nonurban spaces afford him the possibility of exploring forms of intimacy and relationality that cut across the dividing lines of class and generation. Such lines, as he goes on to argue, are too rigidly fixed in urban life: "In the countryside, the young and old come into greater contact, whereas in cities they are quickly separated into groups."[27] In his suggestion that queer urban cultures (and their associated technologies of erotic narrow casting) all too hastily foreclose the possibilities of cross-generational eroticism, we can also identify in this statement an implicitly *temporal* dimension. This point is important to keep in mind because Guiraudie's cinema frequently exploits the decelerated temporalities of nonurban life to articulate moments of queer possibility that are open-ended and distraction-free. Yet given that such moments of erotic contact range from brief and furtive glimpses of cross-generational desire (between a young worker and his older boss in *That Old Dream*) to thoroughgoing explorations of gerontophilia (in *Staying Vertical* and his novel *Now the Night Begins*), Guiraudie also enjoys a complex relation to another spatiotemporal quality that is typically imputed to rural life: "backwardness" (*être en arrière*). Exemplifying the counterstylistic strategy central to Herring's queer critique, Guiraudie's cinema is rarely beholden to logics of propriety. Rather, his films traffic—often ironically and absurdly—in the reductive tropes he ultimately wants to counteract.

Given that his work exists at odds with urban accounts of cruising, his "oblique" perspective engenders a formal creativity in his work. Unable to rely on the flux of city spaces to generate the ambient affects and erotics of cruising, he pursues other ways of marshaling spectatorial attention, creating narrative suspense, and achieving erotic release. The following close readings outline two distinct ways of doing this. First, I turn to *That Old Dream,* a film that invites us to consider how slowness (which is linked to the economic conditions and material milieu of a run-down factory) recalibrates erotic relations on screen. I then explore the rural setting of *Stranger by the Lake,* asking how the film's focus on the spatial practice of cruising might help us to expand the scope of queer ecological thought. I ultimately show that the settings of Guiraudie's films invite us to rethink how male homosocial eroticism is entangled with broader economic and ecological forces, thereby offering substantive possibilities for queer spatial theory.[28]

Slow Cinema's Redundant Narratives: *That Old Dream That Moves*

That Old Dream That Moves is a medium-length film that, on the surface at least, documents the routine of a handful of workers in a steel factory in the small town of Gaillac, in the Tarn, during the week prior to its definitive closure. Beneath this surface, it also documents the machinations of queer desire in a radically circumscribed homosocial environment. One way of accounting for the film's dual status is to turn, perhaps fittingly, to its own mode of production. While the project started its life as a documentary on the renovation of factory buildings, it quickly moved into the fictional domain of social realist drama. Having broadened the film's prior focus on economic development, Guiraudie decided to turn his attention to the space (and subject) of homoerotic desire. As Fabienne Bullot explains, by "moving away from a documentary topos centred on the spaces of work and economic heritage, Guiraudie transformed a factory in the Tarn, which had been shut for six months and appears barely cleared of its metallurgical residue, into a timeless, atemporal setting in which the redefinition of identities and relationships is subsequently explored."[29]

While the film's setting is sharply delimited (we never leave the factory gate: the scenes alternate between the vast expanses of the factory hangar, the tightly framed locker room, and an outdoor yard), *That Old Dream* speaks metonymically to much broader dynamics of postindustrial entropy; this is a film situated squarely within "the grips of liquid modernity."[30] To further underscore the links between the film's economic context and its aesthetic style (or to couch this in squarely Marxian terms, base and superstructure) we might also note how it resonates with Matthew Flanagan's understanding of "slow cinema" as a mode of film practice that indexes the fallout of those "spaces that have been indirectly affected or left behind by globalization."[31] Moreover, it is a film that captures the zeitgeist of early twenty-first century filmmaking by meditating, often nostalgically, on its own historical conjuncture. As Bullot goes on to note, "The film presents an opus that defers to the historical consciousness of workers, searching for a narrative form that accommodates and rehabilitates the residue of a utopian vision centered on community."[32] Lamenting the fact that the modern workplace has grown increasingly atomized, Guiraudie summons a vision of an erstwhile age of camaraderie, fraternity, and—most strikingly—homosociality, and it is the ambivalent sexual politics of this homosocial vision that interest me here.

Before exploring the formal particularities of Guiraudie's slow cinema, let us first outline the film's plot. *That Old Dream* chronicles the final five days of the steel factory's operation. We follow a man in his thirties called Jacques Roudillou (Pierre Louis-Calixte), who has been brought in as a temporary worker to take apart a machine called the Ubitona. While the actual function of the Ubitona remains unknown, the mystical machine acts as a necessary point of anchorage for the film's exploration of the machinations of eroticism. Over the five days, Guiraudie presents the friendship that Jacques strikes up with an older man named Louis (Jean Ségani) and explores his relationship with the slightly younger Jean Donand (Jean-Marie Combelles), the factory's hard-nosed manager who slowly becomes the object of Roudillou's erotic interest. Simultaneously a muted tale of workplace desire and a meditation on the waning of normative masculinity, *That Old Dream* unfolds via a series of loosely scripted conversations between the three men on the factory floor. We learn of a first wave of redundancies six years ago that reduced the workforce by half, which was followed by a second wave of cuts that occurred in the previous six months. The factory's imminent closure was confirmed shortly thereafter, leaving only a skeleton staff. The film documents the drawn-out phase of decommissioning, which is experienced as a slow but steady process of entropy. This gradual decline is captured within a relatively condensed time frame of forty-nine minutes, taking us from Monday morning to Friday evening. The film therefore occupies an ambiguous temporal space: although much of the factory work that transpires on screen seems to lack purpose, and many of the workers are vocal about wanting to leave, a sense of finitude—which is materially underwritten by the associated loss of livelihoods—casts a shadow over any conceivable future.

That Old Dream comprises almost exclusively medium and long takes. In typical Bazinian fashion, Guiraudie maintains a strong depth of field throughout—a formal choice that attains a striking effect when the camera lingers on immense, vacant factory hangars in various states of disrepair. As with *Stranger by the Lake,* as we will see, clocks are rarely on display in Guiraudie's universe. Rather, the succession of narrative events advances by way of repetition. Repeated sequences of establishing shots (a view of the factory entrance followed by a shot of the factory floor) act as a loose metronome in Guiraudie's films, both registering the passing of days and guiding us toward an uncertain end. Though we can guess in advance that *That Old Dream* is likely to conclude with a shot of the workers leaving the factory (thereby replaying a moment that, as Elena Gorfinkel has suggested, constitutes the foundational instant of cinema), the slow, protracted rhythms of the factory labor frustrate this neat telos and convenient narrative arc.[33] For some (notably older) workers, the demand to keep up the pretense of undertaking productive work in the final week of the factory's existence is felt as an egregious affront. Others find themselves caught in a temporal double bind. Laying bare labor's contradictions, Guiraudie shows that there is a self-negating dimension to the speed of work: the more productive the worker becomes, the faster they work themselves out of employment. The only person to be spared this grim fate is Jacques Roudillou, the character around whom gathers the film's threadbare narrative. The itinerant mechanic has been charged with the task of removing the machine that lies at the center of the factory hangar. That this younger queer man is brought to such a fragile space of working-class masculinity (and, moreover, that he is tasked with the job of dismantling a phallic machine) sets out in a fairly heavy-handed manner *That Old Dream*'s allegorical premise. If, as David Pendleton and Roy Grundmann write, the film is chiefly concerned with "the superimposition of eroticism and economics and even architecture," then Guiraudie asks us to consider whether the social scaffolding of normative masculinity can remain intact once untethered from its material foundations.[34] Or, as the filmmaker himself puts it: "Is it still possible to get an erection after the closure of a factory?"[35]

The Dream Factory

The steel factory, which serves as the film's setting, is more than just a backdrop. Its imposing structure dwarfs all human forms, making it perhaps the most crucial element of the film. By maintaining an unwavering focus on the factory's spaces, Guiraudie enjoins us to consider several questions that have been central to recent debates in film theory. For Gorfinkel, there is always already a reflexive dimension to the screening of factory labor.[36] She notes that in the filming of factories (the prototypical example of which remains Louis Lumière's *Workers Leaving the Lumière Factory in Lyon / La sortie de l'usine Lumière à Lyon,* 1895) we encounter several conceptual problems that strike at the heart of cinema's ambivalent aesthetic status. To screen manual work by way of a slow, protractive durational aesthetic, moreover, is to negotiate film's complex relationship to both labor and leisure, which by extension raises broader questions about cinema's simultaneous status as art form (an object of aesthetic disinterestedness) and an industrial product (the output of commercial pressures).

Jean-Louis Comolli also writes at some length about the ability of factory scenes to reflexively foreground the materiality of laboring bodies. In his essay "Mechanical Bodies, Ever More Heavenly," he explores the various associations (technical, kinetic, biopolitical) and homologies between factory films and the cinematic medium. "The fabrication of the visible and the organized visibility of machines" generates "attraction" and "seduction." Comolli describes how cinema transfigures the "arduousness of work in the steel mill"—note that his example fits squarely within the context of our present example—"through cinema's magic."[37] That is to say, the material heft of heavy lifting is somehow sublimated, transformed into an art of "lightness and grace." He invites the theorist–spectator to "witness the industrial films" and notice how "the length of shots, the careful framing, the flow of tracking shots convey something like a cameraman's delight in filming mechanical tools, cranes, car bodies, presses—all that moves in the sheen of metal, everything that slides, strikes, rises and falls in the immutable cadence of the metronomic beat."[38] For Comolli, the operation of this slick machine *en abyme* is not only formally pleasing but exudes something of the erotic, a term I will qualify shortly. Adopting a syntactical structure that formally resembles the chiastic symmetry of the mechanical chain, he writes that "the eroticism of machines is captured to perfection by the cinerotic machine."[39] He goes on to argue that this "cinerotic machine" is most "boldly exemplified" in the 1920s filmmaking of Dziga Vertov. Read from a queer standpoint, there is a slight irony to this claim. For while Comolli's dialectical approach to the image of factory labor hopes to bring to the fore those elements habitually screened from view, he neglects to consider another, altogether more obvious dimension of factory film: its potential gayness. The crucial point of reference here would not be Vertov but his contemporary, Sergei Eisenstein, for whom the Soviet imagery of laboring bodies and homosocial bonding served as an alibi for the queer director and his spectators. (Just consider David Gerstner's analysis of the "tightly framed, muscular, chiseled young men" serving as the—occasionally shirtless—proletarian agitators in Eisenstein's *Strike / Stachka* [1925], or Tom Waugh's account of how the "physical beauty of the male proletarian hero" in Eisenstein's work "arose from a unique confluence of erotic sensibility and political belief.")[40] While for Comolli it is the kinetic synergies and formal correspondences between bodies and machines that produces a generative friction that he calls "erotic," for Eisenstein the erotic charge of this body of filmmaking is linked to the factory space's more obvious function as a locus of homosocial physicality. Yet, while Eisenstein and Guiraudie share an erotic investment in the laboring male form, the cinematographic means by which the French filmmaker explores the carnal density of these "heavenly bodies" is quite different. As I suggested above, this is due in part to Guiraudie's subscription to the tenets of André Bazin who, in the overarching narratives that are often told about film theory at least, is frequently cast as Eisenstein's antagonist.

Suffice to say that in *That Old Dream* eroticism is *not* generated from the pleasing synergy of well-oiled machines (Comolli) or well-oiled bodies (Eisenstein), but rather from cinema's narrative breakdown. Turning his attention to the temporal particularities of the factory in ruin, Guiraudie renders noticeable those moments of what Schoonover, in his writing on the queer temporality of cinematic labor, terms "fallow film time."[41] It is precisely in such moments of narrative uneventfulness that the otherwise latent homoeroticism of the film comes to the fore. As I hope to show by way of close analysis, the queer charge of Guiraudie's factory film comes from its slow and deliberative pace, which both guides our attention toward, and calibrates our anticipation of, the film's eventual erotic climax. Or, to formulate the relation between time, space, and sexuality in simpler terms: the factory setting establishes the temporal conditions of the film, and these temporal conditions create spaces of erotic possibility.

Producing Masculinities

There is a sociological impetus to the film that is perhaps a residual trace of its documentary origin. Guiraudie's primary interest is in showing us how factories produce (or rather produced) the social, cultural, and economic conditions for normative masculinities to thrive in rural France. The crucial difference at the present historical conjuncture, however, is that the steel factory is in a state of decline. In Grundmann and Pendleton's account of the film's setting, which strikes a vaguely elegiac tone, they note that "the structure is there, but it's crumbling, and out of this crumbling structure comes something new."[42] The waning of heteronormative masculinity, they suggest, will give way to a different libidinal economy. Against the striking geometry of the hangar's backdrop, at the forefront of the now-empty factory floor, Guiraudie stages scenes of labor that are processes of not construction but rather deconstruction. Jacques's job is to dismantle a phallic avatar (the mysteriously named Ubitona) while the other workers spend their day killing time in the courtyard. Given that we are never told what this machine does, Guiraudie distances us even further from the utility of Jacques's mechanical movements. In a quasi-structuralist manner, the film's minimal narrative, stiff dialogue, and patient focus on Jacques's slow and laborious gestures have the combined effect of heightening our attention to the materiality of his body. (*What, or even where, is the film's action?* we may wonder, as the film's narrative advancement is held in abeyance.) By staging scenes of "empty cinematic time," to draw on Tiago de Luca's phrasing, the filmmaker "expos[es] in return the calculated temporal mechanisms by which cinema conventionally abides in its production of meaning."[43] Via this subtle transvaluation of narrative eventfulness, and Guiraudie's concomitant phenomenological focus on laboring bodies qua bodies, we are encouraged to read the relation between Jacques and the men around him for legible signs of desire.

In a compelling discussion of the generic traits of contemporary slow cinema, Schoonover notes that this form of "art cinema exploits its spectator's boredom, becoming as much a cinema of expectancies as one of attractions. It turns boredom into a kind of special work, one in which the empty onscreen time is repurposed, renovated, rehabilitated."[44] He continues, "The boringness of art films exposes that genre's insistent disarticulation of the body on-screen from the body offscreen." Drawing on Barthes (whose meditations on boredom and eroticism I explored in chapter 2), Schoonover considers, from a queer materialist perspective, a paradox that may be familiar to those readers well versed in structuralist/materialist film theory, or indeed to those spectators who have sat through a screening of Andy Warhol's *Blowjob* (1964) in its entirety: the less we are given to make sense of, the more we invest in what *is* put on display. This basic principle attains a queer charge for Guiraudie, especially when it is coupled with a minimal narrative that coyly suggests, though rarely speaks explicitly about, the circulation of desire among men.

In one scene, which takes place in the central hangar, Louis tries to find out more about Jacques's personal life: "Why is a good-looking young man like you without a wife?" Louis asks bluntly, eyeing his coworker. When Jacques challenges Louis's heteronormative assumptions, the older man leaves swiftly and tells his boss, Donand, about the interaction. As Michael Korensky writes, "What initially seems like an all-too-common instance of homophobia proves to be something far more complex and impossible to make generic mincemeat from."[45]

In the later scene that finally marks the long-awaited *passage à l'acte,* the circulation of erotic tension on the factory floor becomes more explicit. Jacques and Donand find themselves alone in the hangar. Donand helps to hold up the Ubitona while Jacques kneels to loosen one of the machine's bolts. After an awkward physical encounter with the machine, we notice Jacques slowly starting to touch, and then caress, his boss's crotch. This sequence represents a pivotal moment; it is precisely the point at which the film's muted desire is made tangible. In the shift from manual labor to manual pleasure, the film acquiesces to the lure of sex. While a furtive moment such as this might go overlooked in many other films, Guiraudie leverages the noneventfulness of *That Old Dream* to frame this fleeting graze as something altogether more climactic. From this point on, we are invited to cast a more suspecting gaze over the spaces of the factory.

The locker-room and shower area (where male nudity is presented with a full-frontal matter-of-factness) attains a gay charge. The physical connections between Jacques and Louis start to loosen up, too, as they both become less inhibited. It is only at the end of the film, as the workers finally leave the factory gates, that Louis finally admits to Jacques that "over these last three days, I have been hard simply thinking about you." Jacques, though flattered, is uninterested. While cross-generational sex is a staple of Guiraudie's filmmaking, on this occasion the dream of this particular old man seems unlikely to move toward fulfillment.

Figure 12. *That Old Dream That Moves* (Alain Guiraudie, 2001). Factory manager (Jean) assists a young and handsome mechanic (Jacques) with the dismantling of a phallic machine within an empty factory hangar. Jacques begins to touch his boss intimately.

Figure 13. *That Old Dream That Moves* (Alain Guiraudie, 2001). Jacques emerges from the shower to re-encounter Jean in the locker room.

Writing on the film's setting, Nick Rees-Roberts writes that "the deserted factory floor occupied by the few remaining workers is the setting for an allusive eroticization of the workplace, achieved by decontextualizing the backward glances of gay cruising and transposing them to the unsexy world of production."[46] Though the "unsexiness" he attributes to the film's setting reads here as an impediment to the "allusive eroticization" of place, I argue, on the contrary, that the "unsexy" backdrop is the structural precondition for its articulation of homoeroticism. Moreover, the connotative specificities of the factory setting allow Guiraudie's spectators to tap into a different—and ultimately more cathected—economy of attention. The factory's predisposition toward spatial, temporal, and gestural abstraction is harnessed by the filmmaker to construct a highly original mise-en-scène of gay desire that both nods obliquely to a venerable cinematic tradition of the factory film (exemplified, for instance, in the work of Eisenstein) but reconfigures its terms to address a new postindustrial climate.

Prolétaires de tous les pays, caressez-vous!

By way of closing, it is important to briefly discuss the interrelationship between sexuality and class in the film to offer a fuller account of its "sexual politics of the slow and the boring."[47] While *That Old Dream* comes close to pitting its exploration of working-class masculinities in opposition to queer sexuality, its ending is careful not to privilege individual mobility (embodied by Jacques, the young, itinerant, queer subject) over one of collective solidarity. For Guiraudie, whose cinema, as we noted above, ought to be read as an antidote to a prevalent "metropolitan condescension," his primary ambition here was to articulate the very vision of working-class queerness, or *prolo-pride,* he found lacking in French cinema.

That Old Dream arguably tells us more about the past, including Guiraudie's own politically formative years, than it does about the present historic conjuncture. What the film proposes is a nostalgic vision that implicitly casts a backward glance toward a previous age of gay politics—one in which sexual liberation was enfolded within a broader revolutionary social struggle. Since the filmmaker routinely invokes the history and politics of French queer labor movement in his discussion of the film, *That Old Dream* might be understood as an encomium to the golden age in the 1970s French queer imaginary—a period when the radical leftist and homophile movements became temporary bedfellows in the form of the Front homosexuel d'action révolutionnaire. To be sure, this movement's rallying cry of *Prolétaires de tous les pays caressez-vous!* (Workers of the world, caress yourselves!) is strikingly literalized in the film. The slogan, which queerly reformulates the rousing injunction of Karl Marx and Friedrich Engels, substitutes the imperative *unissez-vous* (unite) for *caressez-vous* (a verb that means "to caress" and, in a somewhat more colloquial and reflexive form, to masturbate). But it also invites further confusion, given that the pronoun *vous* hovers ambiguously between the second-person singular in a formal register and the plural form. In a sense, such attempts to conjugate working-class fraternity and homoerotic bonding hinge on such a strategic elision: just as Guiraudie, after Eisenstein, seeks to bring into the sphere of the visible those queer impulses that otherwise lay dormant on the factory floor, so, too, this erstwhile tradition of queer Marxism, led by vanguard figures such as Daniel Guérin, sought to bring the subversive potential of queer sex into the broader field of social, political, and industrial relations.

As we move away from the factory floor and toward the space of the rural lakeside, I trace the lineaments of the queer thinking that emerged after this critical moment: away from a Marxian ethos of fraternal bonding via masturbation (in French, *branlement*) and toward what Leo Bersani, taking his cue from the negatively inflected writing of Guy Hocquenghem, would later term *ébranlement* or self-shattering. For, as I hope to demonstrate here, the central question that resonates across Guiraudie's varied body of work is how homosociality might be reimagined following its encounter with the erotic. This is seen in terms of both Guiraudie's interest in a vision of *prolo-pride* that is beholden to a logic of positive recognition and, conversely, his later appeal to an antisocial dimension of queerness that, to summon the specter of Hocquenghem, "haunts the normal world."[48] By shifting our focus away from the postindustrial backwaters of the Tarn and toward the lakeside setting in the Verdon Gorge, I now take as my focus the ecological, rather than economic, dimension of his work to ask how queer spatial and sexual practices might occasion new ways of relating to the natural world.

Seeing the Wood for the Trees: *Stranger by the Lake*

Although there is much that separates the postindustrial backdrop of a metallurgical factory in the Tarn and the lapping shores of a lake in Provence, the formal similarities between both films offer a compelling basis for this coupling. As Komljen and Lattimer note, "The factory and the lake are interesting in that they're pre-existing spaces on the one hand, but on the other they're highly constructed, they function almost like a stage for a plot to play out on."[49] To elaborate on this statement, it is important to note that the lakeside setting of *Stranger by the Lake* (hereafter *Stranger*) might be qualified as "man-made" in two different ways. First, the film's location of the lac de Sainte-Croix, which stretches over twelve kilometers and lies at the foot of the Verdon Gorge, is in fact an artificial lake that was engineered in the 1970s. And second, the cruising zone that is the film's setting is one that is "produced" by the spatial and sexual practices of the men who dwell there. In the interviews that followed the release of the film, Guiraudie spoke of a red line of continuity between *Stranger* and his earliest films, *Heroes Are Immortal* and *That Old Dream.* Speaking of his formal ambitions for the film in a dialogue with filmmaker João Pedro Rodrigues, he notes that "after making three feature-length films in which the geography was not very precise, I had the wish to return to a form of filmmaking that was quite simple, a film where one repeatedly returned to the same spaces: the car park, the forest path, the beach. . . . It's a very geometric—or even scenographic film—a natural space with its own architecture."[50] In his comparative reading of *Stranger* and *That Old Dream,* Dennis Lim similarly notes how both "confine themselves to a single location, a rhythmic day-by-day structure, a circumscribed masculine world, and both use a formal language so precise and delimited as to verge on structuralist repetition." Though the formal similarities between both films are clear enough to see, my interest lies in the thematic territory opened up by the concomitant shift from the (post)industrial to the rural. While *That Old Dream* implicitly drew on an economic idiom, here we turn to questions of ecology.

Stranger unfolds over a ten-day period in the middle of summer. It follows Franck (Pierre Deladonchamps), a man in his thirties who spends his days in a lakeside cruising spot in the South of France. On the first day, Franck meets Henri (Patrick D'Assumçao), a portly man in his fifties who is positioned on the periphery of the cruising zone. Unlike the other men by the lakeside, Henri is ambivalent about his sexual preferences. While he is recently divorced from his wife, he holds himself at arm's length from "ces mecs qui sont vraiment homo" (those men who are "really" gay). (It will later transpire that Henri is indeed very fond of Franck but is unwilling to submit to the indignities of unrequited love.) Within the clearly coded spatial economy of the film, Henri is similarly positioned "on the fence." Throughout the film he can be found perched at the furthermost border of the cruising zone that, he explains, is governed by an invisible dividing line; he frequently gestures *là bas* (over there) to the lake's social obverse, a family-friendly zone where he used to spend summer days with his wife. When Franck and Henri strike up a friendship on the first day, the seemingly autonomous gaze of the camera is drawn into the orbit of another man, Michel (Christophe Paou), as if to anticipate his privileged position as the film's object of desire. Michel is a man of around Franck's age with striking athleticism and dark hair. His retro moustache summons an erstwhile golden age of 1970s gay pornography, a period that predates HIV/AIDS.

Over the week and half, Guiraudie diagrams the triangulation of relations between the three men. This day-by-day account of the lakeside's comings and goings will lead, by the end of the second day, to the strangulation and drowning of a fourth man at the hands of Michel. The murder—which occurs late in the evening, once most of the lakeside cruisers have left—is a potent warning sign both to Franck, who witnesses the murder, and Henri. Once a rumor circulates among the regulars that the man, whose corpse is washed ashore, was the victim of a ten-meter catfish, the lakeside setting loses its luster. Police Inspector Damroder (Jérôme Chappatte) gets involved in the case, submitting the spatial and sexual practices of the lake's anonymous community to fierce, forensic, and homophobic scrutiny. Henri later warns Franck against pursuing Michel, the object of his growing affection: "OK, il est bronzé, il est musclé, il est bien foutu, mais je te jure qu'il est bizarre" (Granted, he is tanned, muscular and well-built, but I swear that there is something odd about him).

Following a period of brooding Hitchcockian suspense, the film reaches its narrative climax. Franck does not heed his friend's warning, preferring instead to succumb to Michel's menacing erotic appeal. This pursuit ultimately leads to the death of Henri—Michel unceremoniously slits his throat—and Franck running through the lakeside forest, hiding in among the foliage, and seeking refuge from the man he previously courted. The end of *Stranger*—a film whose temporal unfolding is governed less by the exigencies of narrative eventfulness and more by the spatial practice of cruising and the diurnal rhythms of natural light—fades out slowly into darkness. The crepuscular glow that previously framed the contours of Franck's body gradually subsides, and we hear Franck's tremorous voice cry out for Michel. Is Franck's cry, framed against the backdrop of a black screen, an invitation to his potential murderer? (*A howl in favor of Sade?*) Or are we to interpret his final plaintive cry as an SOS? Offering little by way of an answer, Guiraudie's film resists narrative closure.

What we *are* left with is an empty screen that captures acoustically the sensory plenitude of the natural environment. In a deft and beautiful summary of the film's ending that conveys in textual form the affective charge of this final moment, Saige Walton writes, "Deferring resolution and prolonging our embodied apprehension once more, *Stranger by the Lake* fades to black, accompanied by the sounds of an impervious wind and the night-time cries of cicadas."[51] Indeed, despite its visual impoverishment, this final scene crystallizes a central tension that runs throughout *Stranger:* namely, the relationship between *bios* and *thanatos*. But to get a greater critical purchase on this crucial tension (one that bedevils the fields of queer and ecological theory as much as it does the film in question), it is necessary to make a detour and consider how the practice of cruising is given visual form in the film.

In critical discussions on *Stranger,* much has been made of the film's formal particularities. As with *That Old Dream,* the time of waiting is exploited to create suspense. Yet, within the affective and generic register of the thriller, this suspense is bound up not only with the machinations of eroticism but also the threat of death. There is also a recursive dimension to the film's form that critics have been quick to pick up on. Every day opens with a shot of a parking lot, followed by a shot of the rocky pathway that leads us through the woodland (where many of the sex scenes transpire), and then to the lakeside, where we are greeted by naked men lying around or bathing. In his analysis of the film's cinematography, Gary Needham invokes a rich body of queer film theory that emphasizes the homological relationship between cruising and spectatorship, writing that Guiraudie "uses both a repetitive and durational structure in its narrative in order to capture the sense of waiting inherent in cruising. Specific shots are repeated to underscore the sameness of days and encounters, but for gay men this is not boring—it is utopian since homosexuality's relationship to desire is not that of straight linear time."[52] While this account of the spatiotemporal dynamics of cruising might feel slightly telescoped (for while there is truth to the Barthesian dictum that "boredom is not far from bliss," the distance is narrowed slightly too hastily here), Needham helpfully reorients our attention toward analytic concerns with form and structure.[53] Gay cruising is not only the principal subject matter of *Stranger* (the thing depicted). Rather, given that we are frequently invited to scan the expansive vistas of the setting for signs of profilmic action, cruising is also central to our appreciation of the film's form (how it depicts). Guiraudie, a filmmaker who is known for his fidelity toward Bazinian aesthetics in his more restrained films, experiments here with duration and depth of field to attune spectators to their surroundings. The film's attention to the material environment of the lakeside moves back and forth between appreciating the natural world and the erotic relations between bodies; scenes of unsimulated sex give way to highly aestheticized shots of the sun-dappled forest floor, suggesting a thematic rapprochement between sex and nature.

In his evocation of cruising, there is a further dimension to Guiraudie's experimentation with the economies of spectatorial attention. Speaking on the topic of the film's reception, Guiraudie notes that "people say that the cruising system I show in the film no longer exists. Now it's Grindr and cruising online. . . . But there was something about love in the outdoors which was very hedonistic. That has now sunken into something I find less fun, something that isn't based so much on seduction, on a real encounter."[54] In a compelling reading of the film grounded in a discussion of "postcinematic" sexualities, Damon R. Young draws our attention to these anachronistic details. Cruising, he notes, takes place without smartphones. The film's distraction-free approach to public sex (or what he refers to as "the meeting of partners *dans la vraie vie*") is mirrored by a distraction-free approach to cinematography: namely, Bazinian realism.[55] The film's rendering of the natural world is, if not prelapsarian, then redemptive to a certain degree; as Young notes: "A certain nostalgia permeates [the film's] mise-en-scène."[56] The nostalgia to which he alludes might refer to the film's bucolic setting (connotations of Arcadian idealism abound throughout), its anachronistic vision of queer sex freed from the grip of technology (i.e., Grindr), its nod to "classical" cinematography (Hitchcock, Bazin), or possibly the conjugation of all three.

Cruising the Threshold of Life and Death

The sensory and erotic appeal of *Stranger* hinges on a critical tension. Or to be more precise, the film weaves together numerous interrelated tensions: between *eros* and *thanatos,* the human and the nonhuman, biophilia and the death drive. While many critics focus on the sensory plenitude of the film—achieved through a strong depth of field aided by crisp, wide-angled digital photography, and amplification of ambient natural sounds (the cicadas, the bushes rustling in the wind, the lapping of the shore, the quasi-synesthetic appeal of pebbles crunching under the weight of sandals)—few have sought to understand how this rich, multisensory rendering of the natural world exists in tension with its narrative focus on the death drive.

Guiraudie skillfully manipulates the raw materials of the film's environment to build its affective architecture—in fact, at various moments, these techniques are so striking as to verge on pathetic fallacy. Consider the scene that follows the murder. On the third day, the habitual sequence of establishing shots is omitted. On this occasion, we cut from a view of the parking lot to a medium shot of shoes and a beach towel strewn on a rocky patch of the lakefront. This is followed by a point-of-view shot from the perspective of Franck that pans across the lakefront, surveying the usual suspects. Franck's roaming gaze, which matches our eyeline, reads more as a look of suspicion (*who, among the usual suspects, is missing?*) rather than one of sexual solicitation. The sky is overcast and the color of the lake, typically a striking azure, is drab and desaturated. In this sequence, the film's otherwise idyllic setting is drained of its vitality, mirroring the affective state of Franck who, having recently witnessed the murder, casts an altogether more cautious gaze over the lakefront. Yet as the day unfolds, Franck's more critical and deidealized state of perception reveals itself to be just as transient and capricious as the weather. The penumbral shadow the murder casts over the film fades away, the clouds dissipate, and Franck continues to pursue the dangerous and alluring Michel. An even more striking use of color, lighting, and mise-en-scène can be found in the subsequent scene in which the two men fuck by the lake. Manichean binaries of light and dark, and their attendant connotations of life and death, are used to striking effect. The tightly framed shots of the two silhouetted bodies recall the bistable image of Rubin's vase. Guiraudie exploits this gestalt effect to invite a spectatorial gaze that oscillates between foreground and background, sensual bodies and sublime surroundings, thereby forging an even tighter connection between the film's primary themes.

When set against the conceptual backdrop of queer theory, Guiraudie's exploration of the tension between the life instinct and the death drive presents two elements that have been at the center of—but have regrettably foreclosed the productive possibilities of—queer ecological theory. From the work of Catriona Mortimer-Sandilands and

Bruce Erikson to recent interventions by Nicole Seymour and Sarah Ensor, there exists a growing body of scholarship that has sought to engage queer theory and the environmental humanities in conversation.[57] In *Strange Natures,* Seymour notes that queer theory, especially in its "antisocial" iteration, is predicated on a radical nonfuturity that is difficult to square with ecological concerns.[58] Timothy Morton similarly avers that, on the surface at least, "ecological criticism and queer theory seem incompatible."[59] Not only are environmentalist politics predicated on a future-oriented teleology, they are often symbolically invested in what Lee Edelman notoriously described as the phantasmatic figure of "the Child." If one of the principal aims of queer theory is to scrutinize discourses that naturalize normative assumptions (Edelman's notion of "reproductive futurism" being the example closest to hand), then surely the rhetorical deployment of the term "nature" merits greater consideration.

Here Guiraudie's approach to the natural world does much to complicate this polarized picture. On the one hand, *Stranger* is heavily invested in the lure of the death drive. Guiraudie habitually alludes to Georges Bataille's definition of eroticism as "l'approbation de la vie jusque dans la mort" (the assenting to life even in death) as a philosophical coordinate for film, and he has also described his film in dialogue with Lee Edelman's critique of reproductive futurism.[60] Yet, while the many suggestive links between *Stranger* and queer theory's antisocial turn are clear enough to see (both are interested in how the vicissitudes of queer sex "shatter" subject positions and the social order, and both demand to be read—in Guiraudie's case, allegorically—against the complicated backdrop of HIV/AIDS discourse), the filmmaker nonetheless affirms, pace Edelman, that his film is "more on the side of queer and the life instinct."[61] Resisting what Greg Garrard has named the "debilitating biophobia of queer theory," he sets his sights beyond the conceptual aporias of queer ecological thought to explore how queers relate to (one another in) the natural world in more capacious terms.[62]

In her contribution to discourses of queer ecology, Sarah Ensor finds in the spatial practice of cruising a way of moving beyond the impasses outlined by Seymour and others. Rather than imputing a "queerness" to the nonhuman world, as many thinkers have previously done, Ensor suggests that the spatial practice of cruising might function as an ecological heuristic. In her essay "Queer Fallout," she takes as her point of departure the curious appeal to an "ecological ethics" that Leo Bersani makes in the final paragraphs of his canonical text "Sociability and Cruising."[63] This passage, Ensor argues, is all the more surprising given that Bersani is not known for proposing the kind of vision of collective responsibility, social propriety, and ecological stewardship we typically associate with environmentalism. Nonetheless, she goes on to argue that Bersani's call to "live less invasively in the world," and his broader account of how cruising catalyzes a heightened attention to one's surroundings (both personal and impersonal, human and nonhuman), might be put to ecological use. Ensor's suggestive account of cruising as prompting a "deep . . . attune[ment] to our impersonal intimacies with the human, nonhuman, and elemental strangers that constitute both our environment and ourselves" resonates strikingly with Guiraudie's vision.[64]

By setting its sights beyond an exclusive focus on "death and desire," Rees-Roberts argues that the film harnesses "cinema's perceptual aesthetic" (which I take to mean a broadly Bazinian mode of deliberative spectatorship) to explore "visual correspondence between human and non-human life."[65] For what is *Stranger* if not a dramatization of the sexual subject's struggle to abandon himself to the dark vicissitudes of eroticism, whose Bataillean avatar we find in the figure of Michel? But even in the last moments of the film, Franck never fully acquiesces to the pull of the death drive. Even though the final scene fades to black, the rustling of Franck's body in the wind and humming of the cicadas

Figure 14. *Stranger by the Lake* (Alain Guiraudie, 2013). Franck hooks up with a fellow cruiser among the long grasses.

Figure 15. *Stranger by the Lake* (Alain Guiraudie, 2013). The bodies of cruising men among the dense woodland.

offers a faint acoustic trace of the rich material plenum of the film. This dense soundscape evokes memories of previous scenes in which Franck's cruising for men on the forest floor always already constituted a sensual engagement with the natural world. What Ensor calls the "intransitivity" of the gaze in the act of cruising is mirrored in, and modeled by, Guiraudie's own mise-en-scène of desiring relations. Throughout the film, we watch a choreography of bodies as they come and go through bushes, thickets, and long grasses. They momentarily merge with their surroundings, thereby proposing a kind of ontological equality between bodies, beings, and things that bespeaks Guiraudie's biophilic tendencies.

But while there is always a risk that the lush, bucolic framing of the film's lakeside setting lapses into an uncritical prelapsarian vision, the specter of the enigmatic stranger is never far away. Given that the act of cruising paradoxically requires both a renunciation of subjective self-mastery in an attunement to the impersonal pleasures of one's environment, and a critical alertness toward the potential dangers of these same surroundings, the unnamed strangers lurking in Guiraudie's landscapes keep us—the film's environmentally attuned spectators—constantly attentive and ultimately unsettled. Figuring an alternative to dominant patterns of queer thought, *Stranger* refuses to traffic in discourse of pastoral redemption and Arcadian idealism, nor does it succumb to visions of erotothanatological transgression that are often articulated with equal force. Rather, the film *estranges* us from preexisting ways of aligning the queer and the ecological. Out of this suspension of overdetermined categories comes something new. As we scan the film's fragmentary mise-en-scène in search of objects of desire (whether things, human bodies, bodies of water, or landscapes), we never know what we will find within the dark recesses of the forest. This provisionality, for Guiraudie, makes rural and wild locales into spaces of possibility and proliferation that multiply our ways of relating to objects and others. And while the urban space's flux, movement, and visual sense data have long been used to make arguments for its privileged relation to cruising, the forest ceiling, the sun-dappled forest floor, and other strategies of "perceptual" disorientation offer an alternative way of conceiving the relationships among sexuality, space, and place. A vital dissenting voice beyond the narrow "metronormative" map of French queer cinema, Alain Guiraudie shows us how we might exploit the languorous temporalities of postindustrial and nonurban spaces, and the affective architectures of the natural environment, to propose a formally inventive and unremittingly sensual vision of gay sexual and spatial practices beyond the harsh glare of the city's lights.

The Open Road

By way of conclusion, I want to terminate this book's trajectory by briefly turning to a film that figures a response to *Stranger* by introducing the very elements conspicuously excised from Guiraudie's narrative. For while *Stranger* should be read as part of his overarching ambition to "remap" France, its heterotopian setting nonetheless exists at one remove from the coordinates of contemporary gay life and France's wider sociopolitical landscape. One film that foregrounds the role of technology in the cruising encounter (providing, according to *Positif* critic Bernard Génin, a bracing rejoinder to the Inspector Damroder's comment that queer men have "a strange way of loving one another") is Jérome Reybaud's 2016 drama *Four Days in France* (*Jours de France*).[66]

Reybaud's drama tells the story of Pierre, a gay man in his early thirties who leaves his partner Paul and his comfortable life in Paris without warning to take a road trip through the heartlands of France. Over a four-day period, he goes cruising in two senses of the term: it is the geosocial hookup app Grindr, rather than a more conventional

GPS, that guides his car journey through the winding course of country roads. (His lover Paul will make use of the same app to track him down; the promise of fugitivity is met by the threat of surveillance.) Midway through the film, Pierre pulls into a clearing on a hilltop on the semirural outskirts of Clermont-Ferrand. In a sequence that echoes the opening shots that mark the passing of days in *Stranger,* we glimpse the protagonist's body emerging from a dense patch of shrubbery; the air is once again thick with the sound of birdsong and cicadas. But on this occasion, we are promptly jolted out of this utopic frame: first, with a close-up on a rusty oil can, accompanied by a view of condoms, wrappers, and other forms of postsex detritus; and second, with the distinctive upward trill of a Grindr alert that transports Pierre out of the rural setting and brings him into contact with an online sphere. Reybaud cuts abruptly to a close-up shot of a hand holding a cell phone, notifying Pierre that he has received a nude photo from somebody nearby (it belongs to his partner Paul). Just as abruptly, we are brought back to the woodland surroundings, where he is accosted by the resident of a house just across the way. The older woman interpellates him as a gay man, asking what he is up to. "Are you planning your nightly rounds? Are you doing your choreography alone, already?" She continues with a hyperbolic diatribe that runs thus: "I've become an insomniac thanks to your behavior, doing your rounds at night, the tires that screech. . . . My dog picks up your filth, the trash you toss on the ground when you're finished. . . . I used to be able to breathe, to smell the flowers, but now it smells of piss. You are polluting us, you fags. You are polluting us." While the French pronoun *vous* strikes an ambiguous note that might be hard to parse (understood as a first-person pronoun it suggests a level of formality, while in its plural form it here names an offensive conflation—*vous, les pédés*), her language of course bespeaks an attitude of social conservatism whereby the distancing effects of linguistic propriety and homophobic intent form two sides of the same coin. The blunt monologue can be read as an object lesson in queer ecological thought insofar as it makes explicit the binary distinction between what Mortimer-Sandilands and Erickson describe as "the perverse, the polluted and the degenerate" on the one hand, and "fit, the healthy, and the natural" on the other.[67] Her appeal to nature, that is, serves both to naturalize a normative order and to phobically and prophylactically cast off the aberrance of queer life forms and deviant sexual practices. But while an exegesis of this passage in broad theoretical terms could detain us for quite some time, my interest lies in how the phantasmatic projections to which she gives voice articulate much more local, situated anxieties surrounding the place of the queer in the French countryside.

As ever, a deeper understanding of this scene remains inaccessible without some grasp of the geographical coordinates of Reybaud's film; thus, it is important to note that much of *Four Days in France* takes place in the Massif Central, in the center of France. This scene occurs at the midpoint of the *diagonale du vide* (empty diagonal), a large slice of France's geography that stretches from the Northeast to the Southwest and represents the most sparsely populated part of the country. (That this "heart" of France long stopped beating due to a rural exodus is a point Reybaud is at pains to belabor.) The woman's language of waste and abandon reveals a double bind for rural queers: those who leave behind their native territory are accused of "leaving it to waste," and those who stay are reprimanded for leaving their waste behind. But if this material detritus is to be understood as an index of queer sexual activity, it is—I suggest—a *negative* index: small pockets of space within these vast geographies, often chosen by virtue of their access or proximity to a motorway turnoff, often gain their reputations as active cruising grounds because they represent the only viable spaces of queer encounter for miles on end. Seen from a less myopic perspective, the traffic in queer sex that so aggravates this old woman (and which contributes to her misleading impression of the vibrancy of queer life) more likely indicates the *lack* of such spaces in the Massif Central more broadly. This rough, variegated, and uneven sexual landscape constitutes for Reybaud the film's primary fascination.

Four Days in France is motivated by a simple question: if one were to forego typical automotive navigation systems and venture away from Paris, turning only to a hookup app for one's spatial and sexual bearings every once in a while, then what spaces, places, and landscapes in contemporary France might come into view? As Pierre takes his Alfa Romeo to the road with no destination in mind, his journey is punctuated by hooking up with strangers and picking up hitchhikers. The road movie, understood as a generic category, is often about breaking with the sedimentations of one's daily routine; the tantalizing possibilities of "the open road" represent something more alluring than the dead end of everyday life. Reybaud, it will soon transpire, has little truck with such idealism: we learn that the fantasy of frictionless access to sex promised in, and by, the Grindr grid needs recalibration.

Much like this book, *Four Days in France* takes cruising as a guiding motif to reflect on the many social, cultural, and sexual landscapes of contemporary France. Yet while the film conflates cruising as travel and cruising for sex, this term—and its equally rich and polyvalent French equivalent, *la drague*—has come to name many different things for the filmmakers I've covered. Although I deliberately avoided naming or rigidly defining this term from the outset (largely to avoid the overdetermining effect this might have on the road map that was to follow), it is perhaps time to ask what cruising has come to mean over the course of this book.

For Jacques Nolot and Roland Barthes, the two mercurial figures with whom I started, cruising in the cinema gave rise to two contradictory impulses. When caught in a state of excitement, these spectator–theorists envisaged the auditorium as a site of social and sexual contact; but in other moments (notably those governed by a sense of melancholy and introspection), the minor affects of "cruisiness," to adopt Nicholas de Villiers's term, emanated more from the warm glow of the screen, the ambient effects of the cinematic situation.[68] For Sébastien Lifshitz's protagonist Rémi, the term represented an extension of that more provisional spatial practice of loitering—a gradual shift that we bore witness to in real time as the taciturn teen took his first steps into Paris's sex clubs and underground scenes. Moving beyond the capital's queer zones into what the French colloquially refer to as *la zone,* the ideologically freighted space that exists beyond Paris's center, the protagonist of Christophe Honoré's *Man at Bath* revealed himself to be a seasoned *dragueur.* Emmanuel's sexual escapades brought sharply into view the multiethnic and class-based diversity of the banlieue *cité*—a vision largely at odds with dominant media representations. And while Vincent Dieutre's urban filmmaking sought to bring the figure of the "trick," and the trope of sociosexual itinerancy, into contact with numerous aesthetic, historical, and geographical frames, Alain Guiraudie's rural settings have emerged, by contrast, as less overdetermined spaces. For him, landscapes and bodies of water offer striking raw materials from which to craft a lush and sensory exploration of queer desire in all its erotic complexity and ecological plenitude.

Queer cinema, it is worth stressing, is not reducible to the question of representation; it is also a spatial and perceptual object that trains us how to see. Similarly, cruising is not just a practice that is staged or depicted but it describes—more capaciously—a mode of inquiry. (Or, to reiterate the words of Gary Needham with which this book opened, "a way of seeing" rather than a thing we see). In trying to flesh out the implications of this idea in a specifically French context, this book has been treading a path that was first laid out, however faintly, by Roland Barthes, who, in his 1973 book *The Pleasure of the Text,* proposed the suggestive figure of *la drague* as a hermeneutic trope. Here he asked his readers to envisage the conditions of aesthetic/textual reception as a kind of cruising: "one must 'cruise' readers without knowing where they are," he notes of the "writerly" text.[69] The "textual seduction" elicited by such an encounter (to draw on Emma Wilson's apposite phrasing) generates what Barthes goes on to describe as a "space of jouissance."[70] In *The Logic of the Lure,* a deft theoretical account of the spatiality of queer eroticism written some thirty years later, John Paul Ricco would push this analogy further. In the opening pages of this book, Ricco invited his reader to consider, "What might it mean to substitute an epistemological ground for a cruising ground?"[71]

While this book has unfolded in a very different direction from Ricco's, I note that much like the perambulatory movement the term implies, the trope of cruising has meandered in many directions (and no doubt erred out of its epistemological comfort zone), brushing up against discourses of art history, film theory, queer studies, and the environmental humanities to model some of the speculative possibilities of bringing disparate scholarly traditions into a more promiscuous dialogue.

Yet, while this book been invested in the notion of "space" as a guiding analytic in general, and the idea of sociosexual itinerancy in particular, I have also sought to foreground some of the blind spots and pitfalls we commonly encounter when treading this path. While Dieutre's documentary frames have offered perhaps a stark illustration of the shortcomings of interpreting social space through the prism of the erotic, Barthes's gay récits surely also provide a case in point. In the opening pages of this book I noted, via Bersani, the need to approach queer sexual spaces without preemptively idealizing them or understanding them as de facto politically resistant. Sometimes consciously and sometimes unconsciously, the queer films I have discussed here have contributed to this work of deidealization, either by tackling questions of social marginality or by negatively exemplifying what Nick Rees-Roberts calls the "faultline issues" that continue to underpin the social and political landscape of France.[72]

Keeping this in mind, what future horizons might be opened up if we continue to follow the centrifugal thrust of this book? Where next to consider the entanglements of space and sexuality? One avenue might be suggested if we turn to the final scene of Reybaud's *Four Days in France.* Following a prolonged cat-and-mouse chase between Pierre and Paul, which takes place online and in real life, Paul eventually catches up with his ex-lover. They terminate their journey together overlooking the Cap d'Antibes on the South coast—which is to say, the point at which the hexagon's border abuts the Mediterranean Sea. What the concluding vista of an open horizon calls to mind (though does not bring into view) is a third dimension of cruising. I am referring here to the cruise as *une croisière,* to the boat crossings that historically connect metropolitan France to its network of former colonial territories. While this traffic in sex has long been an important facet of French gay life and cultural production, it has historically been consigned to the *hors-champ* of its sexual geography. What lies beyond the hard limit of the *hexagone* is, to draw on anthropologist İrvin C. Schick's phrase, an "erotic margin."[73] While a cinematic exploration of this sphere would take us well beyond the scope and remit of the present study—and might (productively) disorient or unsettle the cartographies of "French" and "Francophone" queer cultures that have been diagrammed in this book—such a trajectory is surely worth pursuing.

ACKNOWLEDGMENTS

Writing a book is often described as a solitary process. (And the process of writing this one was compounded—not least—by the spatial practice of social distancing that shaped the environment in which it was first conceived.) I therefore count myself immensely lucky to have been sustained by many generous forms of association over recent years that have made writing this book an enjoyable process.

First, I owe a debt of gratitude to the people who have most shaped my academic trajectory. John David Rhodes, my former supervisor and now colleague, has provided wit and wisdom in equal measure. His broad frames of cultural reference and sharp insights expanded my thinking in ways that I could not have imagined in my early days as a graduate student. His deceptively simple injunction to "write the kind of scholarship you want to read" restored to my work a sense of urgency and purpose when it was most needed. Thank you, JD, for your guidance and friendship, your patience and good humor. Emma Wilson met my initial application to study at Cambridge with characteristic warmth and boundless enthusiasm. I join countless others in describing Emma as a model of rigor and generosity; she represents the very best of academia, and I fear that I can never fully requite the kindness she bestowed on me. Many thanks are also due to Nick Rees-Roberts for the unwavering support and kindness he has offered me for well over a decade. When a timetabling mix-up led me into his French cinema class as a second-year undergraduate (rather than toward the *dix-neuviémistes* gathered down the hall) I had little idea of the impact this contingent event would have on what was to follow. That my own program of research represents a sustained dialogue with Nick's own writing and teaching is, of course, far from incidental.

This book began life as a doctoral project at the University of Cambridge and developed into maturity during a postdoctoral fellowship at St John's College. I thank the Wolfson Foundation, Trinity Hall, the Newton Trust, and the Fellows and Master of St John's College for generously supporting my work. Damon Young and Laura McMahon engaged thoughtfully with my doctoral thesis and pushed it to be a more ambitious book. Georgina Evans has been the best colleague and friend I could have asked for at St John's. I also count myself very lucky to have as a mentor and advocate Brian Price, who has been supportive at so many critical junctures. He forms part of a tight-knit editorial team at *World Picture,* whom it has been a joy to work alongside. I have found in the journal's ever-growing network of contributors, readers, and conference attendees a profound sense of intellectual kinship. They offer an annual reminder of why it is that we do what we do.

The past few years in Cambridge would have not been the same without the many evenings spent in pubs or around dinner tables with Victoria Baena, Damien Pollard, and Becca Sugden. Similarly, it would be hard to imagine my time in Paris without the company of Lili Owen Rowlands, McNeil Taylor, or B. Ruby Rich. For their support and counsel at many critical junctures, I also thank Lawrence Alexander, Toby Ashworth, Emma Ben Ayoun, James Cahill, Maite Conde, Jasmine Cooper, Nick Courtman, Martin Crowley, Ben Dalton, Jacob Engelberg, Kareem Estefan, Daria Ezerova, Veronica Fitzpatrick, David Gerstner, Elena Gorfinkel, Diarmuid Hester, Brian Jacobson, Patrick Lyons, Geoffrey Maguire, Isabelle McNeill, Ry Montgomery, Gary Needham, Jeff Scheible, Kyle Stevens, Meghan Sutherland, Leo Temple, and James S. Williams.

My editor at the University of Minnesota Press, Leah Pennywark, has been enthusiastic about this project ever since it landed on her desk. I thank her, and Anne Carter, for their patience, generosity, and sage advice throughout the editing process. The incisive written reports of the Press's anonymous readers have also done much to shape and strengthen this book, although any shortcomings of course remain my own to bear.

Finally, on a personal note, I thank my family. I count myself very lucky to have been afforded the right to be inquisitive when I was growing up. No topic was off the table, no cultural object was maligned. (I would even go so far as to wager that nothing animates discussions about the affective contours of cinematic time and Bergsonian *durée* quite like visceral teenage memories of squirming through French cinema's many seemingly interminable sex scenes in the presence of one's parents.) Thank you to my mother, Marie-Christine, who first taught me how to make and think about art; my father, James, with whom I have spent countless evenings debating the differences between "French" and "Anglo-Saxon" ways of thinking; and my siblings, Élise, Chloe, and Tristan, for keeping me grounded. This book is dedicated to Samuel Bell, whose love, care, and support has sustained me throughout. Thank you for helping me to see the bigger picture in (many) moments of doubt.

NOTES

Introduction

1. R. Bruce Brasell, "My Hustler: Gay Spectatorship as Cruising," *Wide Angle* 14, no. 2 (1992): 54–64.

2. Gary Needham and Cüneyt Çakırlar, "The Monogamous/Promiscuous Optics in Contemporary Gay Film: Registering the Amorous Couple in *Weekend* and *Paris 05:59: Theo & Hugo*," *New Review of Film and Television Studies* 18, no. 4 (2020): 420.

3. Mark W. Turner, *Backward Glances: Cruising the Queer Streets of New York and London* (London: Reaktion, 2003), 10.

4. John Paul Ricco, "The Art of the Consummate Cruise and the Essential Risk of the Common (2/2)," *Feedback,* February 2016, https://openhumanitiespress.org/feedback/sexualities/the-consummate-cruise-2.

5. Edward Welch, *France in Flux: Space, Territory and Contemporary Culture* (Liverpool: Liverpool University Press, 2019), 8.

6. James F. Austin, "Editor's Preface: New Spaces for French and Francophone Cinema," *Yale French Studies,* no. 115 (2009): 3.

7. Manny Farber, quoted in James S. Williams, *Space and Being in Contemporary French Cinema* (Manchester: Manchester University Press, 2013), 1.

8. Henri Lefebvre, *The Production of Space,* trans. Donald Nicholson-Smith (Oxford: Blackwell, 1991), 34; emphasis added.

9. Unifrance, "Dossier de presse: *Théo et Hugo,*" 2016, https://medias.unifrance.org/medias/77/103/157517/presse/theo-et-hugo-dans-le-meme-bateau-dossier-de-presse-francais.pdf. Unless otherwise noted, all translations are my own.

10. The English title of Rivette's film, *Céline and Julie Go Boating* (to which Ducastel and Martineau's French title also makes a passing allusion) does not adequately capture the expression *aller en bateau* (literally "to go boating"), which carries a surplus meaning of getting caught up in mischief or make-believe.

11. From the wandering Mona in Varda's later *Vagabond* (*Sans loi ni toit,* 1985) to the itinerant subjects that populate Leos Carax's cinematic universe, there exists many examples of bodies on the move in French cinema. For an introduction to this topic, see Keith Reader, "Cinematic Representations of Paris: Vigo/Truffaut/Carax," *Modern and Contemporary France* 1, no. 4 (2003): 409–15.

12. Reader, 409; Mike Crang and Nigel Thrift, "Introduction," in *Thinking Space,* ed. Crang and Thrift (New York: Routledge, 2000), 14.

13. Giuliana Bruno, *Atlas of Emotion: Journeys in Art, Architecture, and Film* (New York: Verso, 2002), 224.

14. Michel de Certeau, "Walking in the City," in *The Practice of Everyday Life* (Berkeley: University of California Press, 1984), 91–110.

15. Thierry Devila, *Marcher, créer: Déplacements, flâneries, dérives dans l'art de la fin du XXe siècle* (Paris: Editions du Regard, 2002), 27–43.

16. Turner, *Backward Glances,* 105. On the cruiser/*flâneur* distinction, see also Edmund White, *The Flâneur: A Stroll through the Paradoxes of Paris* (London: Bloomsbury, 2001), 145–70. On the question of embodiment in queer feminist cinema, see Katharina Lindner, *Film Bodies: Queer Feminist Encounters with Gender and Sexuality in Cinema* (London: I. B. Tauris, 2017).

17. Leo Bersani, *Is the Rectum a Grave? and Other Essays* (Chicago: University of Chicago Press, 2006), 12.

18. Damon R. Young, *Making Sex Public and Other Cinematic Fantasies* (Durham, N.C.: Duke University Press, 2018), 182.

19. For clarification, Agnès does not solicit sex in the woods. The Bois refers to the place she meets Hélène and her husband, Jean, for the first time. The title of Bresson's film nonetheless plays on a long-standing association between the Bois and sex work.

20. Emmett Harsin Drager and Lucas Platero, "At the Margins of Time and Place," *TSQ: Transgender Studies Quarterly* 8, no. 4 (2021): 418.

21. Karl Schoonover and Rosalind Galt, *Queer Cinema in the World* (Durham, N.C.: Duke University Press, 2016).

22. Bruce Erickson and Catriona Mortimer-Sandilands, "Introduction: A Genealogy of Queer Ecologies," in *Queer Ecologies: Sex, Nature, Politics, Desire* (Bloomington: Indiana University Press, 2010), 12.

23. Erickson and Mortimer-Sandilands, 13.

24. De Certeau, *Practice of Everyday Life,* 165–76.

25. Lena Haque, "*Au coeur du bois:* Critique du film," *Le bleu du miroir,* 2021, http://www.lebleudumiroir.fr/critique-au-coeur-du-bois.

26. Jules Gill-Peterson, "General Editor's Introduction," *TSQ: Transgender Studies Quarterly* 8, no. 4 (2021): 413.

27. On the relationship between sex work documentaries and discourses of confession, see Nicholas de Villiers, *Sexography: Sex Work in Documentary* (Minneapolis: University of Minnesota Press, 2017).

28. Eve Kosofsky Sedgwick, *Touching Feeling: Affect, Pedagogy, Performativity* (Durham, N.C.: Duke University Press, 2003), 9.

29. I have borrowed the notion of the traveling concept from Mieke Bal, whose work has mutely informed my own approach to, and critical reflection on the stakes of, interdisciplinary inquiry. See *Travelling Concepts in the Humanities: A Rough Guide* (Toronto: University of Toronto Press, 2002).

1. The Seduction of Space in French Queer Film and Theory

1. Nathaniel B. Smith, "The Idea of the French Hexagon," *French Historical Studies* 6, no. 2 (Autumn 1969): 152.

2. Mustafa Dikeç, *Badlands of the Republic: Space, Politics, and Urban Policy* (Oxford: Blackwell, 2007), 8.

3. François Maspéro, *Les passagers du Roissy-Express* (Paris: Seuil, 1990), 24.

4. Mike Crang and Nigel Thrift, "Introduction," in *Thinking Space,* ed. Crang and Thrift (New York: Routledge, 2000), 13.

5. Kristin Ross, *The Emergence of Social Space: Rimbaud and the Paris Commune* (Minneapolis: University of Minnesota Press, 1988), 4.

6. Crang and Thrift, "Introduction," 13–14. While this chapter does not pursue political theory in detail (for reasons of space), it is important to acknowledge the role that the spatial imaginary has played in contemporary French thought. In his account of the political writing of Jean-Luc Nancy and Jacques Rancière, *Space, Politics and Aesthetics* (Edinburgh: Edinburgh University Press, 2017), Mustafa Dikeç notes how "politics implies some form of generative spatial rupture in the established order of things, creating new relations, orders and meanings." Both thinkers, he continues, engage "space as a mode of political thinking" (4).

7. Henri Lefebvre, *The Production of Space,* trans. Donald Nicholson-Smith (Oxford: Blackwell, 1991), 142; James S. Williams, *Space and Being in Contemporary French Cinema* (Manchester: Manchester University Press, 2013), 8 9.

8. Like many umbrella terms, the imperfect designation of "French spatial theory" might be objected to on the grounds that it unites a diverse body

of thinkers who have different viewpoints. (It is not hard to pinpoint antagonisms between different members of this heterogeneous group: de Certeau's *Practice of Everyday Life* was positioned as an explicit critique of Foucault's theorization of power.) Yet, while I acknowledge that the term is a retrospective designation and a discursive construction (one that recalls François Cusset's account of the *institution* of "French theory"), I nonetheless find it a useful shorthand to describe a proximity between thinkers, to impute a national specificity to their work, and to gesture to their broader collective reception in the field of critical theory writ large. See François Cusset, *French Theory. How Foucault, Derrida, Deleuze, and Co. Transformed the Intellectual Life of the United States,* trans. Jeff Fort (Minneapolis: University of Minnesota Press, 2008).

9. Verena Andermatt Conley, *Spatial Ecologies: Urban Sites, State and World-Space in French Cultural Theory* (Liverpool: University of Liverpool Press, 2012), 28.

10. Michel de Certeau, "Walking in the City," in *The Practice of Everyday Life* (Berkeley: University of California Press, 1984), 93.

11. De Certeau, 98.

12. De Certeau, 91.

13. Michael Crang, "Relics, Places and Unwritten Geographies in the Work of Michel de Certeau," in Crang and Thrift, *Thinking Space,* 137.

14. Lefebvre, *Production of Space,* 38.

15. Crang, "Relics, Places and Unwritten Geographies," 138.

16. Phil Hubbard, *Cities and Sexualities* (London: Routledge, 2012), xv.

17. Eden Kinkaid has argued, in a parallel exploration of Lefebvre's thought and the phenomenological tradition, that recent critiques of the phenomenological *epoché*—or the "bracketing" of embodied differences as a precondition for phenomenological inquiry—advanced by scholars of race, gender, and queerness can equally be leveled against spatial theorists. See "Re-encountering Lefebvre: Toward a Critical Phenomenology of Social Space," *Environment and Planning D: Society and Space* 38, no. 1 (February 2020): 167–86.

18. Michael P. Brown, *Closet Space: Geographies of Metaphor from the Body to the Globe* (New York: Routledge, 2000), 59; Claire Colebrook, "Certeau and Foucault: Tactics and Strategic Essentialism," *South Atlantic Quarterly* 100, no. 2 (Spring 2001): 547.

19. Victor Burgin, *In/Different Spaces: Place and Memory in Visual Culture* (Berkeley: University of California Press, 1996), 27–30.

20. J. Jack Halberstam, *In a Queer Time and Place: Transgender Bodies, Subcultural Lives* (New York: NYU Press, 2005), 10.

21. Gayle S. Rubin, "Thinking Sex: Notes for a Radical Theory of the Politics of Sexuality," in *Deviations: A Gayle Rubin Reader* (Durham, N.C.: Duke

University Press, 2012), 137; Judith Butler, "Merely Cultural," *Social Text* 52/53 (Autumn/Winter 1997): 268.

22. Lefebvre, *Production of Space,* 50.

23. Lefebvre, 49–50.

24. The term "reproductive futurity," which I address substantively in chapter 5, is derived from Lee Edelman's *No Futures: Queer Theory and the Death Drive* (Durham, N.C.: Duke University Press, 2004), 3.

25. George Chauncey, *Gay New York: Gender, Urban Culture, and the Making of the Gay Male World, 1890–1940* (New York: Basic Books, 1994), 23.

26. Michel Foucault, "Of Other Spaces," trans. Jay Miskowiec, *Diacritics* 16, no. 1 (Spring 1986): 22.

27. Williams, *Space and Being,* 9.

28. Michel Foucault, "The Gay Science," *Critical Inquiry* 37, no. 3 (2011): 399; Michel Foucault, "Friendship as a Way of Life," in *Ethics: Subjectivity and Truth,* ed. Paul Rabinow (New York: New Press, 1994), 138.

29. This passage from Foucault is reproduced in the following texts: Sara Ahmed, *Queer Phenomenology: Objects, Orientations, Others* (Durham, N.C.: Duke University Press, 2006), 107; Leo Bersani, *Is the Rectum a Grave? and Other Essays* (Chicago: University of Chicago Press, 2006), 59–60; J. Jack Halberstam, *In a Queer Time and Place,* 10–11; and John Paul Ricco, *The Logic of the Lure* (Chicago: University of Chicago Press, 2003), 5.

30. Philip Howell, "Foucault, Sexuality, Geography," in *Space, Knowledge and Power: Foucault and Geography* (Farnham, UK: Ashgate, 2007), 296; Paul B. Preciado, "Architecture as a Practice of Biopolitical Disobedience," *Log* 25 (2012): 121. This Foucauldian reading of eroticized space is subsequently extended in Preciado's book-length project *Pornotopia: An Essay on Playboy's Architecture and Biopolitics* (New York: Zone Books, 2014).

31. Hubbard, *Cities and Sexualities,* xv.

32. Mehammed Amadeus Mack, *Sexagon: Muslims, France, and the Sexualization of National Culture* (New York: Fordham University Press, 2017), 2.

33. Mack, 10.

34. Emmanuel Redoutey, "Drague et *cruising,*" *EchoGéo* 5 (2008): 1–12, https://doi.org/10.4000/echogeo.3663; George Lakoff and Mark Johnson, *Metaphors We Live By* (Chicago: University of Chicago Press, 1980), 31.

35. David Bell and Gill Valentine, "Introduction: Orientations," in *Mapping Desires: Geographies of Sexualities,* ed. Bell and Valentine (London: Routledge, 1995), 4.

36. Jasbir K. Puar, "A Transnational Feminist Critique of Queer Tourism," *Antipode* 34, no. 5 (2002): 936.

37. Bell and Valentine, "Orientations," 2.

38. Bell and Valentine, 2.

39. Bell and Valentine, 16.

40. Lisa Duggan, *The Twilight of Equality? Neoliberalism, Cultural Politics, and the Attack on Democracy* (Boston: Beacon Press, 2003), 179.

41. Larry Knopp, "From Lesbian and Gay to Queer Geographies: Pasts, Prospects and Possibilities," in *Geographies of Sexualities: Theory, Practices and Politics,* ed. Kath Browne, Jason Lim, and Gavin Brown (Farnham, UK: Ashgate, 2007), 22.

42. Leo Bersani, "Sociability and Cruising," in *Is the Rectum a Grave?,* 45–62; Foucault, "Friendship as a Way of Life," 137.

43. Heather Love, "Bersani on Location," in *Leo Bersani: Queer Theory and Beyond,* ed. Mikko Tuhkanen (Albany, N.Y.: SUNY Press, 2014), 39; Lauren Berlant and Michael Warner, "Sex in Public," *Critical Inquiry* 24, no. 2 (Winter 1998): 547–66.

44. Michel Foucault, "Sex, Power, and the Politics of Identity," in *Ethics: Subjectivity and Truth,* ed. Paul Rabinow (New York: New Press, 1997), 164.

45. Ricco, *Logic of the Lure,* xxi.

46. Leo Bersani and Ulysse Dutoit. *Forms of Being: Cinema, Aesthetics, Subjectivity* (London: BFI, 2004), 165.

47. John Paul Ricco, "Jacking Off: A Minor Architecture," *Keep It Dirty,* vol. a (2016): ii–iii, https://web.archive.org/web/20190624190918/http://keepitdirty.org/a/jacking-off-a-minor-architecture. Indeed, Ricco's writing articulates with greater acuity a problem that scholars in geography had only treated superficially: the question of how understandings of queer space might move beyond the sphere of the visible to consider the representational aporias associated with queer life and death. For a discussion of how spaces come to bear the residues of prior times, practices, and bodies, see also José Esteban Muñoz, *Cruising Utopia: The Then and There of Queer Futurity* (New York: NYU Press, 2009), 33–48.

48. Ricco, *Logic of the Lure,* 149.

49. Halberstam, *In a Queer Time and Place,* 6.

50. Ahmed, *Queer Phenomenology,* 6.

51. Ahmed, 67.

52. Michael Moon, *A Small Boy and Others: Imitation and Initiation in American Culture from Henry James to Andy Warhol* (Durham, N.C.: Duke University Press, 1998), 15–30.

53. Ahmed, *Queer Phenomenology,* 3.

54. Ahmed, 70.

55. Eve Kosofsky Sedgwick, *Tendencies* (Durham, N.C.: Duke University Press, 1993), xii.

56. In a sharp and perceptive essay, Valerie Traub notes similar techniques at play in the cognate field of "queer temporality." Working against the grain of much of this work, Traub notes how "the rejection of 'straight temporality' forges a tight metonymic chain among the alleged operations of sex, time, and history. They link these operations through rhetorical manoeuvres whereby difference and sameness are constellated with concepts that stand in as near cognates: not only hetero and homo but also difference and similitude, distance and proximity, multiplicity and self-identity, change and stasis, disidentification and mimesis. These close cognates allude to both abstract theoretical principles and specific material realities. Yet drawn as they are from different epistemological registers—psychic, social, temporal, formal, historiographic—and abstracted from contexts of space or time, they are rhetorically deployed to cross seamlessly from one conceptual domain to another." Such rhetorical moves, I suggest, are also at play in queer spatial discourse. See "The New Unhistoricism in Queer Studies," *PMLA* 128, no. 1 (January 2013): 30.

57. Halberstam, *In a Queer Time and Place,* 6.

58. The ease with which the two notions can become disconnected is, I wager, due to the spatial connotations of the term queer itself, which seem perfectly capable of constituting their own object of study. Sedgwick famously traced the word's etymology back to the "Indo-European root *-twerkw,* which also yields the German *quer* (transverse), Latin *torquere* (to twist), [and] English athwart," while the term's contemporary meaning has been subject to a similar process of "twisting" (*Tendencies,* xii). In this resignification of queer from the slanderous to the slantwise, there is a divestiture of negative affect that lays open the possibility for positive resignification. On these processes of resignification, see Judith Butler, "Critically Queer," *GLQ* 1, no. 1 (Fall 1993): 19–21.

59. James Penney, *After Queer Theory: The Limits of Sexual Politics* (London: Pluto Press, 2014), 19.

60. Michel Warner, "Queer and Then?," *Chronicle of Higher Education,* January 1, 2012, https://www.chronicle.com/article/QueerThen-/130161.

61. Natalie Oswin, "Critical Geographies and the Uses of Sexuality: Deconstructing Queer Space," *Progress in Human Geography* 32 (2008): 90; emphasis added.

62. Teresa de Lauretis, "Queer Theory: Lesbian and Gay Sexualities. An Introduction" *differences* 3, no. 2 (1991): iv; Teresa de Lauretis, "Habit Changes," *differences* 6, no. 2 (1994): 297.

63. Leo Bersani, *Homos* (Cambridge, Mass.: Harvard University Press, 1996), 2.

64. David Halperin, "The Normalization of Queer Theory," *Journal of Homosexuality* 45, no. 2–4 (2003): 341–42; Tim Dean and Oliver Davis, *Hatred of Sex* (Lincoln: University of Nebraska Press, 2022).

65. James Agar, "Queer in France: AIDS Disidentification in France," in *Queer in Europe,* ed. Lisa Downing and Robert Gillett (London: Routledge, 2016), 64.

66. Oliver Davis and Hector Kollias, eds., "Queer Theory Returns to France," special issue, *Paragraph* 35, no. 2 (2012): 139–301; Tim Dean, "Queer Theory without Names: A Response to *Queer Theory's Return to France,* edited by Oliver Davis and Hector Kollias, *Paragraph* 35:2 (July 2012)," *Paragraph* 35, no. 3 (2012): 421.

67. See Jacques Aumont, Pascal Bonitzer, Pascal Kané, Jean Narboni, Sylvie Pierre, and Jacques Rivette, "L'espace: Table ronde autour de Jacques Rivette," *1895: Mille huit cent quatre-vingt-quinze* 79 (Summer 2016): 104–35. While the proceedings of this roundtable were not published at the time for reasons that will become apparent, they eventually saw the light of day almost half a century later, thanks to the archival labors of film historian and translator Daniel Fairfax.

68. Aumont et al., 105.

69. Eve Kosofsky Sedgwick, *Touching Feeling: Affect, Pedagogy, Performativity* (Durham, N.C.: Duke University Press, 2003), 9.

70. Williams, *Space and Being,* xv.

71. Williams, xiii.

72. Williams, 2.

73. Elena Gorfinkel and John David Rhodes, "Introduction: The Matter of Places," in *Taking Place: Location and the Moving Image,* ed. Gorfinkel and Rhodes (Minneapolis: University of Minnesota Press, 2011), viii.

74. Elena Gorfinkel, "Tales of Times Square: Sexploitation's Secret History of Place," in Gorfinkel and Rhodes, *Taking Place,* 55–76; Ricco, *Logic of the Lure,* 51–60.

75. Nick Rees-Roberts, *French Queer Cinema* (Edinburgh: Edinburgh University Press, 2008); Nick Rees-Roberts, "*Hors milieu:* Queer and Beyond," in *A Companion to Contemporary French Cinema,* ed. Alistair Fox, Michel Marie, Raphaëlle Moine, and Hilary Radner (New York: Bloomsbury, 2015), 439–60.

76. Rees-Roberts, "*Hors milieu,*" 458.

77. Karl Schoonover and Rosalind Galt, *Queer Cinema in the World* (Durham, N.C.: Duke University Press, 2016).

2. Coming and Going in Jacques Nolot's Cinema

1. Roland Barthes, "Leaving the Movie Theatre," in *The Rustle of Language* (New York: Farrar, Straus and Giroux, 1986), 346. Further citations of this work are given in the text.

2. "Jacques Nolot Sicilia Queer 2018," YouTube, September 24, 2018, https://youtu.be/X5DA_OGtHfc?.

3. James S. Williams, "His Life to Film: The Extreme Art of Jacques Nolot," *Studies in French Cinema* 9, no. 1 (2009): 178.

4. A scene bearing a striking resemblance to Daïga's instant of nonrecognition unfolds in "Times Square Blue," Samuel Delany's essay on Manhattan's cruising culture. Here Delany recounts an instance in which his friend Ana accompanied him to an erotic movie house. Focusing her gaze on the screen, she is largely impervious to the multiple uses of the auditorium spaces and how spectatorial attention circulates otherwise. As well as raising the gap between the implicit and explicit uses of theater space, the passage also renders explicit the latent culture of misogyny that stubbornly lingers in the cinema. See *Times Square Red, Times Square Blue* (New York: NYU Press, 1996), 26–31.

5. Williams, "His Life to Film," 178.

6. The notion of autofiction is rich and complex. This neologism was coined in 1977 by Serge Doubrovsky to designate a hybrid text that comprises a blend of autobiographical and fictive elements. For a genealogy of the term, and its contemporary application in French literature and culture, see Johnny Gratton, "Autofiction," in *Encyclopedia of Life Writing: Autobiographical and Biographical Forms, I: A–K,* ed. Margaretta Jolly (London: Fitzroy Dearborn, 2001), 86–87.

7. Guy Hocquenghem, *Le gay voyage: Guide et regard homosexuels sur les grandes métropoles* (Paris: Albin Michel, 1980).

8. David Caron, *The Nearness of Others: Searching for Tact and Contact in the Age of HIV* (Minneapolis: University of Minnesota Press, 2014), 212–13.

9. Roland Barthes, "Soirées de Paris" in *Incidents,* trans. Richard Howard (Berkeley: University of California Press, 1992), 68. Barthes's exploits at Le Dragon are also addressed in Dan Callwood's excellent article on the rise of gay pornography in 1970s France, "Anxiety and Desire in France's Gay Pornographic Film Boom, 1974–1983," *Journal of the History of Sexuality* 26, no. 1 (January 2017): 36.

10. Williams, "His Life to Film," 178.

11. James Quandt, "Just a Gigolo," *Artforum* 46, no. 10 (2008): 93. Indeed, this auditorium would later serve as the inspiration for the setting of Christophe Honoré's recent play *The Sky of Nantes* (*Le ciel de Nantes*).

12. In a pornotopia, Steven Marcus argues, the pornographic imaginary informs the governing logic of actual spatiotemporal arrangements, thus blurring the line between the textual and extratextual space. See *The Other Victorians: A Study of Sexuality and Pornography in Mid-Nineteenth-Century England* (London: Corgi, 1964), 268–74.

13. José B. Capino, "Homologies of Space: Text and Spectatorship in All-Male Adult Theatres," *Cinema Journal* 45, no. 1 (Fall 2005): 52.

14. The ambivalent status of Barthes's own sexuality has been the subject of two notable studies: D. A. Miller, *Bringing Out Roland Barthes* (Berkeley: University of California Press, 1992); and Nicholas de Villiers, *Opacity and the Closet: Queer Tactics in Foucault, Barthes, and Warhol* (Minneapolis: University of Minnesota Press, 2012), 63–88.

15. James S. Williams, "At the Reader's Discretion: On Barthes and Cinema," *Paragraph* 21, no. 1 (February 1998): 49.

16. Philip Watts, *Roland Barthes' Cinema* (Oxford: Oxford University Press, 2016), 67.

17. Watts, 67.

18. Jocelyn Szczepaniak-Gillece, "In the House, In the Picture: Distance and Proximity in the American Mid-Century Neutralized Theatre," *World Picture* 7 (2012): 1–2. Le Méry is located at the intersection of the Place de Clichy and rue Biot, and the building's checkered history is itself indicative of the commercial pressures and patterns of entertainment consumption over the theater's eighty-year history. The theater, originally named Le Clichy, opened in 1935 and subsequently turned into a small-scale cinema (*cinéma de quartier*) in the mid-1960s. Between 1980 and 1991, the space took the form that is recognizable in the film—a porn theater. By the time Nolot shot his film, Le Méry was facing an uncertain future; the auditorium was used intermittently for small theatrical productions and screenings before closing definitively in 2005. More recently, in 2016, a banner appeared above the building's entrance indicating plans for the cinema to be rechristened as the Théâtre Métropole. The signage, complete with pseudo art deco flourish, hung below the traces of the theater previously housed there. Despite efforts to remove the original sign, the dirt gathering under the previous lettering conspicuously indicated the building's obdurate historicity.

19. Watts, *Roland Barthes' Cinema,* 4.

20. Roland Barthes, *The Pleasure of the Text,* trans. Richard Miller (New York: Farrar, Straus and Giroux, 1975), 10.

21. Roger Cardinal, "Pausing Over Peripheral Detail," *Framework* 30/31 (1986): 124.

22. Cardinal, 124.

23. Paul Willemen, "Postscript: Terms for a Debate," *Framework* 30/31 (1986): 131.

24. Olivier Cheval, "Le cinéma pur: Sur deux utopies pornographiques," in *Pornographiques,* ed. Emmanuelle Andre and Laurent Zimmermann (Paris: Hermann, 2015), 139–40. See also Jean-Louis Baudry, "The Apparatus," trans. Jean Andrews and Bertrand Augst, *Camera Obscura* 1 (1976): 117.

25. Avery Tompkins, "Asterisk," *TSQ: Transgender Studies Quarterly* 1, no. 1/2 (May 2014): 27.

26. Watts, *Roland Barthes' Cinema,* 47.

27. I draw this term from Judith Butler, who makes an argument for the necessity of self-reflexive critique in the field of queer theory in their essay "Critically Queer," *GLQ* 1 (1993): 17–32.

28. Williams, "His Life to Film," 179.

29. Roland Barthes, *How to Live Together: Novelistic Simulations of Some Everyday Spaces,* trans. Katie Briggs (New York: Columbia University Press, 2014), 6–10; Susan Harrow, "Living Alone Together: Barthes, Zola, and the Work of Letters," *L'esprit créateur* 55, no. 4 (Winter 2015): 21.

30. Williams, "At the Reader's Discretion," 48.

31. Kadji Amin, *Disturbing Attachments: Genet, Modern Pederasty, and Queer History* (Durham, N.C.: Duke University Press, 2017), 10.

32. Hocquenghem, *Le gay voyage,* 135.

33. Williams, "His Life to Film," 188.

34. Lesley Stern, "Paths That Wind through the Thicket of Things," *Critical Inquiry* 28, no. 1 (Autumn 2001): 345.

35. Barthes, *Pleasure of the Text,* 26.

36. Watts, *Roland Barthes' Cinema,* 67.

37. Watts, 72.

38. Philip Rosen, *Narrative, Apparatus, Ideology: A Film Theory Reader* (New York: Columbia University Press, 1986), 282.

39. D. A. Miller quoted in Callwood, "Anxiety and Desire," 36.

40. Williams, "His Life to Film," 181.

41. Nick Rees-Roberts, "*Hors milieu:* Queer and Beyond," in *A Companion to Contemporary French Cinema,* ed. Alistair Fox, Michel Marie, Raphaëlle Moine, and Hilary Radner (New York: Bloomsbury, 2015), 446; Williams, "His Life to Film," 181.

42. Dennis Lim, "Jacques Nolot: An Examined Life of Wicked Pleasure," *New York Times,* July 16, 2008, https://www.nytimes.com/2008/07/16/arts/16iht-13lim.14537619.html.

43. Williams, "His Life to Film," 189.

44. Williams, 189.

45. Rees-Roberts, "*Hors milieu,*" 446.

46. John David Rhodes, *Spectacle of Property: The House in American Film* (Minneapolis: University of Minnesota Press, 2017), 32.

47. Pamela Robertson Wojcik, *The Apartment Plot: Urban Living in American Film and Popular Culture, 1945 to 1975* (Durham, N.C.: Duke University Press, 2010), 8.

48. Rhodes, viii.

49. Victoria Rosner, *Modernism and the Architecture of Private Life* (New York: Columbia University Press, 2005), 2.

50. Wojcik, *Apartment Plot,* 5.

51. Lee Wallace, *Lesbianism, Cinema, Space: The Sexual Life of Apartments* (London: Routledge, 2008), 14.

52. Wallace, 14. In a recent study, Olivier Vallerand argues that theorizations of queer spatiality ought not to be limited to the "public" sphere. Rather, queer thinking should be productively brought to bear on the domestic, if only to complicate commonsense understandings of public/private distinction that are tacitly shaped by normative gender constructs, and to gain greater critical purchase on the ideological dimensions of the architectural design with which we engage most frequently. See *Unplanned Visitors: Queering the Ethics and Aesthetics of Domestic Space* (Montreal: McGill-Queen's University Press, 2020).

53. "Jacques Nolot Sicilia Queer 2018."

54. A Parisian *chambre de bonne* refers to modest dwellings in the top floor of a Haussmannian building, historically functioning as a studio apartment in the maid's quarter. Commenting on the particular class connotation of these rooms in France, Richard Keller situates them within "a long history of poverty, marginalization, and disenfranchisement in contemporary Paris. They are an artifact of deep economic inequalities in the city." See *Fatal Isolation* (Chicago: University of Chicago Press, 2015), 112.

55. Yann Gonzalez, "Entretien avec Jacques Nolot," L'association du cinéma indépendant pour sa diffusion, accessed November 9, 2007, https://web.archive.org/web/20071109132020/http://www.lacid.org/fichesfilms/presse/dp-nolot-bd.pdf.

56. Hugues Perrot and Laura Tuillier, "Éprouver la vie: Entretien avec Jacques Nolot," *Cahiers du cinéma,* no. 721 (April 2016): 91.

57. Quandt, "Just a Gigolo," 93; Williams, "His Life to Film," 187.

58. Gonzalez, "Entretien avec Jacques Nolot."

59. Roland Barthes, *La chambre claire* (Paris: Gallimard, 1980), 129.

60. "Jacques Nolot Sicilia Queer 2018."

61. Quandt, "Just a Gigolo," 94.

62. This question has also sustained the attention of critical theorists in the last half century, from Jean Baudrillard's *The System of Objects,* trans. James Benedict (London: Verso, 1996) and Peter Schwenger's *The Tears of Things: Melancholy and Physical Objects* (Minneapolis: University of Minnesota Press, 2006) to Lesley Stern's "Paths That Wind."

63. Quandt, "Just a Gigolo," 94.

64. Rhodes, *Spectacle of Property,* 4.

65. Sarah Schulman, *The Gentrification of the Mind: Witness to a Lost Imagination* (Berkeley: University of California Press, 2013), 37.

66. Schulman, 39.

67. Schulman, 39.

3. *Quartiers chauds*

1. Ann Laura Stoler, *Duress: Imperial Durabilities in Our Times* (Durham, N.C.: Duke University Press, 2016), 123.

2. Mehammed Amadeus Mack, *Sexagon: Muslims, France, and the Sexualization of National Culture* (New York: Fordham University Press, 2017); Nick Rees-Roberts and Maxime Cervulle, *Homo exoticus: Race, class et critique queer* (Paris: Armand Colin, 2010), 79–109.

3. Mustafa Dikeç, *Badlands of the Republic: Space, Politics, and Urban Policy* (Oxford: Blackwell, 2007), 4.

4. John David Rhodes, *Spectacle of Property: The House in American Film* (Minneapolis: University of Minnesota Press, 2017), 5–6.

5. On the trope of the difficult Arab boy, see Mack, *Sexagon,* 130–79.

6. For a sensitive exploration of queerness and grief in *Wild Side,* see David Caron, "Queer Relationality and the Dying Mother: Waiting and Caring in Sébastien Lifshitz's *Wild Side* and Jacques Nolot's *L'arrière-pays,*" *L'esprit créateur* 61, no. 1 (Spring 2021): 13–25.

7. Kyle Stevens, "Headphones, Cinematic Listening, and the Frame of the Skull," in *Oxford Handbook to Film Theory,* ed. Stevens (Oxford: Oxford University Press, 2022), 338.

8. Joe Hardwick, "Bodies That Loiter: Genre, Generation and Subjectivity in *Les corps ouverts,*" *Australian Journal of French Studies* 41, no. 3 (2004): 75–87.

9. Ross Chambers, *Loiterature* (Lincoln: University of Nebraska Press, 1999), v.

10. Chambers, 32.

11. Hardwick, "Bodies That Loiter," 79–80.

12. Chambers, *Loiterature,* 255.

13. Chambers, 254.

14. Chambers, 258.

15. Cervulle and Rees-Roberts, *Homo exoticus,* 15.

16. La Marr Jurelle Bruce, "Shore, Unsure: Loitering as a Way of Life," *GLQ: A Journal of Lesbian and Gay Studies* 25, no. 2 (April 2019): 352.

17. Bruce, 353.

18. Bruce, 353.

19. Bruce, 353.

20. Indeed, as Loïc Wacquant warns us, we should not expect terms related to precarious and racialized urban dwelling to travel seamlessly across the transatlantic divide. See "French Working-Class Banlieues and Black American Ghetto: From Conflation to Comparison," *qui parle* 16, no. 2 (Spring/Summer 2007): 5–38.

21. Sarah Cervenak, *Wandering: Philosophical Performances of Racial and Sexual Freedom* (Durham, N.C.: Duke University Press, 2014), 4.

22. Cervenak, 4.

23. Todd Reeser, *Queer Cinema in Contemporary France: Five Directors* (Manchester, UK: Manchester University Press, 2022), 182.

24. Reeser, 182.

25. Merl Storr, "The Reproduction of 'Race': Bisexuality, History and Racialization," in *The Bisexual Imaginary: Representations, Identity, Desire,* ed. Phoebe Davidson, Jo Eadie, Clare Hemmings, Ann Kaloski, and Merl Storr (London: Cassell, 1997), 85.

26. Marlon Ross, "Beyond the Closet as a Raceless Paradigm," in *Black Queer Studies: A Critical Anthology,* ed. E. Patrick Johnson and Mae G. Henderson (Durham, N.C.: Duke University Press, 2005), 161–89.

27. Clare Hemmings, "What's in a Name? Bisexuality, Transnational Sexuality Studies and Western Colonial Legacies," *International Journal of Human Rights,* 11, no. 1 (2007): 14. In *The Homoerotics of Orientalism* (New York: Columbia University Press, 2014). Joseph Boone addresses the specifically Franco-Arab articulation of this logic when he points to a contradiction in Western (mis)perceptions of Arab men as always already bisexual and also presumably homophobic.

28. Carrie Tarr, *Reframing Difference:* Beur *and* Banlieue *Filmmaking in France* (Manchester, UK: Manchester University Press, 2005), 18.

29. Isabelle McNeill, "Music and Spatial Injustice in Banlieue Cinema," *French Screen Studies* 20, no. 3/4 (February 2020): 319.

30. James F. Austin, "Destroying the *Banlieue*: Reconfigurations of Suburban Space in French Film," *Yale French Studies* 115 (2009): 82–83.

31. Dikeç, *Badlands of the Republic,* 4.

32. Eric Fassin, "Homophobic City, Homophobic Banlieue?," trans. Christina Mitrakos, *Metropolitics,* no. 9 (March 2011), https://www.metropolitics.org/Homosexual-City-Homophobic.html.

33. Fassin.

34. Denis M. Provencher, *Queer Maghrebi French: Language, Temporalities, Transfiliations* (Liverpool: Liverpool University Press, 2017), 14.

35. Franck Chaumont and Fouad Zeraoui, "Kelma beur gay: Débat dans tetu," *Kelma,* December 19, 2009, https://web.archive.org/web/20140326095643/https://www.blog-gay.kelma.org/gays-en-banlieue.

36. Chaumont and Zeraoui.

37. Nick Rees-Roberts, *French Queer Cinema* (Edinburgh: Edinburgh University Press, 2008), 13; see also Cervulle and Rees-Roberts, *Homo exoticus.*

38. Mack, *Sexagon,* 30–31.

39. Mack, 23–24.

40. Christophe Honoré quoted in "Christophe Honoré: An Interview," trans. David Powell, in *Christophe Honoré: A Critical Introduction,* ed. David A. Gerstner and Julien Nahmias (Detroit: Wayne State University Press, 2016), 198.

41. David E. James, *Allegories of Cinema: American Film in the Sixties* (Princeton, N.J.: Princeton University Press, 1989), 12.

42. Christophe Honoré quoted in press release for *Man at Bath,* accessed July 31, 2024, https://medias.unifrance.org/medias/72/131/99144/presse/man-at-bath-presskit-english.pdf.

43. Honoré quoted in press release for *Man at Bath*; emphasis added.

44. Rees-Roberts, *French Queer Cinema,* 14.

45. Mack, *Sexagon,* 225.

46. Will Higbee, "Re-presenting the Urban Periphery: Maghrebi-French Filmmaking and the 'Banlieue' Film," *Cinéaste* 33, no. 1 (Winter 2007): 40.

47. Tarr, *Reframing Difference.*

48. On Sagat's ambiguous racial presentation see Gabriel Ojeda-Sagué, "The Whiteness of François Sagat," *Porn Studies* 8, no. 1 (June 2021): 107–20.

49. Honoré quoted in press release for *Man at Bath.*

50. Honoré.

51. Leo Bersani, "Is There a Gay Art?," in *Is the Rectum a Grave? and Other Essays* (Chicago: University of Chicago Press, 2009), 34.

52. Mack, *Sexagon,* 226.

53. Honoré quoted in "Interview with Christophe Honoré," in Gerstner and Nahmias, *Christophe Honoré,* 200.

54. On the shifting use of the "we" in queer theory, see the prologue to Leo Bersani's *Homos* (Cambridge, Mass.: Harvard University Press, 1996), 1–10.

4. A Queer Window onto the World?

1. For a transcript of this extract see François Zourabichvili, "Deleuze contre la bêtise," *France Culture,* March 18, 2005, https://www.franceculture.fr/emissions/macadam-philo/deleuze-contre-la-betise.

2. Gilles Deleuze, "The Problem of Stupidity," in *Difference and Repetition,* trans. Paul Patton (New York: Continuum, 2004), 149–53.

3. While the term "acousmatic" was first used by Pierre Schaeffer, its ubiquity in film studies can be attributed to the work of Michel Chion. Chion's subsequent coinage of the *acousmêtre*—from *acous-* (hear) and *être* (being)—is used to describe the ambivalent "place" of the voice-over in film, as a "mysterious" presence clearly felt but whose source of emission is not visible in the profilmic space. See Michel Chion, *Audio-Vision: Sound on Screen,* trans. Claudia Gorbman (New York: Columbia University Press, 1994), 221.

4. The enmeshing of autobiographical and documentary film practices has been much discussed by scholars in recent years. In *The Personal Camera,* Laura Rascaroli explores forms of essay filmmaking that resist documentary film's habitual suppression of authorial subjectivity and readily assume the first-person position. She draws parallels between the essay film and other forms of textual self-inscription, such as the diary, the travelogue, and the self-portrait. In the introduction to *The Cinema of Me,* Alisa Lebow similarly focuses on the role of the enunciating subject in the interpellation of a community of cospectators. The subjective mode of address of a documentary film, she argues, is key to understanding its "grammar"—or *how* it effects a declension from the first-person singular (*I*) to the first-person plural (*we*). See Rascaroli, *The Personal Camera: Subjective Cinema and the Essay Film* (London: Wallflower Press, 2009); and Lebow, *The Cinema of Me: The Self and Subjectivity in First Person Documentary* (London: Wallflower Press, 2012).

5. Emma Wilson, "Pathos as Queer Sociality in Contemporary European Visual Culture: François Ozon's *Time to Leave,*" in *What's Queer about Europe? Productive Encounters and Re-enchanting Paradigms,* ed. Mireille Rosello (New York: Fordham University Press, 2014), 151.

6. Renaud Camus, *Tricks: 45 récits* (Paris: POL, 1988).

7. Vincent Dieutre, "'Et plus si affinités . . .': Le trick comme figure de la modernité au cinema," in *La rencontre: Au cinéma toujours l'inattendu arrive,* ed. Jacques Aumont (Rennes, Fra.: Presses universitaires de Rennes, 2013), 28.

8. The disarming simplicity and economy of Camus's is discussed amply by Roland Barthes in his preface to the book (12–18).

9. Dieutre, "'Et plus si affinités . . . ,'" 29.

10. Boyd McDonald, *Cruising the Movies: A Sexual Guide to Oldies on TV* (South Pasadena, Calif.: Semiotext(e), 2015).

11. Henning Bech, *When Men Meet: Homosexuality and Modernity,* trans. Teresa Mesquit and Tim Davies (Chicago: University of Chicago Press, 1997), 118.

12. Tom Cuthbertson, "In/Out: Fictionalising Autobiography in Vincent Dieutre's *Jaurès* (2012)," *Studies in French Cinema* 17, no. 3 (2017): 266.

13. Cuthbertson, 266.

14. Laurent Guido, "'Entre lyrisme esthétique et pessimisme culturel': Vincent Dieutre et les nouvelles voies autobiographiques de l'Europe," *Cinémas* 21, no. 1 (Fall 2010): 21.

15. Jean Pierre Carrier, "A comme abécédaire: Vincent Dieutre," *Le cinéma documentaire de A à Z,* August 4, 2019, https://dicodoc.blog/2019/08/04/a-comme-abecedaire-vincent-dieutre.

16. Carrier.

17. Mitterrand was an early proponent of the autobiographical travelogue in French cinema, but his contribution to French queer cinema has been eclipsed by a scandal resulting from the publication of his 2005 autobiography *La mauvaise vie* (Paris: Éditions Robert Laffont) in which he wrote with disarming frankness about his experiences of sex tourism in Thailand. Nick Rees-Roberts and Maxime Cervulle have usefully situated the ensuing *affaire Mitterrand* within overlapping debates about sexual and racial politics in France (whose intersections, they note, have been largely overlooked). In the aftermath of the Mitterrand scandal, the authors note that "the gay community preferred to close that debate rather than lifting the lid on the 'distinguished' culture of exoticism and pederastic elegance that we find in the real and fictional travelogues of André Gide, Roland Barthes, Hervé Guibert, and Jean Sénac." See Cervulle and Rees-Roberts, *Homo exoticus: Race, class et critique queer* (Paris: Armand Colin, 2010), 13–14.

18. Roger Odin, "Le documentaire intérieur: Travail du JE et mise en phase dans *Lettres d'amour en Somalie,*" *Cinémas* 4, no. 2 (Winter 1994): 89.

19. Rascaroli's appeal to the space of the voice importantly revises and reassesses many orthodoxies in documentary theories of the voice that, following Michel Chion, tend to impute to the voice-over the status of omniscience. See *How the Essay Film Thinks* (Oxford: Oxford University Press, 2017), 116.

20. Dieutre uses the term "dialectical" to qualify his own approach to verbal/visual relations in his cinema. See UniverCiné, "Vincent Dieutre présente son film *Jaurès,*" Dailymotion, last modified April 12, 2016, https://www.dailymotion.com/video/x3c8zb1.

21. Vincent Ostria, "*Bonne Nouvelle,*" *Les inrockuptibles,* January 1, 2001, https://www.lesinrocks.com/cinema/films-a-l-affiche/bonne-nouvelle.

22. Karlheinz Stierle reminds us that Baudelaire takes as his generic foil the late eighteenth-century tradition of the *tableau de Paris,* a literary subgenre comprising "short texts which give fragmentary views of the common life of Paris, especially of those aspects of it which have not yet been objects of literary description." See "Baudelaire and the Tradition of the *Tableau de Paris,*" *New Literary History* 11, no. 2 (1980): 347.

23. Dieutre, "Et plus, si affinités . . . ," 28.

24. Ostria, "*Bonne Nouvelle.*"

25. UniverCiné, "Vincent Dieutre présente son film *Jaurès.*"

26. Cuthbertson, "In/Out," 270.

27. Gilles Deleuze, *Cinema 1: The Movement-Image,* trans. Hugh Tomlinson and Barbara Habberjam (Minneapolis: University of Minnesota Press, 1986), 109.

28. Deleuze, 109.

29. Deleuze, 208.

30. Deleuze, 109.

31. Deleuze, 109.

32. Gilles Deleuze, *Foucault,* trans. Seán Hand (1988; repr., New York: Continuum, 1999), 54.

33. Greg Youmans, "France in Autumn*: Race d'Ep!* and the End of the Seventies," *Dirty Looks,* May 2012, https://www.gregyoumansfilm.files.wordpress.com/2018/01/race-dep-screening-publication_may-2012_dirty-looks-nyc_final.pdf.

34. Simon Ofield, "Cruising the Archive," *Journal of Visual Culture* 4, no. 3 (Winter 2005): 351.

35. Fiona Anderson, "Cruising as a Method and Its Limits," *LUX,* August 23, 2017, https://www.lux.org.uk/writing/cruising-method-limits-fiona-anderson.

36. Centre Pompidou, "Selon Patricia Falguières: Let's Queer Art History!," Dailymotion, May 25, 2011, https://www.dailymotion.com/video/xiwjl2.

37. Given the thematic affinities between the writing of Leo Bersani and the filmmaking of Vincent Dieutre—both of which coalesce around common interests in art history, French culture, and gay cruising—Bersani's short interview in the film represents something of a missed encounter. In his contribution to *Tenebrae Lessons,* Bersani explores aesthetic questions about the lighting of bodies in Caravaggisti artwork, rather than tackling questions about the legibility of homosexuality at stake in *Caravaggio's Secret* (Cambridge, Mass.: MIT Press, 1998), the book he coauthored with Ulysse Dutoit.

38. Cuthbertson, "In/Out," 270.

39. Martine Beugnet, *Cinema and Sensation: French Film and the Art of Transgression* (Edinburgh: Edinburgh University Press, 2007), 1–9; Marlène Monteiro, "The Body as Interstitial Space between Media in *Leçons de ténèbres* by Vincent Dieutre and *Histoire d'un secret* by Mariana Otero," *Acta Universitatis Sapientiae, Film and Media Studies* 7 (2013): 111–26.

40. Monteiro suggests that Ágnes Pethő's application of ekphrasis to film offers a promising framework for thinking about intermedial relations in Dieutre's work. Yet her use of the term to name a process of "embedding" of one

form of visual media into another continues to privilege the visual over the auditory. (Indeed, defined in these terms, the notion of "cinematic ekphrasis" might be coextensive with "remediation" or "transmediality"). While indebted to her previous reading of the film, I aim to reframe Dieutre's ekphrastic impulse in a broader conceptual, literary, and queer theoretical framework. See "Body as Interstitial Space," 122–23.

41. Vincent Dieutre, "Abécédaire pour un tiers-cinéma," *La lettre du cinéma,* no. 21 (2003): 75–85; also available on the *pointligneplan* website, https://www.pointligneplan.com/document/abecedaire-pour-un-tiers-cinema-vincent-dieutre-2.

42. Ágnes Pethő, "Media in the Cinematic Imagination: Ekphrasis and the Poetics of the In-Between in Jean-Luc Godard's Cinema," in *Media Borders, Multimodality and Intermediality,* ed. Lars Elleström (Basingstoke, Eng.: Palgrave McMillan, 2010), 211–22.

43. Sarah Cooper, *Film and the Imagined Image* (Edinburgh: Edinburgh University Press, 2019), 40.

44. Brian Glavey, *The Wallflower Avant-Garde: Modernism, Sexuality and Queer Ekphrasis* (Oxford: Oxford University Press, 2016), 4.

45. W. J. T. Mitchell, "The Politics of Genre: Space and Time in Lessing's *Laocoon,*" *Representations* 6 (Spring 1984): 108.

46. Glavey, *Wallflower Avant-Garde,* 8.

47. Glavey, 9.

48. Glavey, 6.

49. François Bonenfant, "Les invasions de la voix," *Vertigo* 26, no. 2 (2004): 74.

50. Emma Wilson. "*Etat présent:* Contemporary French Women Filmmakers," *French Studies* 59, no. 2 (April 2005): 222.

51. Elizabeth Freeman, *Time Binds: Queer Temporalities, Queer Histories* (Durham, N.C.: Duke University Press, 2010), 127.

52. Saige Walton, *Cinema's Baroque Flesh: Film, Phenomenology and the Art of Entanglement* (Amsterdam: Amsterdam University Press, 2016), 21.

53. In a succinct gloss of Bal's notion of the "pre-posterous," Wayne Andersen notes that "even when juxtaposing, rewriting, over-painting, reworking, or recasting, Bal proposes putting what came chronologically first ('pre') as an after-effect behind ('post') its later recycling, thus fashioning a preposterous history—a vision of how to re-vision the Baroque contrary to proper sense." See "Mieke Bal's Preposterous Art History," *European Legacy* 6, no. 3 (2001): 354.

54. Glavey, *Wallflower Avant-Garde,* 3.

55. Both in its mode of address—an apostrophe to a lost lover—and the suggestive affinities it draws between nude male cruiser and the sphere of

painting, Dieutre's *Tenebrae Lessons* recalls an earlier French queer film, Philippe Valois's *Johan: Mon été 75* (*Johan: My Summer 1975*). *Johan* tells the story of a filmmaker, played by Vallois, who intends to make a film about his lover—the eponymous Johan—but is unable to do so because he is in jail. The film chronicles the filmmaker's attempts to make a film, using various substitutes for Johan—many of whom he encountered while cruising in Paris. For a detailed account of this film, and a rigorous and theoretically illuminating introduction to Vallois's filmmaking more generally, see David A. Gerstner, "Choreographing Homosexual Desire in Philippe Vallois's *Johan*," *Camera Obscura* 28, no. 3 (December 2013): 125–57.

56. W. J. T. Mitchell, *What Do Pictures Want? The Lives and Loves of Images* (Chicago: University of Chicago Press, 2005), 58.

57. For example, in *French Queer Cinema* (Edinburgh: Edinburgh University Press, 2008), Nick Rees-Roberts writes that Dieutre's "lofty references to Schubert and Caravaggio" are integral to his "artistic self-fashioning" (129). Though the charge of bad faith is not explicitly leveled against the filmmaker, what seems to be implied is that Dieutre's citation of a rarefied artistic canon serves to soften the film's less salubrious moments, providing aesthetic respite from its otherwise "downbeat account of queer sexuality" (130).

58. André Bazin, "Painting and Cinema," in *What Is Cinema? Volume 1*, trans. Hugh Gray (Berkeley: University of California Press, 1967), 166.

59. The limit of the film frame, or what Anne Friedberg calls the "ontological cut," has been the source of disagreement between French film theorists in the 1970s, most notably Jean-Louis Comolli and Jean Narboni. See Friedberg, *The Virtual Window: From Alberti to Microsoft* (Cambridge, Mass.: MIT Press, 2006), 157. For a lively discussion of the borders of the cinematic frame, see also Des O'Rawe, "Toward a Poetics of the Cinematic Frame," *Journal of Aesthetics and Culture* 3, no. 1 (2011), https://doi.org/10.3402/jac.v3i0.5378.

60. Jacques Aumont, *Esthetique du cinéma* (Paris: Armand Collin, 2016), 15.

61. Pascal Bonitzer, "Hors-champ (un espace en défaut)," *Cahiers du cinema*, no. 234/35 (1971): 16.

62. Georges Perec, *Une tentative d'épuisement d'un lieu Parisien* (Paris: Christian Bourgois, 1982). The aim of Perec's exercise was to access the realm of the "hyperordinary" by registering every movement, gesture, and change in the urban landscape that would otherwise fall below the radar of remarkability.

63. Cuthberton, "In/Out," 274.

64. *Vincent Dieutre, la chambre et le monde*, DVD, dir. Fleur Albert (Paris: INA Éditions, 2013).

65. UniverCiné, "Vincent Dieutre présente son film *Jaurès.*"

66. Toby Ashraf, "Discover This: *Jaurès,*" *Stil in Berlin,* August 8, 2013, https://www.stilinberlin.de/blog/2013/08/discover-this-jaures.html.

67. Cuthbertson, "In/Out," 266.

68. Cuthbertson, 276.

69. Marc Siegel, "How Do I Look (Now)?," *Sissy* 25 (2015): 29.

70. Siegel, 29.

71. Jean-Louis Comolli, "Mots et images," *Ces films à part qu'on nomme "documentaires,"* October 5, 2012, https://www.cesfilmsapart.wordpress.com/2012/10/05/mots-et-images.

72. Comolli.

73. Kimberlé Crenshaw, "Mapping the Margins: Intersectionality, Identity Politics, and Violence against Women of Color," *Stanford Law Review* 43, no. 6 (July 1991): 1241–99.

74. Patricia Hill Collins, *Intersectionality as Critical Social Theory* (Durham, N.C.: Duke University Press, 2019), 27.

75. James S. Williams, "From Migration to Drift: Forging Queer Migrant Spaces and Transborder Relations in Contemporary French Cinema," in *Queering the Migrant in Contemporary European Cinema,* ed. Williams (London: Routledge, 2020), 171.

76. Marianne Blidon, "Reception and Use of Intersectionality: A Reading from French Perspective" [*sic*], trans. Patsy Baudoin, *Gender, Place and Culture* 25, no. 4 (April 2018): 599. The reference to "reading grids" appears as a hasty translation of the French *grille de lecture,* which might be more accurately translated as "interpretative framework."

77. Rees-Roberts, *French Queer Cinema,* 145. For a comprehensive account of the intersections between sexuality, race, and ethnicity in France see Rees-Roberts; Cervulle and Rees-Roberts, *Homo exoticus;* and Mehammed Amadeus Mack, *Sexagon: Muslims, France, and the Sexualization of National Culture* (New York: Fordham University Press, 2017).

78. Sarah Cooper, *Selfless Cinema? Ethics and French Documentary* (Oxford: Legenda, 2006), 8.

5. Sex beyond the City

1. Vincent Dieutre, "Abécédaire pour un tiers-cinéma," *La lettre du cinéma,* no. 21 (2003): 75–85; also available on the *pointligneplan* website, https://www.pointligneplan.com/document/abecedaire-pour-un-tiers-cinema-vincent-dieutre-2.

2. Dieutre.

3. Karl Schoonover and Rosalind Galt, *Queer Cinema in the World* (Durham, N.C.: Duke University Press, 2016), 215.

4. Frédéric Majour, "Lieux dits: Entretien avec Alain Guiraudie," *Vertigo* 30, no. 1 (2007): 28.

5. Majour, 28.

6. Scott Herring, *Another Country: Queer Anti-Urbanism* (New York: NYU Press, 2010), 17.

7. Cruising Pavilion, "Cruising Occitanie," *Fireflies* 6 (2018): 56–65; Nathan Friedman, "Diagram of the Amorous Search: Generating Desire with Guiraudie's *L'inconnu du lac,*" *Scapegoat: Landscape, Architecture, Political Economy* 9 (Winter/Spring 2015): 183–88; Jean-Marc Fournier, "Effet de lieu, frontières et territoires sur un lieu de drague," *Géographie et cultures* 95 (2015): 13–28.

8. Frédéric Jaeger, "Running, Waiting, Hoping," *Fireflies* 6 (2018): 35.

9. Majour, "Lieux dits," 34.

10. Nick Rees-Roberts, "Queer and Upright: Sex, Age, and Disorientation in Alain Guiraudie's *Staying Vertical,*" in *Cross Generational Relationships and Cinema* ed. Joel Gwynne and Niall Richardson (Basingstoke, Eng.: Palgrave McMillan, 2020), 137.

11. The recipient of 2014's prix Sade—a telling mark of approbation—this transgressive novel's narrative represents a hybrid of themes from *Stranger by the Lake* (summer escapades, lakeside cruising, police violence) and *Staying Vertical* (cross-generational relationality, gerontophilia). See Alain Guiraudie, *Ici commence la nuit* (Paris: POL, 2014).

12. Enda McCaffrey, "(Im)personal Relationality in Alain Guiraudie's *Ici commence la nuit,*" *Review critique de fixxion française contemporaine* 12, no. 7 (June 2016), https://doi.org/10.4000/fixxion.7440.

13. Roland Barthes, "The Light of the Southwest," in *Incidents, trans.* Richard Howard (Berkeley: University of California Press, 1992), 4.

14. Philippe Dubois, "Révélations intimes: Vers une cartographie queer du Sud-Ouest," *French Literature Series: Queer Sexualities in French and Francophone Literature and Film* 34 (2007): 164.

15. Jaeger, "Running, Waiting, Hoping," 31.

16. Dane Komljen and James Lattimer, "I Desire Something?," *Fireflies* 6 (2018): 39.

17. Henning Bech, *When Men Meet: Homosexuality and Modernity,* trans. Teresa Mesquit and Tim Davies (Chicago: University of Chicago Press, 1997), 98; Bech, "Citysex: Representing Lust in Public," in *Sexualities: Critical Concepts in Sociology,* ed. Ken Plummer (London: Routledge, 2002): 30.

18. David Bell, "Eroticizing the Rural," in *Decentring Sexualities,* ed. Richard Phillips, David Shuttleton, and Diane Watt (New York: Routledge, 2000), 84.

19. J. Jack Halberstam, *In a Queer Time and Place: Transgender Bodies, Subcultural Lives* (New York: NYU Press, 2005), 12.

20. J. Jack Halberstam, *Wild Things: The Disorder of Desire* (Durham, N.C.: Duke University Press, 2020), 30.

21. Herring, *Another Country*, 10.

22. Herring, 10.

23. Herring, 6.

24. Nick Rees-Roberts, "Down and Out: Immigrant Poverty and Queer Sexuality in Sébastien Lifshitz's *Wild Side*," *Studies in French Cinema* 7, no. 2 (January 2007): 151; Roy Grundmann and David Pendleton, "Sunshine for the Scoundrels: Interview with Alain Guiraudie," *Cinéaste* 39, no. 3 (Summer 2014): 16.

25. Cyril Neyrat, "J'ai envie de refaire la France: Entretien avec Alain Guiraudie," *Vertigo* 2, no. 29 (2006): 26.

26. Neyrat, 26.

27. Neyrat, 27.

28. It is important to acknowledge that my treatment of Guiraudie does not aspire to be comprehensive. Critics have routinely distinguished two tendencies in his work. The first aligns with the freewheeling energy of his fantastical films, including *No Rest for the Brave* (*Pas de repos pour les braves*, 2003); *Time Has Come* (*Voici venu le temps*, 2005); and *The King of Escape* (*Le roi de l'évasion*, 2009). In these films, which according to Dennis Lim are "prone to extravagant flights of fancy," cinematic space is notoriously diffuse. A second tendency can be identified in Guiraudie's more "sober and rigorously contained" work, first seen in his early 16 mm films, and subsequently *That Old Dream* and *Stranger by the Lake*. This chapter focuses on the second strand of films because they reveal three critical junctures in Guiraudie's career—his first attempt at filmmaking, his first art house success, and his international breakthrough.

29. Fabienne Bullot, "L'usine vide comme imaginaire cinématographique," *Contemporary French and Francophone Studies* 18, no. 3 (May 2014): 314–15.

30. Bullot, 314.

31. Matthew Flanagan quoted in Tiago de Luca and Nuno Barradas Jorge, "Introduction," *Slow Cinema*, ed. de Luca and Barradas Jorge (Edinburgh: Edinburgh University Press, 2015), 13.

32. Bullot, "L'usine vide," 314.

33. Elena Gorfinkel, "The Work of the Image: Cinema, Labor, Aesthetics," *Framework* 53, no. 1 (Spring 2012): 43.

34. David Pendleton and Roy Grundmann, "Sunshine for the Scoundrels: An Interview with Alain Guiraudie," *Cinéaste* 39, no. 3 (Summer 2014): 17.

35. This question is raised in the context of a post-screening discussion of the film documented in Chloé Scialom's documentary *Après la lutte* (Marseille, Fra.: Shellac Sud, 2001).

36. Gorfinkel, "Work of the Image," 43.

37. Jean-Louis Comolli, "Mechanical Bodies, Ever More Heavenly," trans. Annette Michelson, *October* 83 (Winter 1998): 21.

38. Comolli, 20–21.

39. Comolli, 20.

40. David Gerstner, "In Excess of the Cut: Peter Greenaway's *Eisenstein in Guanajuato*," *Los Angeles Review of Books*, April 15, 2016, https://www.lareviewofbooks.org/article/in-excess-of-the-cut-peter-greenaways-eisenstein-in-guanajuato; Thomas Waugh, "A Fag-Spotter's Guide to Eisenstein," in *The Fruit Machine: Twenty Years of Writings on Queer Cinema* (Durham, N.C.: Duke University Press, 2000), 64.

41. Karl Schoonover, "Wastrels of Time: Slow Cinema's Laboring Body, the Political Spectator, and the Queer," *Framework* 53, no. 1 (Spring 2012): 65.

42. Grundmann and Pendleton, "Sunshine for Scoundrels," 17.

43. Tiago de Luca, "Slow Time, Visible Cinema: Duration, Experience, and Spectatorship," *Cinema Journal* 56, no. 1 (Fall 2016): 31.

44. Schoonover, "Wastrels of Time," 70.

45. Michael Koresky, "Passing Through," *Fireflies* 6 (2018): 48.

46. Nick Rees-Roberts, "*Hors milieu:* Queer and Beyond," in *A Companion to Contemporary French Cinema*, ed. Alistair Fox, Michel Marie, Raphaëlle Moine, and Hilary Radner (New York: Bloomsbury, 2015), 451.

47. Schoonover and Galt, *Queer Cinema in the World*, 277.

48. Guy Hocquenghem, *Homosexual Desire*, trans. Daniella Dangoor (Durham, N.C.: Duke University Press, 1993), 50.

49. Komljen and Lattimer, "I Desire Something?," 38.

50. "Sex, Death, and Geometry: A Conversation between Alain Guiraudie and João Pedro Rodrigues on *L'inconnu du lac*," *Cinema Scope* 55 (Summer 2013), https://cinema-scope.com/features/sex-death-and-geometry-a-conversation-between-alain-guiraudie-and-joao-pedro-rodrigues-on-linconnu-du-lac.

51. Saige Walton, "Cruising the Unknown: Film as Rhythm and Embodied Apprehension in *Stranger by the Lake* (2013)," *New Review of Film and Television Studies* 16, no. 3 (2018): 260.

52. Gary Needham, "Cruising as Another Way of Looking," *Wuxia* 1–2 (2014): 49–50.

53. Roland Barthes, *The Pleasure of the Text*, trans. Richard Miller (New York: Farrar, Straus and Giroux, 1975), 26.

54. Nicholas Elliot, "Interview: Alain Guiraudie," *Bomb*, January 21, 2014, https://bombmagazine.org/articles/alain-guiraudie.

55. Damon R. Young, *Making Sex Public and Other Cinematic Fantasies* (Durham, N.C.: Duke University Press, 2018), 230.

56. Young, 229.

57. Catriona Mortimer-Sandilands and Bruce Erickson, eds., *Queer Ecologies: Sex, Nature, Politics, Desire* (Bloomington: Indiana University Press, 2010); Nicole Seymour, *Strange Natures: Futurity, Empathy, and the Queer Ecological Imagination* (Urbana: University of Illinois Press, 2013); Sarah Ensor, "Queer Fallout: Samuel R. Delany and the Ecology of Cruising," *Environmental Humanities* 9, no. 1 (May 2017): 149–66.

58. Seymour, *Strange Natures*, 7.

59. Timothy Morton, "Guest Column: Queer Ecology," *PMLA* 125, no. 2 (March 2010): 273.

60. Guiraudie quotes Bataille in Nicolas Azalbert and Jean-Philippe Tessé, "Jusqu'au bout du désir: Entretien avec Alain Guiraudie," *Cahiers du cinéma*, no. 690 (2013): 52. For Guiraudie's invocation of Edelman's writing, see Giovanni Marchini Camia, "Interview with Alain Guiraudie," *Fireflies* 6 (2018): 101.

61. Alain Guiraudie quoted in Marchini Camia, 101.

62. Greg Garrard, "How Queer Is Green?," *Configurations* 18, no. 1 (Winter 2010): 79.

63. Leo Bersani quoted in Ensor, "Queer Fallout," 149.

64. Ensor, 149.

65. Rees-Roberts, "*Hors milieu*," 457.

66. Bernard Génin, "*Jours de France*," *Positif*, no. 673 (March 2017): 50.

67. Catriona Mortimer-Sandilands and Bruce Erickson, "A Genealogy of Queer Ecologies," in Mortimer-Sandilands and Erickson, *Queer Ecologies*, 3.

68. Nicholas de Villiers, *Cruisy, Sleepy, Melancholy: Sexual Disorientation in the Films of Tsai Ming-liang* (Minneapolis: University of Minnesota Press, 2022), 7–8.

69. Roland Barthes, *The Pleasure of the Text*, trans. Richard Miller (New York: Hill and Wang, 1975), 4.

70. Emma Wilson, *Sexuality and the Reading Encounter: Identity and desire in Proust, Duras, Tournier, and Cixous* (Oxford: Clarendon Press, 1996), 9.

71. John Paul Ricco, *The Logic of the Lure* (Chicago: University of Chicago Press, 2003), xix.

72. Nick Rees-Roberts, *French Queer Cinema* (Edinburgh: Edinburgh University Press, 2008), 2. Here, Rees-Roberts is invoking the terminology of Alan Sinfield.

73. İrvin C. Schick, *The Erotic Margin: Sexuality and Spatiality in Alterist Discourse* (New York: Verso, 1999).

INDEX

abjection, 69
acousmatic, 114, 119, 131–35, 139, 206n3. *See also* voice-over
aesthetic judgment: of bodies, 110–13; of cinema, 107–8; across cultural registers, 102–3, 108, 127–28, 136–37, 210n57; intermedial, 133, 137–38
affect, 1, 9, 31, 44, 55–58, 66, 120, 122, 129–36, 139, 155, 161, 175, 184
aging, 68–71, 81
Ahmed, Sara, 31, 37–39, 155
Akerman, Chantal, 76–78, 119
Amin, Kadji, 62
anachronism: architectural, 57, 63–65, 200n18; art historical, 110, 129, 135–37, 209n53; and media forms, 63–65, 176; retro aesthetics, 104, 174
any-space-whatever (Deleuze), 126
apartments, 68–82, 139–45
apparatus theory, 55–60, 67
archives, 118, 127–29, 138
art history: baroque, 131, 135–38, 208n37; and curation, 127–30; modernist, 78, 110; nineteenth century, 109, 116. *See also* aesthetic judgment; painting
Aumont, Jacques, 42, 115, 139
Aurélia Steiner (Melbourne) (1979, dir. Marguerite Duras), 134
autofiction, 48–50, 74, 114, 118, 199n6

Bal, Mieke, 137
banlieue, 81, 85–86, 98–111. See also *cinéma de banlieue*
Barthes, Roland: *Camera Lucida,* 51, 76; on cinematic spectatorship, 55–61, 66–68, 168; on cruising, 115, 128, 185; on the movie theater, 47, 55–58, 84; and Jacques Nolot, 50, 82, 186; race in, 91–93, 185; "Soirées de Paris," 52, 63, 91–93; on the Southwest, 155–56
Bataille, Georges, 178–79

bathhouse, 10. *See also* sex: clubs
Baudelaire, Charles, 9, 116, 122, 207n22
Baudry, Jean-Louis, 58, 60
Bazin, André: on painting, 138–39; realist aesthetics of, 44, 76, 152, 164, 175–76, 179
Bech, Henning, 116, 158–59
Before I Forget (2007, dir. Jacques Nolot), 68–84
Bell, David, 33–34, 159
Belmadi, Yasmine, 88–90, 98
Benjamin, Walter, 9, 122
Berlant, Lauren, 35
Bersani, Leo: on aesthetic forms, 31; art history of, 110, 114, 131; ecocritical reading of, 178–79; on new relational modes, 2, 36; on queer's lack of specificity, 40; on self-shattering, 172; "Sociability and Cruising," 35, 178–79
beur, 86, 88–93, 100–102
bisexuality, 96–98, 173
Blow Job (1964, dir. Andy Warhol), 66, 168
body: in cruising encounter, 1–3, 7, 33; in Dieutre, 131, 134–38; and film theory, 6, 56–60, 166; in Guiraudie, 157, 168–70, 176–81; in Honoré, 108–111; in Lifshitz, 90, 93–96; in Nolot, 53–66, 69–71, 79–84; and queer theory, 12, 15, 33–39; and spatial theory, 24, 26, 33, 155; of spectator, 44, 47–60, 128
Bonitzer, Pascal, 42–43, 139
Bonne Nouvelle (2001, dir. Vincent Dieutre), 121–26
boredom, 61–67, 157, 168, 175
Bresson, Robert, 11, 78
Burgin, Victor, 27, 122
Butler, Judith, 28, 36, 60, 197n58

Cadinot, Jean-Daniel, 127–28
Caillebotte, Gustave, 109–10
Camus, Renaud, 91, 115, 124
Cardinal, Roger, 59
Caron, David, 51, 203
Cavell, Stanley, 138
Céline and Julie Go Boating (1974, dir. Jacques Rivette), 8, 192n10
Cervenak, Sarah, 94
Chambers, Ross, 91–92
Chaumont, Franck, 97, 100–103
Chauncey, George, 29
Chion, Michel, 120, 139
cinéma de banlieue, 103, 107–8
cinéma du corps. See New French Extremity
cinéma verité, 14, 122
cinephilia, 8, 66, 68
city: on screen, 8, 10–11, 47–48, 88–98, 121–26, 140–49, 161; and sexuality, 98–101, 158–61; and spatial theory, 22–29. *See also* metronormativity; Paris
Cléo from 5 to 7 (1962, dir. Agnès Varda), 8–10
closet, 32, 101–2, 143, 173
Cold Lands (1999, dir. Sébastien Lifshitz), 88–89
Colebrook, Claire, 27, 29
coloniality: banlieue and, 98–99; and bisexuality, 96–97; "post-colonial pornography," 86, 102; and queer space, 33; sex work and, 11, 92; and spatial description, 22–23, 31, 186; and white gay culture, 81, 88, 92

communautarisme, 87. *See also* Republicanism, French
Comolli, Jean-Louis, 146, 165–66
Cooper, Dennis, 104, 110
Cooper, Sarah, 133, 146
Crang, Michael, 8, 22, 24, 26, 28
Crenshaw, Kimberlé, 147
crossdressing. See *travesti*
cross-generational relations, 68, 79–82, 155–56, 161, 169
cruising: as archival engagement, 113, 128–9, 134–38, 209–10n55; of art galleries, 127–28, 138; choreography of bodies in, 2–3, 125, 167–70; digital, 33, 107, 176, 181–84; ecological dimension of, 178–81; ephemerality of, 3–4, 123–25; and *flânerie,* 9–10, 116, 158; grounds, 11, 47–48, 95–96, 172–73, 183; and loitering, 91–94; in movie theaters, 51–68, 83–84, 199n4; and nostalgia, 82, 171, 176; in queer theory, 35–36; as reading practice, 8, 15, 115–16, 185; as spectatorship, 1–2, 115–16, 175–76; and travel, 134–35, 186; urban bias of discourses on, 158–59
Cusset, François, 41

dark rooms, 1–3, 95–96. *See also* sex: clubs
Davis, Oliver, 40–41
Dean, Tim, 40–41
death: drive (Freud), 176–79; and mourning, 51, 70, 75–76, 82; murder, 174; and still life, 77–78
Debord, Guy, 9, 24, 55
de Certeau, Michel: and Foucault, 194n8; on poaching, 13, 29; queer potentiality of, 27–29; space/place distinction in, 34–35; spatial semiotics of, 25, 30, 94; "Walking in the City," 9, 15, 26, 94
Delany, Samuel R., 37, 52, 199n4
Deleuze, Gilles, 114, 126–27, 133
Denis, Claire, 48–50
depth of field, 152, 164, 176
Dieutre, Vincent: and Chantal Akerman, 119; art history in, 129–31, 135–39; Leo Bersani, 131; biography of, 117; *Bonne Nouvelle,* 121–26; cinematic writing of, 115–16, 118, 132; *Jaurès,* 140–49; on migration and clandestinity, 121–26, 143–48; and Frédéric Mitterrand, 119–120; and Nolot, 113–14; painting, 129–32, 134–38; and Parisian space, 118, 121–26; race in, 121–26, 140–48; *Tenebrae Lessons,* 117–39; travel in, 119, 131, 134–35; voice-over in, 113–14, 120–26
Dikeç, Mustafa, 22, 26, 87, 99–100
documentary, 10–14, 116–49
domestic space. *See* apartments
Down There (2006, dir. Chantal Akerman), 119
drag, 54, 58–62, 83. See also *travesti*
Drexel, Claus, 10–15
Ducastel, Olivier, and Jacques Martineau, 1–10
Duras, Marguerite, 76, 118, 127, 134

Edelman, Lee, 56, 178
Eisenstein, Sergei, 166, 171

ekphrasis, 132–34, 209n40
Ensor, Sarah, 178–80
environmental politics, 156
Erickson, Bruce, 12, 178, 182
essay film, 120–21, 129, 206n4

factory, 162–70
fado (lyrical genre), 11
Fassbinder, Rainer Werner, 78
Fassin, Eric, 100–101
figure/ground relation, 66, 177
film theory: of Barthes, 52, 55–58, 84; of Deleuze, 125–27; documentary, 120–21, 149, 206n4; haptic, 59–60; and labor, 165–68; phenomenological, 90, 131, 134–35, 168; psychoanalytic, 55–68; queer, 1–3, 45, 55, 96, 115, 152; realist, 44, 76–78, 84, 152, 164, 175–76, 179; and sound, 90, 120, 139, 206n3; spatial, 42–45, 71–74, 198n67; structuralist, 66–67, 173. *See also* apparatus theory
financing, of films, 74, 104–5, 156
flâneur, 8–10, 91, 94, 158
Four Days in France (2016, dir. Jacques Reybaud), 181–84
Fox and His Friends (1975, dir. Rainer Werner Fassbinder), 78
frame: cinematic, 42–44, 210n59; documentary framing, 116, 143, 145–49; empty, 77, 125–26, 134, 162; painting, 137–39
French theory, 41–42
From Somalia with Love (1982, dir. Frédéric Mitterrand), 119–20
Front homosexuel d'action révolutionnaire (FHAR), 171–72. *See also* Marxism

gallery spaces, 127–29, 135–38
Galt, Rosalind, 45, 152
garçon arabe, le, 86. See also *beur*
gentrification, 81–82, 107
Gerstner, David, 166, 209–10n55
Glavey, Brian, 133–34, 137
Godard, Jean-Luc, 129, 152
Gorfinkel, Elena, 44–45, 58, 164–65
Grindr, 107, 176, 181–84
Guiraudie, Alain: biography of, 156–58; boredom in, 157, 166–71; class politics of, 156, 161, 164–65, 171–72; death drive in, 175–81; and ecology, 173–81; and labor, 165–70; linear metaphors in, 154–55; *Now the Night Begins* (novel), 155; Occitanie, 155–56; and psychoanalysis, 154–55; relation to city, 151, 153, 160–62; slow cinema of, 162–68, 171; *Stranger by the Lake,* 172–81; *That Old Dream That Moves,* 162–72

Halberstam, J. Jack, 27–28, 36–39, 159
Halperin, David, 40
Hate (La haine) (1995, dir. Mathieu Kassovitz), 102
Haussmann, Georges-Eugène (Baron), 23, 28
Heroes Are Immortal (1990, dir. Alain Guiraudie), 156–57
Herring, Scott, 153, 159–60
heterotopia, 30
hexagone, 21, 31–32
Hill Collins, Patricia, 147
Hinterland (1998, dir. Jacques Nolot), 51, 69, 79

Histoire(s) du cinéma (1989–98, dir. Jean-Luc Godard), 129
HIV/AIDS: and allegory, 178; history, 16, 63–64, 81–82, 117, 178; living with, 66, 70, 131, 135; seroconversion, 7–8
Hocquenghem, Guy, 50, 62, 127, 172,
homelessness, 124, 143–45
homonationalism, 32, 148
homonormativity, 34
Homosexual Century (Race d'Ep!), (1979, dir. Lionel Soukaz and Guy Hocquenghem), 127–28
Honoré, Christophe: and art history, 109–11; on banlieue, 105–6, 109–11; experimentalism of, 104; film production, 104–6; *Man at Bath,* 103–11; pornography in, 102–3; on sexual types, 107
housing projects, 86, 98–99, 105. *See also* banlieue
human geography, 34–35

I Can't Sleep (1994, dir. Claire Denis), 49–50
indexicality, 76–78, 84
intermediality, 118, 131–34, 137
intersectionality, 147–48
intertextuality, 8, 49, 66, 79

Jaurès (2013, dir. Vincent Dieutre), 140–49

labor: and film theory, 165–68; manual, 164–69; migrant, 98; sex work, 10–14, 53–54, 79–81, 88–90, 109; undocumented, 121, 124
La chambre (1972, dir. Chantal Akerman), 77
La Chatte à deux têtes. See *Porn Theatre*
Ladies of the Woods (2021, dir. Claus Drexel), 10–15
La matiouette ou l'arrière-pays (1983, dir. André Téchiné), 48, 79
Lefebvre, Henri, 7, 15, 23–31
lesbianism, 65, 73–74
Liftshitz, Sébastien: as actor, 96; on bisexuality, 96–98; *Cold Lands,* 88; *Open Bodies,* 88–98; race in, 88, 90–98; *Wild Side,* 11, 88–89
lighting: cinematic, 7, 14, 177; in painting, 131, 208n37
lived space (Lefebvre), 24–25, 77
loitering, 89–98

Mack, Mehammed Amadeus, 32–33, 86, 100–103, 111
Man at Bath (2010, dir. Christophe Honoré), 103–11
Manège (1986, dir. Jacques Nolot), 47–48
Marxism: queer, 171–72; and spatial theory, 27, 162. *See also* working class
McDonald, Boyd, 115
Mediterranean, 186
metronormativity, 158–61
Metz, Christian, 58
Miller, D. A., 68, 200n14
Mitchell, W. J. T., 133, 138
Mitterrand, Frédéric, 119–20, 207n17
Mortimer-Sandilands, Catriona, 12, 182
mourning. *See* death

My City's Gonna Crack (1997, dir. Jean Paul Ricquet), 103
My Hustler (1965, dir. Andy Warhol), 66

Needham, Gary, 1–2, 175, 185
neorealism, Italian, 77
New French Extremity, 48, 57, 69
new wave, French, 8, 64–65, 102
Nolot, Jacques: as actor, 48–50; and Roland Barthes, 50–52; *Before I Forget,* 68–84; on death, 70–71; and Claire Denis, 49; and domestic space, 74–78; film production, 74; inheritance in, 78–82; *Porn Theatre,* 49–68; race in cinema of, 63, 79–81, 85–86; on sex work, 53–54, 70
North Africa, 79–81, 88–92, 100. See also *beur*
nouvelle vague. See new wave, French

Occitanie, 155
opacity, 93–94, 98, 101–2
Open Bodies (1998, dir. Sébastien Lifshitz), 88–98
orientation, 30–33, 37–40, 152, 197n56
Ozon, François, 48, 88, 156

painting, 77, 109, 130–38. *See also* art history
Paris: and banlieue, 85–86, 101, 105–7; in the cinema, 8, 10–11, 47–48, 122, 161; in cultural theory, 8–9, 11–13, 22–23, 52; and political power, 22–23, 28; and provinccs, 89, 151, 157, 161; and urban planning, 13–4, 21–22, 143. *See also individual film titles*
Paris 05:59 (2016, dir. Olivier Ducastel and Jacques Martineau), 1–10
parks, 11–14
Pasolini, Pier Paolo, 81, 85, 88, 110
Peirce, Charles Sanders, 84
Perec, Georges, 141
phenomenology, 37–39, 90, 194n17
poaching (de Certeau), 13, 29
pornography, 49, 83, 86, 95, 102–9, 111, 123, 127–28, 174. See also *Porn Theatre*
Porn Theatre (2002, dir. Jacques Nolot), 49–68
postmodern geography, 27–30, 159
Preciado, Paul B., 31
production of films, 53, 74, 104–5, 117, 156
projection booth, 57
props, 77, 79
psychoanalysis, 55–60, 69, 97, 155
psychogeography, 9, 155
Puar, Jasbir, 32–33

queer theory: ecological, 12–13, 177–78, 182; and etymology, 155, 197n58; French reception of, 41; phenomenology and, 37–39; and spatiality, 35–39; and temporality, 36–37, 96, 130, 166, 197n56

race: and bisexuality, 96–98; exoticism, 85–86, 123–24; and French republicanism, 32, 86–88, 147–48; in gay culture, 81, 86–87, 123–24, 147–48; and police, 61, 93; and spatial relations, 37–38, 87–111, 140–46
Rancière, Jacques, 26, 129
red-light district, 10–15, 48, 51

Rees-Roberts, Nick, 68, 81, 106, 138, 148, 155, 160, 170, 179; and Maxime Cervulle, 86, 88, 93, 102
refugee, 140–46
representations of space (Lefebvre), 24–25
Republicanism, French: and difference, 28, 32, 41, 98–100, 148; and spatial relations, 5, 87. See also *communautarisme*
Reybaud, Jérome, 181–86
Rhodes, John David, 44, 72, 79, 87–88
Ricco, John Paul, 4, 35–36, 45, 185
Rifkin, Adrian, 129
Rivette, Jacques, 8, 42–43
Rosen, Philip, 67
Rosner, Victoria, 72–73
Ross, Kristin, 23

Sagat, François, 102–11
Salò or the 120 Days of Sodom (1975, dir. Pier Paolo Pasolini), 110
Schoonover, Karl, 45, 152, 166–68
Schulman, Sarah, 81–82
screen: cinematic, 47, 53–58, 63–66, 96, 184; "dream screen," 60; as synonym for concealment, 62, 166; television, 95; as temporary architecture, 13
Sedgwick, Eve Kosofsky, 32, 38, 44, 101, 156
separatism. See *communautarisme*
sex: anal, 3, 123; clubs, 1–3, 7, 10, 95–96, 143; fisting, 135; group sex, 2, 58–62; hand job, 168; oral, 3, 66, 79–80; tourism, 92–93, 124, 207n17; work, 10–14, 53–54, 79–81, 88–90, 109
shot: close-up, 2, 53, 58–59, 77, 95–96, 123, 130, 136, 182; dorsal, 70, 84; establishing, 1–2, 11, 52–53, 70, 89–90, 105, 108, 123, 164, 175–77; handheld camera, 105; high-angle, 89, 139–40, 143; long, 143, 176; medium, 75, 77, 79–80, 83; panning, 64, 123; point-of-view, 1, 77, 90, 108–9; shot–reverse, 109; tracking, 119, 165; wide-angle, 176. *See also* depth of field
Simone Barbès or Virtue (1980, dir. Marie-Claude Treilhou), 65
Situationists, 9, 55, 122
Smith, Jack, 66
Soukaz, Lionel, 127–28
Southwestern France, 155–56
spatial practices, 7, 15, 25–26, 88, 91–96, 128
spatial theory: in cinema, 42–45, 71–74, 198n67; French, 6–7, 22–31, 99
spectatorship: and attention, 66–67, 166–70, 174–76; deliberative, 43–44, 57, 167, 175–79; erotic, 44–45, 54–67, 115, 128, 136; as labor, 125, 165–68; mise-en-abyme of, 54–67, 139–45
Stern, Lesley, 65–66
Stoler, Ann Laura, 86
Straight Ahead until Morning (1994, dir. Alain Guiraudie), 152–56
Stranger by the Lake (2013, dir. Alain Guiraudie), 172–81
suburbs. *See* banlieue

Téchiné, André, 48, 50, 79, 156
temporality: cinematic slowness, 152–53, 157, 163–68; and dead

time, 66, 75–78; and *durée,* 8; queer, 36–37, 96, 130, 166, 175, 197n56; relation to spatiality, 44
Tenebrae Lessons (1999, dir. Dieutre), 129–38
That Old Dream That Moves (2001, dir. Alain Guiraudie), 162–72
theater: as art form, 53, 104; movie theater, 45, 47–68, 82–84, 200n18. See also *Porn Theatre*
Thrift, Nigel, 8, 22, 24, 28
time. *See* temporality
trans: aesthetics, 14; allegory, 60; geographies, 12; sex work, 11–15, 89
Traub, Valerie, 197n56
travelogue, 119, 131–35
travesti, 11–14, 53–66, 132
Treilhou, Marie-Claude, 65
trick (Camus), 91, 115, 124, 184
Turner, Mark W., 3, 10

Umberto D. (1952, dir. Vittorio de Sica), 77

Valentine, Gill, 33–34
Valois, Philippe, 210n55
Varda, Agnès, 8–10, 122
Vertov, Dziga, 166
voice-over, 119–26, 134–49, 206n3, 207n19

Wallace, Lee, 73–74
Warhol, Andy, 66, 168
Warner, Michael, 35, 39–40
Watts, Philip, 56–60, 67
Willemen, Paul, 59
Williams, James S.: on cinematic space, 25, 30; on Dieutre, 148; on Nolot, 49, 69
Williams, Linda, 66
Wilson, Emma, 114–15, 135, 185
Wojcik, Pamela, 72
working class: queer, 78, 161–64, 167; and race, 32, 85, 103; rural, 161. *See also* Marxism

Young, Damon R., 10, 176

Zeraoui, Fouad, 101, 107

Jules O'Dwyer is teaching associate in film studies and French at the University of Cambridge.

Zeitfracht Medien GmbH
Ferdinand-Jühlke-Straße 7
99095 Erfurt, Deutschland
produktsicherheit@kolibri360.de